Germany, Russia, and the Rise of Geo-Economics

Germany, Russia, and the Rise of Geo-Economics

Stephen F. Szabo

Bloomsbury Academic
An imprint of Bloomsbury Publishing Plc

B L O O M S B U R Y
LONDON • NEW DELHI • NEW YORK • SYDNEY

Bloomsbury Academic
An imprint of Bloomsbury Publishing Plc

50 Bedford Square	1385 Broadway
London	New York
WC1B 3DP	NY 10018
UK	USA

www.bloomsbury.com

BLOOMSBURY and the Diana logo are trademarks of Bloomsbury Publishing Plc

First published 2015

© Stephen F. Szabo, 2015

British Library Cataloguing-in-Publication Data
A catalogue record for this book is available from the British Library.

ISBN: HB: 978-1-4725-9632-1
PB: 978-1-4725-9631-4
ePDF: 978-1-4725-9634-5
ePub: 978-1-4725-9633-8

Library of Congress Cataloging-in-Publication Data
A catalog record for this book is available from the Library of Congress.

Typeset by Newgen Knowledge Works (P) Ltd., Chennai, India
Printed and bound in Great Britain

To Karl Cerny, teacher and mentor

Contents

Acknowledgments

This book is the product of my career as a Germany watcher, which began in the 1970s and has resulted in a number of books and articles, including one on the diplomacy of German unification and another on the United States–German split over the Iraq war. Both of these books came out of my interest in the contemporary German–American relationship and how it has evolved from its highpoint with the peaceful unification of Germany in 1990 through the lowpoint of the split over the Iraq war. This split seemed to presage the end of the close relationship that had prevailed through the Cold War and the decade after unification. It also signaled a new kind of Germany, not only now unified but one that was become less a subject and more an actor internationally. It was a Germany that represented a new kind of power, an economic power, which is replacing the old type of military-based power embodied by the type of power the United States still is. Germany is a geo-economic power, the most successful export economy in the world, a country that now ranks as the most popular in many global opinion polls, and yet a power that downplays military power. Germany is a precursor of other emerging powers in the era of globalization, powers like Brazil, India, Indonesia, Singapore, which are gaining influence in global politics through economic prowess.

I was also interested in the changing Russian–German relationship that seemed to me to be in flux ever since the government of Gerhard Schröder coalesced with it against the George W. Bush administration over the Iraq war. This was something new, the first time that a postwar German government sided with Russia against the United States on a matter of national security that the US administration deemed vital. The language of Schröder and his team, which stressed the independence and sovereignty of Germany and its need to be taken seriously, as well as implication that the American administration was treating Germany less as a partner and more as a satellite was also significant and indicated the return of Germany as an important independent player on the world stage. When the Grand Coalition government of Angela Merkel continued to split with the Bush administration over the Russia–Georgia war and the policy of enlarging NATO to Georgia and Ukraine, it became clear how important Russia could be in the future of the German–American relationship.

I wanted to explore the motivations and interests of Germany in its relationship with Russia to better understand where Germany was headed. I came to see that the Russian relationship was a case of a larger strategic approach, that of a geo-economic power, which presaged a major alteration of the traditional German approach as a civilian power. This approach requires a different type of foreign policy analysis, one that not only looks at the roles of political policymakers and opinion shapers, but also that of the private sector and lobbyists. Germany's Russia policy cannot be understood without an understanding of the dynamics of economic relationships and the role of German business. Here again, Germany is one case in a larger trend already identified by such writers as Steve Coll, Anne Marie Slaughter, Thomas Friedman, and Hans Kundnani to name a few. This is a new type of statecraft that is the product of the era of globalization and marketization, which will define the twenty-first century.

This book, then, is an examination of Germany and how it is changing. While Russia is the case chosen, given that geo-economics are so predominant in the relationship, this is a book about Germany not so much about Russia. I am not a Russia specialist and am not trying to assess Russia as Russia but more how Russia is viewed by the leading power in Europe today and the implications for Germany, Europe, and the United States.

This book is the product of two years of research conducted while I was directing the Transatlantic Academy in Washington. The views and analysis are purely my own and do not in any way reflect the views of the Transatlantic Academy or its partners. I am grateful to many people who assisted in the research of this volume, especially to my two main research assistants, Judit Vásárhely-Kondor and Thedore Reinert, both former students at the Nitze School of Advanced International Studies, Johns Hopkins University, an institution I have been proud to have been associated with for two decades and to Jessica Hirsch for her help with the bibliography. In addition, thanks to Edward Berlin, Caroline Mükusch, Leonie Willenbrink and Joana Allamani for their research assistance. Thanks also to Samuel Charap, Bartek Nowak, Ralph Thiele, Rolf Nikel, and Ash Jain for their comments on portions of the manuscript. Special thanks to Pia Bungarten and the Friedrich Ebert Stiftung for including me in a study group on Germany, Russia, and the United States, which provided invaluable insights for this study. Thanks to Karl Cerny my Professor and Doktorvater at Georgetown who directed me toward a life long interest in Germany. Finally thanks to my wife Joan, whose patience and support was, as always, crucial.

1

The Foreign Policy of Germany Inc.

Drang nach Osten

It is July 2010. The venue is sunny Yekaterinburg, and the occasions is the annual Petersburg Dialogue between German and Russian leaders. Yekaterinburg is an industrial town behind the Ural Mountains and is the place where the tsar and his family were murdered in 1918 and where Boris Yeltsin began his early career. Its German name was changed back from the Soviet "Sverdlovsk." Standing in front of the cameras are Angela Merkel, the German chancellor, and Dmitry Medvedev, the Russian president. Merkel's relationship with Russia is complicated. She grew up in communist East Germany and became a fluent Russian speaker during her schoolgirl days. While she developed a sympathy for Russian culture, her experience in the former East Germany seems to have made her a Russia skeptic. She, like Barack Obama, is an unemotional realist, who understands the nature of Russian power, the immutable nature of Russian authoritarianism, and that country's central importance to Germany.

While Medvedev represented the outward looking, friendly face, the real power player, Russian prime minister Vladimir Putin, had a deep connection with Germany. He joined a German language club while a young student in Russia, surprising his teachers who thought he was not interested in anything academic. He picked up the language easily and used this background to become a KGB agent in Dresden, and when he visits Saxony he speaks of "returning home." He sent one of his children to a German school in Russia and has employed several former members of the East German secret service, the Stasi, in Russian enterprises. When he meets German leaders, he speaks with them in fluent German and he impressed the Bundestag with his command of the language. He thought he knew how to manipulate the former East German schoolgirl now turned German chancellor. At one of their early meetings, knowing that Merkel, who as a child had been bitten by a dog, has a strong aversion to big dogs, Putin brought his black Labrador Retriever Koni, apparently with the intention of both intimidating the chancellor and letting her know how much he knew about her. This must have been an unpleasant moment for her, bringing back memories of Russian tactics in her former homeland.[1] Merkel would later recount that when she hears Putin speak German, she is reminded of listening to an interrogator.

Once Merkel came to power, much was made of her desire to promote democracy and human rights in Russia. She told American politicians that her background in East Germany made her an especially strong advocate of democracy and liberty. During her first trip to Moscow, she met with human rights and democracy activists to the consternation of Putin. This was in sharp contrast to her predecessor Gerhard Schröder, who was a particularly close friend of Putin, having celebrated Christmas and birthdays together and using nicknames such as "Gerd" and "Volodya." Putin had sent a Cossack chair to Schröder for his private home, and Schroeder adopted two Russian girls through Putin's intervention. After leaving office, Schroeder became a key executive in a European consortium dominated by Gazprom, the massive Russian energy concern. He referred to Putin as a "flawless democrat" and was careful not to criticize his policy in public while being openly critical of President George W. Bush.

Yet, on this July day in Russia, Merkel is standing with the leader of Russia's new generation. Behind her is a phalanx of 25 German businessmen, with a deep interest in the Russian market as she signs major economic agreements with Medvedev. The businessmen are a virtual Who's Who of German business— Peter Löscher of Siemens, Martin Winterkorn of Volkswagen, Thomas Enders of Airbus, Martin Blessing of Commerzbank, and Johannes Teyssen of the energy giant, EON, among others. At the meeting, Siemens signed deals worth a billion euro. The chancellor stated, "We will also discuss domestic political problems and various issues which have to do with human rights," as well as "research, education and health." But she pointedly added that the thrust of the meeting was "that we do business, that we make profits and that we cooperate more intensively."[2]

Like her Social Democratic predecessor, Merkel seems to have a better relationship with the Russian president than with his American counterpart. All of these signify the major changes occurring in Germany's foreign policy. Germany is the key player in Europe on dealing with Russia. Given the lack of consensus in Europe over Russia, Berlin plays a decisive role in shaping a coherent and successful Russia policy. Yet, while Germany is crucial to any

Western policy consensus on Russia, there are real differences in interests, cultures, and approaches between Berlin and Washington, as well as between Berlin and Warsaw, Brussels, and other key European capitals that have led to divisions. There is a real possibility that without a common approach, Germany will increasingly play the role of mediator among Russia, the United States, and Europe.

There are voices in the West that have raised concerns about Germany's reliability as a partner in dealing with Russia. The conservative *Weekly Standard* warned, "Berlin has entered a new era of shared interests with Moscow and divergence from Washington. Incoming administration officials would be wise to recognize that on issues ranging from the gas dispute to Eastern Europe to Afghanistan and Iran, the Germany of today is not the partner the United States once had."[3] Zbigniew Brzezinski believes, "If the romance between Russia and Germany goes too far, it could strike a blow against European integration,"[4] and Edward Lucas, international editor of *The Economist* and author of a book on Russia titled *The New Cold War*, argues that the German-Russian relationship is "the most puzzling and troubling feature of modern European politics."[5] Philip Stephens from the *Financial Times* reports that "Mr. Obama's aides fret that Ms Merkel sometimes prefers the company of China and Russia over that of the US in the UN Security Council. She is too soft on Moscow. German exports trump allegiance to the western alliance."[6]

There has long been an undercurrent of worry about Germany's reliability as a partner, dating back to the Rapallo complex of the 1920s, when Germany and the Soviet Union signed a treaty of reconciliation, and more recently with then Polish defense minister Radek Sikorski's, references of the Nord Stream Russia-German gas pipeline as a new Molotov-Ribbentrop pact. The future of the German-American relationship and of Europe itself will hinge, in part, on how Germany, Europe, and America manage their approaches toward Russia. What then are the sources of both divergence and convergence of interests between Berlin and key Western capitals on Russia and how can a Western strategy be developed?

Trading state versus civilian power

The place to begin to answer these questions is in business. The German genius[7] has been manifest in philosophy, music, social and natural sciences, military affairs, and economics long before its late national unification in the nineteenth century. Germans have been much less impressive in the realm of politics and diplomacy, with, at times, disastrous results both for themselves and for others. After the monumental catastrophe of Hitler's Reich, Germans decided to put their energies, intelligence, and organizational skills into the economic sphere, largely ceding the military and diplomatic fields to the Americans in the Cold War. Divided, discredited, and demoralized, they succeeded in creating the most powerful economy in Europe and the fourth largest in the world. The Deutsche Mark became for the Germans what the nuclear arsenal was for the French, a symbol of national pride. During the 44 years of national division, West Germany was a semi-sovereign power in military affairs, a subcontractor to the United States in defense policy, more a consumer than a provider of security.

The West German grand strategy relied on its economic prowess for its influence and was brilliantly successful. The German approach came to be one of a "civilian power." As developed by the political scientist, Hanns Maull, this strategy relied on Germany exerting its influence through its economic resources rather than on the more traditional instruments of statecraft. The Germans took away the German threat from their neighbors by stressing their European vocation and multilateral diplomacy. West Germany slowly regained its sovereignty by submerging much of it in the European Union and NATO. It regained both respect and legitimacy by developing a post-national and postmodern identity, which minimized national identity. It openly confronted its "unmasterable past"[8] in a forthright and admirable manner, in contrast to that of the other leading civilian power, Japan, and succeeded in lowering the fears and distrust of its neighbors.

With the unification of Germany in 1990, this strategy continued and was adapted to the new era of globalization ushered in by the end of bipolar world. The German military participated in the NATO alliance in wars in Kosovo and later Afghanistan, but it continued to shrink in size, budget, and public acceptance. The opening of new markets to German industry in Asia, Eastern Europe, and the Middle East reinforced the export orientation of the German economy. Today, Germany is moving from being the center of Europe to the center of the global economy.[9]

Germany as a reemerging power

The German economy has always stood out from those of other advanced industrial economies in many aspects. First is its heavy reliance on exports.

Germany, a country of only 80 million inhabitants, ranks third in the world in exports, just behind China and America with a population five times its size. In 2013, exports made up 41 percent of the German GDP, with exports have accounted for two-thirds of GDP growth during the past decade. Second, Germany is more reliant on manufacturing than is the United States and other advanced industrial economies.[10] Industry makes up almost one-quarter of Germany's GDP, employing more than five million people. Four sectors dominate German industry: cars, machinery, chemicals, and electronics. Merkel once told Tony Blair that the secret of the German economy is that "we still make things."

The German economic success can be attributed to a highly calibrated "business cycle chain" that starts with initial demand stimulus in the form of strong exports, which in turn drives corporate investment and ultimately drives employment and private consumption. Unlike the United States, Germany does not depend on household spending to drive its economy, with private consumption in Germany being largely level during the past five years. This leaves Germany increasingly dependent on foreign sales. On the positive side, the combination of moderate consumption and high savings rate has kept the inflation rate in check and limited the growth of private debt. It has, however, created tensions with the United States and its southern European neighbors, leading the US Treasury Department to chastise it in its 2013 report with the following analysis:

> Germany has maintained a large current account surplus throughout the euro area financial crisis, and in 2012, Germany's nominal current account surplus was larger than that of China. Germany's anemic pace of domestic demand growth and dependence on exports have hampered rebalancing at a time when many other euro-area countries have been under severe pressure to curb demand and compress imports in order to promote adjustment. The net result has been a deflationary bias for the euro area, as well as for the world economy. Stronger domestic demand growth in surplus European economies, particularly in Germany, would help to facilitate a durable rebalancing of imbalances in the euro area.[11]

In the 2010 KOF Globalization Index, Germany ranked eighteenth in the world, which exceeded most of its European competitors as well as the United States. A number of factors are at the heart of Germany's global competitiveness. First, German industry has managed to maintain high worker productivity and high level of plant capacity utilization relative to its European competitors. This fact has been attributed to the quality of its educational system and its willingness to reinvest capital in areas of high productive capacity. Second, German industry has been able to retain its higher industrial investment rate because of a decreasing corporate debt and net interest burden. In the 1990s, the country chose to retain its core industrial capacity, forswearing the process of "deindustrialization," which has undercut US and UK global industrial competitiveness. Finally, a government-funded short-time working scheme, *Kurzarbeit*, helped keep employees, who otherwise would have been laid off during the financial crisis, on the job during the depths of the crisis. This enabled Germany companies to retain skilled labor and expertise.[12]

A key factor in the new German economy is its movement outside the euro zone to markets in Eastern Europe, Russia, the Middle East, and Asia. This is due to both the implications of unification and globalization. While Germany formally unified in 1990, unification took two decades to reach what might be called an approximation of completion. During the period, Germany transferred over $1.9 trillion to eastern Germany in investment and subsidies, an enormous burden that slowed productive investment. It is only now, with this costly transition mostly behind it, that the German economy has been able to flex its muscles and start to punch at its own weight. German trade still depends on European markets. In 1991, the EU area absorbed 51.3 percent of total German exports. While the euro zone still accounts for the largest source of German trade, growth is coming from the outside. In 2010, German exports to the euro zone had fallen to 41 percent, while Asia accounted for 16 percent (up by 4% from the year before). By the end of 2012, the effects of the European recession were being felt, and while exports to the EU remained stagnant, exports to non-EU nations jumped by more than 10 percent. German exports totaled over €1 trillion by the end of 2013. German investment has followed similar patterns. By 2014, German manufacturers invested in and imported more from China than France, and while France remains Germany's largest export market, China ranks fifth in exports and second in imports (see Figure 1.1).

German business thinks globally, and it is the German private sector that is pushing German foreign policy in many areas. Today, the business of Germany is leading, and politics follows behind. The best and brightest can be found in business rather than in politics. This has major implications for the civilian power paradigm. While economic power has always been a main component of this approach, its strategic dependence on the United States and its orientation toward western markets tempered the conflict between its political values and its economic interests. During this period, Germany emerged as what former

Import				Export
Netherlands	87	104		France
China	77	87		United States
France	65	72		United Kingdom
United States	51	71		Netherlands
Italy	49	67		China
United Kingdom	44	58		Austria
Russian Federation	42	56		Italy
Belgium	38	49		Switzerland
Switzerland	38	45		Belgium
Austria	37	42		Poland

Preliminary result:
© Statistisches Bundesamt, Wiesbaden 2013

Figure 1.1 Germany's major trading partners, 2012 in EUR bn.

chancellor Helmut Schmidt described as an economic giant but a political dwarf. With unification and the end of the Soviet Union, Germany emerged from a semi-sovereign status with less dependence on the United States and NATO for its security and growing interdependence in both Europe and globally. Germany became primarily a trading state with a strong geo-economic approach. Its role in global economic institutions, such as the G-20, the IMF, the WTO, and the World Bank, grew while it became a secondary player in NATO and within European security policy. When the Greek and other weak European economies came to Germany for bailouts, the Germans were far less "European" than they were when they were West Germans. German business and banking are also relatively less concerned with the European market as they expand into the wider world.

Germany as a geo-economic power

In my assessment, we are on the way—including German society in a broader sense—to understanding that a country of our size, with such an export orientation, that in an emergency, military deployments are necessary in order to protect our interests, for example, securing free trade routes or preventing regional instabilities, which would definitely negatively influence our trade, jobs, and incomes. This all has to be discussed, but I think we are not on such a bad track.[13]

German President Horst Köhler resigned shortly after making these remarks, yet, what he said was both accurate and unremarkable. As a trading state lacking many of the key raw materials needed to fuel its manufacturing machine, it is imperative that Germany has predictable and stable access to these raw materials, especially minerals and energy. It is also imperative that it maintains its reputation as a reliable supplier, especially in the age of just-in-time production in a global chain of production. What the former German president said is also stated in the German defense ministry's official White Book on defense policy. All of these highlight the tension between Germany the Civilian Power and Germany Inc. the export-driven economy.

The global German trading state will give priority to stable economic relationships over other considerations such as the political record of its partners, including the state of democracy, human rights, and labor rights in economic partner countries. This is an economic form of realism known as geo-economics or commercial Realpolitik, similar to that of political realism, which puts the national economic interest as the ultimate value in a state's foreign policy.[14] So, if a large trading partner, like China, exercises pressure on German business to avoid meetings with Dalai Lama, political actors will comply. When Chancellor Merkel did meet with him, all the major economic players in Germany, as well as the Social Democratic opposition's leadership, criticized her for risking German exports and jobs. She subsequently toned down her remarks on Tibet.

Edward Luttwak and a few other strategists began to recognize at the beginning of the 1990s that geo-economics was replacing geopolitics in the core or center of the globalizing international system.[15] The French analyst, Pascal Lorot, notes,

> Nations are engaged—alongside their national companies—in offensive policies to conquer external markets and to take control of sectors of activity considered to be strategic. For nations today the quest for power and assertion of their rank on the world stage depends more on their economic health, the competitiveness of their companies and the place they occupy in world trade.[16]

Globalization has only accelerated these tendencies into a zero-sum world. The increasing porousness of borders, the growing role of multinational corporations with global strategies, and the decline of the national security state have led to a switch from the territorial state to the trading and investment state. The key concerns of political leaders are with prosperity and competitiveness, not with security in the central global core. Security remains a problem in what Robert Cooper calls the premodern and modern world, and the post-9/11 focus on terrorism is an example of the threats emanating from the periphery, but the American response with its exaggeration of military power and the security nature of threats has led it to fall behind in the real competition of the twenty-first century. Germany, in contrast, has forged ahead as one of the most successful contemporary geo-economic states.[17]

This approach is in tension with the civilian power emphasis on human rights, multilateralism, and "Moralpolitik." Given contemporary Germany's historical legacy, it has been incumbent on German leaders to stress the moral high ground in foreign policy and to continuously atone for the sins of the Third Reich. The clash between these two major imperatives has been most visible in the Middle East where German companies have aggressively sought markets in a manner that has alarmed Israel. German companies have been accused of providing materials to Iraq, Libya, and Iran that could be turned against Israel in a military attack and continues to sell tanks to Saudi Arabia. German companies were heavily involved in selling the Assad regime components for their chemical weapons capability. Germans have had a special sensitivity to their moral and historical responsibility to Israel, given the Holocaust. As a nonnuclear power, it has a strong stake in a stable nonproliferation regime. Thus, while the German economic stake in Iran was substantial, it nevertheless supported economic sanctions on the Iranian government to halt its pursuit of a military nuclear capability.

As Germany moves further away from its horrific past and as a new generation of leaders born after German unification assume greater power and responsibility, the geo-economic aspect of its foreign policy will likely increase. The German geo-economic model of foreign policy is characterized by the following:

- A definition of national interest in economic terms.
- A shift from multilateralism to selective multilateralism.
- A predominant role of business and especially export-oriented business in the shaping of German foreign policy.
- The elevation of economic interests over human rights, democracy promotion, and other noneconomic interests.
- The use of economic power to impose national preferences on others.[18]

This shift has some important implications. First, it cedes overall grand strategy to business interests, especially those associated with the export market and natural resources, and reduces the role of political and administrative leaders. Within the government, this model enhances the role of the chancellor's Office, The Finance, Economics, and Technology ministries and reduces that of the Foreign and Defense ministries. At the same time, the symbiosis between business and politics is deepened in those cases in which German business has to deal with state-dominated economies, most notably in China, Russia, and the Middle East.

Second, a geo-economic approach clearly subordinates *Moralpolitik* or the concept of Germany as a normative power and lowers the priority of noneconomic values in German policy at the expense of human rights, democracy, and related considerations.[19] Stability, predictability, and reliability of Germany's reputation as a stable economic partner are paramount. In this sense, risk aversion, already a deeply embedded trait in the German political culture, is reinforced.[20]

The nature of hard security and of the military as an instrument of state influence is also transformed. As former president Köhler's remarks indicate, given the centrality of economic and especially trading interests, the military's primary role will be to protect German access to raw materials and to keep secure sea lines of communications and other key trading routes. The old roles of protecting the German homeland from invasion or of deploying forces for missions defined by NATO are clearly downgraded. In Edward Luttwak's characterization, "methods of commerce are displacing military methods."[21] At the same time, Germans can continue to comfort themselves as being antimilitarist, even pacifist, and exceptional in their rejection of the use of military force a la the United States, France, and the United Kingdom. However, as the American role in European security recedes and German industry becomes more vulnerable to threats to its lines of supply and commerce, the notion of comprehensive security will have to be redefined.

Finally, globalization in all its broad implications has reinforced these tendencies. Globalization has begun to pull Germany out of Europe as its markets have expanded and Europe has faltered as a competitor. It has also promoted a much deeper and significant shift in the distribution of power and the emergence of new non-European powers while weakening the significance and influence of the United States, a trend that was accelerated by the financial crisis and the dysfunctions of the American political system. All of these trends have weakened the anchors of Germany's foreign policy that had been founded on its ties to the West. Finally, globalization has brought with it a "zero-sum world," in which competition for markets, technology, and natural resources has accelerated.[22]

Adapting *Ostpolitik* to globalization

A major question facing Germany in this new era of zero sum competition is whether the economics *über alles* approach and the risk averse style that it encourages is compatible with strong leadership. Does Germany want to be what a former national security advisor to Chancellor Kohl calls "a greater Switzerland, where foreign policy supports commercial aims and military engagements are avoided."[23] When former German foreign minister, Joschka Fischer was asked in 2010 to characterize contemporary German foreign policy, he responded:

> The current foreign policy is essentially foreign economic policy and follows almost exclusively domestic political considerations. What is useful in the election campaign? What brings consent and what brings rejection? Where is the domestic political risk, can I take that, what does it cost me? I would call this "refusal to lead." Thereby we lose more and more of what used to be at the core of German foreign policy in the future; and what should also be at the core in the future.[24]

The advent of the strategic culture of the geo-economic state is in many ways an extension of Germany's approach to the world since the *Ostpolitik* that began in the late 1960s. The legacy of 1989 is central to the German strategic culture and its approach toward Russia. It is also an important part of the German-American divergence on Russia and lies in the lessons learned from the end of the Cold War. Germans tend to believe the Cold War ended peacefully and Germany was reunified because of détente and engagement with the other side. The German public has consistently credited Gorbachev and then foreign minister, Hans Dietrich Genscher, and not Ronald Reagan, for the peaceful ending of east-west hostilities. The lesson drawn for future policy was that dialogue, diplomacy, mutual trust, and multilateralism were the best approach for dealing with seemingly intractable opponents. When Helmut Kohl decided to support the enlargement of NATO in the 1990s, he did so with the precondition that Russia would be included through the NATO-Russia Council. Gerhard Schröder stressed diplomacy and multilateralism in contrast to the Bush approach to Iraq and formed a coalition with Russia against the Bush policies, while Angela Merkel has linked sanctions against Iran to active engagement with Iran in negotiations.

The policy of "Change Through Rapprochement" allowed it to gain the confidence of the Soviet leadership to the point that Gorbachev could accept the unification of Germany in 1990 without fear of revanchism. This approach is not only compatible with the political culture of democratic Germany but also with the imperatives of an EU Europe and the world beyond. In short, soft power and a multilateral approach enhanced German influence, prestige, and room for maneuver. Thus, the geo-economic grand strategy is an adaptation and transformation of this approach, which was shaped largely not only by the division of Germany but also by its relationship to the then Soviet Union, now Russia. The implications for Germany's relationships with contemporary Russia will be an important part of this evolution and adaptation to the new international conditions. It implies that German ties with Moscow will increase and the priority of Russia, China, and other new powers will also rise in German foreign policy. Germany will be the leading power in defining European policies toward Russia and China as well, given its growing economic power and influence in Europe.

Germans and Russians

German images of Russia

An exhibition mounted in Berlin in 2008, titled, "Our Russians, Our Germans: Images of the Other 1800–2000" explored German and Russian stereotypes of each other. It revealed long-standing German and Russian clichés about the other nation and concluded that this has been a volatile love-hate relationship on both sides. From the German perspective, war has occupied a central place in these images, as has a view of Russia as a reactionary and authoritarian society, which is often placed in stark contrast to idealized German views of themselves. During the time of Bismarck, Germans viewed Russians as Asiatics who had little to do with European culture, although some intellectuals such as Thomas Mann were taken with "the Russian soul." After World War II, West Germans viewed the USSR as a direct military and ideological threat while East Germans were presented with an image of the Russians as liberators and as a model for the new society.

Gorbachev and his reforms were supported by most East Germans, who wanted a liberalization of the moribund Honecker system. Both East and West Germans praised Gorbachev's role in the reunification of the country.[1] Another exhibition held in 2013 played out similar themes. "Russen & Deutsche" held in Berlin's Neues Museum attracted over hundred thousand visitors after a run the previous summer in Moscow.

Historical context

As these exhibitions demonstrate, Germans have been dealing with the Russians for a long time. As a description of the 2012 exhibition notes:

> The theme is established from the beginning by an intricately carved woodcut, dating to 1360 or 1370, that shows Russian hunters armed with axes, bows

and arrows, and sticks. Once they have caught their prey, they select the finest furs and hides. The Russians then approach German traders who stand, arms folded, waiting to bargain. It is clear who has the upper hand. The elegant dress and demeanor of the Germans contrast with the simple clothes of the peasant hunters. The allure of things German—money, business savvy, confidence and culture—marks the entire exhibition.[2]

As one German journalist observed in 1989, "The Russians have always played a special role in the fantasies of the Germans and the Germans in the fantasies of the Russians; that is the history of almost a thousand years which has carried over from two gruesome wars."[3] The historical memories of the two nations is a complex one, with a mixture of both horrible memories of war combined with German gratitude to Gorbachev for allowing the peaceful unification of their country. "Rome or Moscow?," this was the choice posed by Alfons Paquet, a German writer in 1920 reacting to the Bolshevik revolution. Russia was part of the never ending debate over German identity. Should Germany be a western country (Rome) or an eastern one (Moscow), a debate which comprised what Gerd Koenen has labeled the German "Russia Complex," "a long running shift between angst and admiration, a phobic defense and empathetic contribution which characterized both sides."[4]

Germany from unification in 1871 until the Bolshevik revolution was of greater importance to Russia than the other way around, providing modernization to a poor Czarist Russia in return for raw materials to feed the dynamic German industrial machine. As Angela Stent points out, "Germany became Russia's most important partner and remained so irrespective of the vagaries of diplomacy."[5] During the Weimar Republic and up to the German invasion of Russia in 1941, Germany and the USSR collaborated against the Versailles Treaty powers that had excluded them, most famously by signing the Rapallo Treaty of 1922, which "symbolized for the Western powers the ultimate act of perfidy—the Soviet state . . . making a separate deal with Germany, persuading Germany to reject its western and eastern neighbors and collaborate with Russia to the detriment of European security."[6]

At the same time there was also "The Red Menace" that was linked by the Nazis to "The Russian Menace" and a virulent anti-Communism. The linkage between the Soviet Union and an Asiatic threat to the West survived World War II and was revived during the 1980s German historian's debate in which revisionist historians relativized the crimes of Hitler with those of Stalin and causally linked Communism with Fascism.[7] There was also "a constant fear of being overrun" by Russia based on its demographic growth, "With no natural frontiers, and therefore no physical barriers in the central landmass, the threat they posed seemed very real."[8]

This fear was most immediate during the Cold War and German division with over four hundred thousand Soviet troops stationed in East Germany. The division of Germany left West Germany both threatened by and dependent upon the USSR. The key to the German question, meaning the national division, lay ultimately in Moscow. So while a key member of NATO, the Federal Republic was also a leader in developing relationships with the East as a way of ameliorating and then overcoming the division of both Europe and Germany. As Stent points out, "In this asymmetrical relationship, the USSR had more to offer the two German states than either had to offer the Soviet Union."[9]

It was the rise of Mikhail Gorbachev and his policies, which finally allowed German unification in a peaceful manner, and the Russian image benefitted greatly. Gorbachev rather than Reagan or even Helmut Kohl, was given the most credit for this historic change, a change that altered the balance in the relationship back to Germany and reopened a period similar to that of Peter the Great or Catherine in which Russia looked to Germany as the key partner in the modernization of a backward country.

All this history has left a number of legacies and images in the German consciousness. There is the legacy of geography, of a proximity that does not allow Russia to be ignored: Russia as the big neighbor. There is also the legacy of economic complementarity of a resource-rich and technology-poor Russia complementing the resource-poor, technology-rich Germany. There is a legacy both of cooperation and destruction, which is continuing to generate fear in its neighbors. Clearly the legacy of cooperation has been the dominant one since German unification in 1990.

Today Russia is not regarded as either a military or a demographic threat. Both its population and that of Germany are shrinking at a rapid and escalating pace and the Russian military threat has been displaced from the heart of Germany to a geographic remove of over a thousand kilometers. The German military no longer considers the Russian military a threat to the German homeland and has restructured its forces away from this old threat to new ones posed in the post–Cold War world. However, among German security services, Russian gangs, and transnational crime remain a serious concern as does the Russian intelligence service. Proximity remains both a problem and an opportunity.

Both Russia and Germany are in demographic decline. In 1937 there were 80 million people living in Germany, and probably around 162 million in the USSR. The projected figures for 2030 are 70 million in Germany and 131 million in Russia. Prior to World War II, close to two million Germans lived in what was the territory of the former Soviet Union. With the end of the Cold War and the disintegration of the USSR, many of these people emigrated to Germany to the point that there are now over 2.4 million immigrants from the former USSR living in Germany.[10] Of this number about 225,000 are Jews who emigrated from the former Soviet Union between 1989 and 2011, ranking Germany third only to Israel and the United States in terms of the size of its Jewish population. It is not clear what impact these immigrants have on the Russian image in Germany, but it is doubtful that it is a positive one given that they voted with their feet to leave once they could. Germans, who are world-class travelers, do not pick Russia as a tourist destination. While Germany is the number one sender of tourists to Russia with 375,285 German tourists traveling to Russia in 2012 out of a total of over 671,676 total German visitors, Russia is not among the top 15 German tourist destinations. Most who do visit the country go to St Petersburg or to Moscow. On the other hand, there has been an almost three-fold increase in the number of Russian tourists visiting Germany since 2007 to 713,000 out of a total of 1,385,365 visiting Germany in 2012.[11]

Contemporary German public opinion on Russia

German views today of that complex and ever-changing country change, but a few constants seem to remain.[12] Germans have highly ambivalent views about the Russian character and history. They view Russia today as a reemerging, potentially great power. They admire Russian culture, and many aspects of Russian history. They feel emotionally and, to some extent, culturally closer to Russians than they do to Americans. They also see Russia's untapped resources and vast market as a great opportunity for German industry and the German economy. They also believe that Russians are weak on organizational skills, tend to be highly emotional, undisciplined and in need of German leadership in technology. The image of Catherine the Great and the role of Germans in modernizing Russia has not really changed much in the twenty-first century.

While Russia to Germans is big it is also unruly and unreliable. Only about one quarter of Germans say they like Russians. When asked what they associate with Russia and Russians, vodka, alcoholism, corruption, and criminality were frequently cited along with the poor state of Russian democracy and of the Russian state. A survey conducted in 2013 found that Germans accept Russians as colleagues at work, as neighbors but only minorities would accept them as friends, bosses, or as a son or daughter-in-law.[13] Few Germans regard Russia as a democracy, a dependable partner, or as a favorable place to invest. Germans are also divided on whether Russia is a European country. They still have a concern for Russia's power based not only on its size, but also on the memory of the destruction that Russia rained on Germany in World War II.

Memories depend upon where in Germany you go. Former West Germans and East Germans have very different experiences and memories with Russians over the past 50 years. East Germans lived with over 400,000 Soviet military forces in their small country for 50 years and were fed a constant diet of propaganda by the East German authorities exalting them to "learn how to win from the Soviet people." Russian was the required foreign language and Angela Merkel was so good at it that she won a Sputnik prize as a teenager. Dissidents were arrested and deported to West Germany for hard currency and almost all of those who remained, in the assessment of a West German paper, "had a good experience" with the Russians.[14] They supported Glasnost and Perestroika and credited Gorbachev for German unification. They were continually fed anti-American propaganda and after unification became neutralists rather than supporters of NATO. Today those differences are muted and few differences can be found on east–west grounds regarding Russia, the United States, and NATO. However a Pew survey conducted in September 2013 found that while German views of Russia were negative, only 50 percent of eastern Germans had unfavorable opinion compared to 63 percent of western Germans.[15] A entire generation of eastern Germans has grown up since unification and have no historical memory of the former German Democratic Republic or of Gorbachev. Both eastern and western Germans are as ambivalent about US influence on their country as about Russian influence.[16] There was not much divergence on key demographic or political variables among Germans regarding views of Russia.[17]

German views of Russia today have to reconcile two dimensions of the strategic culture, the dimension of a trading state and that of a country that emphasizes human rights, democracy, and global norms. The German public remains skeptical and critical about the Russian state and the nature of the Russian political system but remain realist in its expectations.

On the realist side, Germans believe that Russia is a world power and that Germany has to work with it no matter the nature of its politics. Allensbach Institute polls in 2008 revealed that 62 percent of Germans regarded Russia as a world power and 45 percent believed that Russia is a land which Germany should work with as closely as possible. By 2013, in a Bertelsmann survey, the public was split over whether the German–Russian relationship was good or bad and over whether Germany should cooperate with Russia and find compromises or whether it should strongly defend its own interests in the relationship. The desire for cooperation with Russia has dropped during the Putin years and the demand for Germany to stand up to Russia has increased.

The image of the Russian polity has been negative for a while. Only 2 percent of Germans in 2008 regarded Russia as a firm democracy, 11 percent as a dependable partner, and 21 percent as a favorable place to invest.[18] The Transatlantic Trends surveys have found a substantial minority of Germans would limit cooperation with Russia in international organizations. It needs to be noted that such skepticism seems to be mutual. While Russians in general have a more favorable view of Germans, in 2008 only 30 percent thought that Germany was a firm democracy, 24 percent saw it as a dependable partner, and 24 percent as a favorable place to invest.

The Transatlantic Trends surveys have also found that Germans were worried about Russian behavior toward its neighbors, its role in providing weapons to the Middle East and its role in the Balkans, with a majority supporting security assistance to the Ukraine and Georgia (prior to the Russian actions in August 2008). Germans were concerned about Russia's role as an energy provider even before the Russian–Ukrainian energy dispute of late 2008 and early 2009, although this concern was not shared among German leaders. The German public has worried that Russia would use its energy resources as a lever, but still they see the need for energy cooperation. This reflects the realist or trading state side of the German strategic culture and provides a check on the democratic or human rights emphasis.[19]

Germans may be realists on Russia's international role, but they are exceptionally skeptical and critical of Russia's domestic politics. Germans are among the most concerned of all European publics about the weakening of democracy in Russia.[20] A Pew 2012 survey found that 64 percent of Germans had a unfavorable view of Russia, levels higher than those in Poland, the Czech Republic, and most other European states and the

United States.[21] In the 2013 edition of Transatlantic Trends only 21 percent of Germans polled had a favorable image of Russia compared to a robust 74 percent who had an unfavorable image. The EU 11 county average was 29 percent favorable and 62 percent unfavorable.[22] The Pew Research registered a marked deteroriation in the German public's opinion after Vladimir Putin's return to the Kremlin. However, the Allensbach Institute found that Germans were highly skeptical already at the beginning of Dmirti Medvedev's presidency. According to the German institute's poll, in 2008 only a quarter of Germans liked the Russians while 35 percent did not and 40 percent were undecided.

There had been a "Medvedev Effect" in German views of Russia when Medvedev assumed the Russian President's office. The Russian image has softened somewhat due to the face the young Russian projects to the outside world as compared to the macho and threatening Putin. The so-called "reset" of United States–Russian relations under the Obama administration also softened the Russian image both in Germany and the United States. The 2010 and 2011 Transatlantic Trends surveys found an improvement in the German image of Russia but kept German opinion within the European norm.[23] Similarly, a BBC 2010 poll concluded that, "Although views on Russia's influence are still predominantly negative worldwide, these have softened in the past year, after having worsened between 2008 and 2009. In the 27-country average for that survey, 37 percent held negative views and 30 percent hold positive views. Seventeen countries give Russia's influence a negative rating, seven give it a positive rating, and three are divided. Negative attitudes also moderated notably in the United States, Germany, and France, though these countries held still predominantly negative views of Russia."[24] The return of Putin to the Presidency in 2012 following the clearly rigged parliamentary elections put the Russian image into a new tailspin.[25]

As the Table 2.1 illustrates, a range of public opinion surveys come to the surprising result that Americans, and in some cases even Poles, have a less negative image of Russia than do Germans.

Pew surveys have found that in June 2007, 35 percent of Americans had an unfavorable view of Russia compared to 62 percent of Germans. By 2012 the difference had narrowed but Germans were still more negative than Americans by between 15 and 24 percent. This continued to be the case in 2013 with the German public holding a more negative view of Russia than Americans and all European publics surveyed except Sweden. A Chicago

Table 2.1 Transatlantic trends 2012/2013 German, American and European views of Russia

Views on Russia	Favorable		Unfavorable		Comment
	Very favorable	Somewhat favorable	Somewhat unfavorable	Very unfavorable	
... in Germany 2012 2013	2 2	32 31 19	50 58	63 12 16	- Unfavorable rose from 62 to 74 in a year - Sweden (76) is the only country with higher share of unfavorable - 70% is favorable about the US - 71% of Russians are favorable about Germany - only country the Germans like less are Iran (87%) and Greece (75% unfavorable), Israel also comes close (60%)
... EU	4 (2012) 3 (2013)	36 (2102) 29 (2013) 32 (2012) 26 (2013)	55 (2012) 62 (2013) 41 (2012) 43 (2013)	14 (2012) 19 (2013)	Less negative than German opinion but also declining
... US	6 (2012) 3 (2013)	42 (2012) 28 (2013) 36 (2012) 25 (2013)	48 (2012) 59 (2013) 29 (2012) 39 (2013)	19 (2012) 20 (2013)	- More favorable than the Germans but also declining over previous year

Views on Russia playing a leading role in world affairs	Desirable		Undesirable		Comment
	Very desirable	**Somewhat desirable**	**Somewhat undesirable**	**Very undesirable**	
... in Germany	33 (2012)		63 (2012)		The German image of Russia playing a leading world role tracks closely with the Russian favorability image
	27 (2013)		69 (2013)		
	3 (2012)	30 (2012)	45 (2012)	17 (2012)	
	3 (2013)	24 (2013)	49 (2013)	20 (2013)	
... EU	25 (2012)		67 (2012)		- Spain (81), Poland (74), are the only two countries with a more negative view than Germany
	26 (2013)		65 (2013)		
	4 (2012)	21 (2012)	39 (2012)	28 (2012)	
	4 (2013)	22 (2013)	37 (2013)	28 (2013)	
... US	45 (2012)		43 (2012)		- More Americans think its desirable than Germans!
	40 (2013)		46 (2013)		
	17 (2012)	28 (2012)	24 (2012)	19 (2012)	
	12 (2013)	18 (2013)	25 (2013)	21 (2013)	

Council on Global Affairs survey in 2008 found that Americans, like Germans, support talking with leaders of countries and hostile or unfriendly nations, with up to two-thirds of those surveyed supporting talks with North Korea, Cuba, and Iran.[26] This and other surveys indicate a resurgence of a realist approach to Russia and the world following the debacle of the Iraq war and the growing strains on the American economy. Even prior to the election of Barack Obama as president, polls were showing a growing American public fatigue and disenchantment with the Bush administration's approach and legacy in foreign policy, including skepticism about the ability of the United States to export democracy.[27]

The results of repeated surveys are closely related to developments in the highest levels of politics in Russia. Moreover, the majority of those asked on either side of the Atlantic do not seem believe that elections represent the Russian people's will. These suggest that the public opinion polls about a given nation's perception of Russia and Russians is heavily influenced by its public's views about President Putin. So if there is a policy gap between the United States and Germany, it is to be found at the elite level rather than with the general public in both nations and this negative attitude allowed Chancellor Merkel to take a tougher line against Putin.

The Russian image in the German media

The picture of contemporary Russia projected by the German media begins with skepticism and moves on to pronounced negative images. Covers (Figure 2.1) from the leading German weekly news magazine, *Der Spiegel*, are illustrative of the changing image of Putin's Russia.

The emphasis on Putin's role in the KGB, the Gazprom state, and his aggressive nationalism provide a sharp contrast to the idolization of Mikhail Gorbachev and the Gorbymania, which characterized German views of the leader who allowed Germany to be peacefully unified. Boris Yeltsin tended to fit the German's image of Russians as friendly alcoholics. Putin's continuing ties with former East German secret service agents has left the impression of a Russian–Stasi network operating within Germany promoting Russian interests.

These connections, which will be detailed later in this volume, have been picked up by the German media and reinforced Putin's image as a ruthless and clever operator who is only too willing to use energy as a tool of foreign policy. The German media have portrayed Putin as a "new Andropov." The Russian image hit low points during the murder of the Russian journalist Anna Politkovskaya in 2006, the war in Georgia in 2008 and the gas crisis with Ukraine in early 2009. Even during the rebound under the Medvedev presidency, the media continued to portray Putin as the real power in Russia.

Despite its own negative view, the German public believes that the image of Russia portrayed by its media is not objective and is rather negative. In a poll taken at the end of 2007, 36 percent believed the German media reported on Russia in an objective manner while 49 percent thought it did not and 44 percent thought the media portrayed Russia in a negative way compared to only 10 percent who thought it was portrayed in a positive light. However 44 percent thought the media conveyed a neutral image.[28] This view is shared by Germany's Russia watchers who view German media coverage of Russia as negative and critical, although documentaries and travel coverage are more positive. They lament the decline in the number of German journalists in Russia and the impact of budget cuts on their coverage.[29]

Russians and pro-Russian Germans have actively tried to influence media coverage of Russia. The Berlin exhibitions on Germany and Russia were

Figure 2.1 The covers from upper left to lower right read *Who Is Putin: Russia's New Alliance between KGB and capital; Russia's Energy: Return to World Power; The Gazprom State: Putin's Energy Empire; The Dangerous Neighbor: Vladimir Putin and the Powerlessness of the West;* Covers used with the permission of Der Spiegel.

sponsored by German energy concerns with extensive dealings with Russia, Wintershall and later E.ON. WINGAS Chairman Dr Rainer Seele explained the rationale:

> It is quite natural that Germany not only maintains good business relations with Russia, but also cultivates a political exchange. At WINGAS, with our German-Russian background, we consider it our social and political responsibility to encourage people to think about stereotypes and deep-seated ideas . . . It is our wish that our commitment to the exhibition and the studies will trigger a debate on stereotypes and prejudices between Germans and Russians and provide a forum for these discussions. The ultimate goal is to promote understanding and openness towards each other.[30]

The public opinion survey conducted at the time by the polling group Forsa, was paid for by Wintershall as well. The 2012–13 exhibition, which focused on energy ties, evoked the following comment from *Die Welt*: "This exhibition is being sponsored by the energy company E.ON, which is a reminder of which energies really tie Russia and Germany together."[31] The depiction of the German–Russia relationship was very selective and excluded mentions of the partition of Poland, the Molotov-Ribbentrop Pact or the suppression of the 1953 uprising of East Germans. As the *Tagesspiegel* observed, "This is an appalling gap. Both sides must face the truth that in the past they were never closer to each other than during this moment of the most awful policy of violence."[32]

The views of German business tend to be more upbeat about Russia than those of the general public or the think tanks and media. German business groups are more prominent and present in Russia than NGOs and with over six thousand German firms present in Russia, their concerns center around the safety and reliability of their investments. The rule of law and enforcement of contracts seem to be their main concern. Bribery and corruption are a continual problem. A survey conducted of their members by the Ost-Auschuss business lobby conducted in January 2013 found that German business remained upbeat over prospects in the Russian market. Half of those surveyed had experienced an improvement in the business climate in Russia, and 83 percent expected more positive developments in 2013 and believed that the climate in Russia was better than in the EU. Almost two-thirds planned on increasing their investments leading to a total of 800 million euro in new investments. Eighty percent wanted an end to the visa requirement between the EU and Russia and the majority expected the Russian government to do something to address the deficiencies in the Russian work force. Energy, raw materials, and automobiles were the branches with the highest expectations. Bureaucracy, corruption, and customs regulations were the areas seen to be in greatest need of reform in the view of those surveyed. Only 14 percent saw any negative effects of the third Putin presidency.[33]

Germans and Russian democracy

The German approach to the problem of Russia's democratic deficit has been to apply its tried and time-tested approach of change through engagement. The term "modernization partnership" characterizes this approach and was formally announced by Frank Walter Steinmeier when he was Foreign Minister in the first Grand Coalition government with Angela Merkel. It was reaffirmed by his successor, Foreign Minister Westerwelle, in a speech commemorating the landmark speech of Egon Bahr at Tützing, which began the Ostpolitik. Westerwelle reaffirmed the Bahr approach in the age of globalization, arguing that close economic networks can contribute to overcoming remaining lines of division with "change through trade" ("*Wandel durch Handel*").[34]

This approach is compatible with the promotion of German economic interests while offering a rationale to those concerned about human rights. As with the Ostpolitik, the modernization partnership is based on the concept of modernization through interdependence. It assumes that Russia cannot be changed through pressure from the outside but only through continual and nonthreatening interaction and interdependence, which will lead to change from within. This is the mantra of German business leaders who claim that through their presence they are gradually introducing the rule of law and the beginnings of a *Rechtstaat*. It is the approach reinforced by Westerwelle in 2013:

> German foreign policy is value bound and led by interests. Very often these are often two sides of the same coin. . . . When we represent German economic interests abroad responsibility driven German concerns can act as examples of microcosms of western values. They bring affluence and set standards in rising countries. In this way the introduction of a self conscious middle class, the rule of law and political participation is promoted.[35]

This approach is based in part on Germany's path to democracy, which began in the Wilhelminian period as a state based on the rule of law that was evolving into a parliamentary democracy when World War I broke out. The Weimar experience also influences German views of Russia today. The German historical consciousness recalls the experience of a new democracy burdened with the weight of economic bad times and imposed by outside powers. There is a substantial part of German elite opinion, which believes that Russia is almost genetically an authoritarian society and which tends to look to the strong leader for guidance. Alexander Rahr, perhaps Germany's most influential Russia watcher, has characterized Russian political culture as one in which the rule of law is a foreign concept. Russians, he contends, have no positive association with democracy and are deeply convinced that their politicians are corrupt and accept this. Russians suffer from a "Weimar Complex," in which democracy translates into corruption and anarchy.[36] Germans think that they know Russians better than any other Europeans and much better than Americans, who are regarded as well-meaning but naïve in their approach to Russia. Democracy cannot be imposed from without but only slowly and gradually through working with those in power.[37] This experience both shaped and was reinforced by the EU enlargement approach to spreading democracy. Germany was a major advocate of the enlargement of both the EU and NATO to east central Europe and saw this as a noncoercive way of expanding democratic norms.

These impressions seem to be widely shared at the elite level. A survey of German Russia watchers taken in the fall of 2009 found the majority, while believing Russia is more open than at any time in the last three to four hundred years, did not believe that Russia is a democracy in the Western sense but is rather something between an authoritarian system, a defective democracy with authoritarian characteristics, a guided democracy, or a sham democracy.[38] They rated the political system as stable and believed that a rapid democratization would threaten stability and even result in a social explosion. However even in 2009, Germany's Russia specialists worried about the growing division between society and state, fostered by rampant corruption, growing income inequalities, a lack of rule of law, and an economy too reliant on energy and other raw material exports. Russia was in need of a thorough modernization but the obstacles in the bureaucracy and the political elite may be too great. The chances for democratization were not assessed as good because democracy was associated with disorder and decline.[39] The protest movements that emerged in Russia in 2011 have challenged this view but has not fundamentally altered it.

There are two main schools of thought in Germany on dealing with this Russian dilemma: one that believes that more networking with Russia will lead to its Westernization and another that believes that it is an authoritarian country, which cannot be integrated or embedded in Western structures.[40] Added to this is a broad discussion on what modernization means. Most Germans still believe that Russia will only be modern when it modernizes its society and political system and they differentiate between Putin's technological definition of modernization and Medvedev's, which includes both political and social modernization. As one Christian Democratic parliamentarian put it, "modernization requires democracy and the security of the law."[41]

There is, however, a debate within Germany on the impact of passivity on Germany's view of itself. A lead on a leading German television news program following the Petersburg Dialogue meeting of 2010 declared, "A Lot of Business and a Little Human Rights." Gernot Erler, a leading Social Democrat parliamentarian and close advisor on Russia policy in the Steinmeier Foreign Office, and thus one of the architects of "modernization through interdependence," agreed that "Human rights, the development of society in Russia and what Germany can contribute to it have been pushed into the background in recent years."[42]

The Greens have been outspokenly critical of the human rights situation in Russia and Germany's economic accommodation to the realities of Putin's Russia as has the Federal Commissioner for Human Rights, Markus Löning, an Free Democrat parliamentarian. The parliamentary coordinator for German–Russian relations, Andreas Schockenhoff, has also been critical of political and human rights abuses in Russia as has the leading Christian Democrat Russia critic, Eckart von Klaeden. Yet the view remains in both major parties that continued engagement with Russia is the only option. There is a consensus that Putin's system still has broad public support, perhaps more than the regime in Beijing, and that the opposition is weak and divided.

German political foundations and NGOs remain active in Russia but have been limited by the sanctions imposed on NGO activities by Russian legislation. The Green's foundation, The Heinrich Böll Stiftung, issued a statement strongly critical of the state of Russian democracy following the 2011 Petersburg Dialogue meeting and has undertaken numerous efforts to work with Russian civil society. The FDP affiliated Naumann Stiftung has also been critical, stating that Russian rhetoric on democratization, including that of Medvedev, is "only rhetoric."[43] A new law that went into effect in November 2012 required organizations operating in Russia and receiving funds from abroad to register as "foreign agents." It not only revived a term used by Stalin, but a law that has had tangible adverse effects on international NGOs. The U.S. Agency for International Development was expelled from Russia weeks before the law even came into effect, the police have conducted "tax raids" in the offices of several other organizations and some of them are or have faced charges for their failure to register as "foreign agents" in front of the court.[44] The crackdown on foreign NGOs not only affected globally well-known international organizations, such as the Human Rights Watch or Amnesty International, but also German political foundations. In March 2013, prosecutors launched investigations at the offices of both the CDU-affiliated Konrad Adenauer Foundation and SPD-affiliated Friedrich Ebert Foundation.[45]

A major problem facing German civil rights advocates is the disjointed nature of Russian civil society. In the estimate of the Friedrich Ebert Stiftung:

> "In Russia there are both engaged citizens and NGOs. However, in a Russia-specific expression: engaged and organized civil society are not linked to each other, but are growing apart. The amendment of the NGO law of 2006 has further increased the latently hostile attitude of the state apparatus towards the NGOs. In Russia, unlike in West European countries, there are no state or tax incentives for engagement in organizations that serve the common good." [46]

The director of the Ebert office in Moscow summed up the situation following the Khodorkovsky trial as: "legal nihilism."

The official German government reactions to the human rights and democracy deficits in Russia has tended toward the Realpolitik and Russia is fundamentally authoritarian approaches until late 2012. A close look at the statements on Russia coming out of the Foreign Office and the Chancellor's Office show that while human rights issues were mentioned, the tone remained noncommittal. State Secretary Werner Hoyer of the Foreign Office warned in 2009 against "anti Russian hysteria while on the other side, saying to our Russian friends what goes and what doesn't." He went on to argue that Russia is "more a European country than one thinks," and should consider itself a part of Europe and embed itself in European structures. In other statements Hoyer argued for avoiding "charges from the Cold War period," and Foreign Minister Westerwelle referred to the "strategic partnership" with Russia and that human rights "are always a theme" in his visits to Russia. These statements contrasted with those of the Commissioner for Human Rights in the Foreign Office, Markus Löning, who was more direct and outspoken referring to the Khodorkovsky verdict as "a farce," which "raises considerable doubts on the legal justice system," and promising to support human rights activists in the future. This contrasted with Westerwelle's reaction which spoke of "a setback on the way toward the modernization of the country." These statements also stood in contrast to those made regarding Belarus, where much more direct and harsh language was used.[47]

The same patterns held for statements by the chancellor who spoke of "having built a completely new partnership with Russia . . . in spite of all the human rights questions," or of her "disappointment" over the Khodorkovsky verdict. In her remarks before the Ost-Auschuss in October 2010, she referred to Russia as "our great partner in the region," and went on,

> I believe our relations with Russia have radically changed over the past twenty years. I will very clear say that I have the strong conviction that Russia is not just a strategic partner on paper, but that Germany and the entire European Union have an immense interest to bind Russia more strongly to Europe . . . I believe the modernization strategy that President Medvedev is pushing with the government and Prime Minister Putin, is the key to success.[48]

In contrast in referring a few months earlier to the murder of the human rights activist Natalia Estremirova, Merkel noted, "It is important that more is done to clarify what happened." In the same statement she referred to the round six thousand German firms active in Russia and the potential for economic cooperation.[49] At a press conference with President Medvedev on July 15, 2010 she stated, "We naturally discussed the murder of Natalia Estemirova. I understand that the investigation is on- going and that we can't disturb it, and that it will be carried out in a reasonable manner." There was a pattern in the statements by the Chancellor and her press spokesman to simply react in a noncommittal way to obvious incidents picked up by the media but to generally downplay them and stress areas of cooperation with Russia. This remained the case in the face of growing public protests in Russia in December 2011 against electoral fraud in the December parliamentary elections. While US secretary of state, Hilary Clinton was quite clear in calling the elections "neither free nor fair," at a meeting of the Organization for Security and Cooperation in Europe, German Foreign Secretary Westerwelle said "we have taken note of the reports by OSCE election monitors in Russia with concern."[50]

The tone of Merkel and Westerwelle sharpened significantly as the vestiges of Russian democracy were eliminated by Putin in 2013. Westerwelle in his June 2013 speech on Ostpolitik and globalization referred to the German relationship to Russia in more balanced terms than were the case prior to 2012.

> Our cooperation with Russia is broad and diverse. Trade has reached record levels, while cultural and academic exchange is more intensive and closer than ever before. On a political level, Russia and Germany, Russia and the EU, are working together in a strategic partnership. We're bound by numerous common interests and we're cooperating closely in many spheres, from the G8, Afghanistan and the efforts to combat piracy off the Horn of Africa to the E3+3 talks on Iran. However, there are also differences and many observers currently believe that what divides us is growing at a faster pace than what we have in common. We're

concerned about the treatment of political opponents and civil society, about selective criminal prosecution and about the discrimination against homosexual people. We aren't ignoring these concerns and differences. For we have a common frame of reference, jointly agreed standards on democracy, the rule of law, and the protection of human dignity. Russia and Germany are both members of the OSCE, we're both members of the Council of Europe. A policy of confrontation toward Russia would achieve nothing. We have to speak frankly but with respect with one another. What we need is strategic patience and political creativity.[51]

Yet the pull of both economic interests and the German political culture have prevented any major changes in policy, as opposed to rhetoric. This tug of war between interests and values continues. While Westerwelle contended that there is no such distinction and that interests are closely related to values, others argue that Germany should push its values in order to promote its interests. As one keen observer of the German political scene, Constanze Steltzenmueller put it,

> Germany will have to understand that this new approach is not just about interests and strategy but also about solidarity, namely, defending the rights of countries that seek safety, prosperity, and democratic values and freedoms: the aspirations Obama spoke of in Berlin last summer and that the United States once protected in West Germany. To the extent that Russia acts to deny these essential rights, Germany and all of Europe must comprehend that they are being confronted with an authoritarian challenge to liberal Western democracy. For reasons of moral self-preservation as much as solidarity, balancing is then no longer an option. That, in the end, is the answer to the new German question.[52]

The Moscow correspondent for the liberal weekly, Die Zeit, while exploring all the violations of the democratic constitution of Russia, concluded:

> Establishing human rights in Russia will take longer than many in the West hope. Doubts about the universality of Western values will still dominate the discussions in which "Russia's own way" is evoked. The unease with "values imperialism" is often mixed with political practicality as Putin's system of "autocracy light" reacts with hostility to any sort of organized opposition. Democracy has to be "directed" in accordance with the ideas of the political elite. It must not be out on the streets, but should be a like a play in the powerless Parliament. However, the real decisions in the Kremlin are hardly transparent. This could change if the emerging middle class would call for political participation and basic rights. So far there has been little evidence of this.[53]

The challenge of this new authoritarianism, what Johannes Vosswinkel calls authoritarian light, is part of a larger challenge to the Western liberal order. It can be seen in the "Beijing consensus," "Asian values," and closer to Europe not only in Russia but also in Hungary. Simply put, can authoritarian systems that deliver economic growth and stability, and allow their subjects (they cannot be called citizens) to travel freely pose a viable alternative the liberal model? Ivan Krastev has raised this problem in a compelling way.

First, Russia is a light version of authoritarianism in that, as Krastev rightly points out, "most Russians today are freer than in any other period of their history. They can travel, they can freely surf the Web . . . and they can do business if they pay their 'corruption tax.'"[54] Second, it is not an ideological regime but rather one which "presents itself as a variant of, not as an alternative to, Western democracy." Finally it is, unlike China, not a success but rather a dysfunctional and uninspiring place, characterized by Krastev as "zombie authoritarianism."

The German response to this challenge is likely to be muted because the "German idea of freedom" has also put a great emphasis on what political scientists call positive freedom rather than the American emphasis on "negative freedom." Germans have emphasized, at least since the beginning of Bismarck's welfare state, the positive role of the state in providing economic security and social equality. The American model, in contrast, emphasized the freedom of the individual and the negative freedom associated with limiting the role of the state.German Liberalism in the European sense has been weak while a social democratic approach modified by Christian Democracy after World War II has resulted in a consensus around the social market economy.[55] In addition, as Ralf Dahrendorf taught, Germans have always had a preference for an apolitical, neutral state run by bureaucratic or technocratic "experts."[56] German political history in the twentieth century reinforced these tendencies. Finally the risk-averse nature of German culture has placed a high priority on predictability and reliability. It is no accident that Germans are the world's best engineers. All of this means that in assessing the state of Russian democracy, Germans are likely to be more sympathetic to a stable and calculable system that may be short on democratic liberties to one that is unstable and unpredictable. Throw in a jaundiced view of the Russian character with its emotionalism and violence and you have a tendency to prefer a soft authoritarian Russia, with a version of a market economy, to an open but wild and unpredictable one. The legacy of the George W. Bush Administration in its efforts at democracy promotion and the failure of American efforts to reform Russia or to impose democracy in Iraq have left most Germans even more skeptical about pushing democracy in authoritarian countries, especially those with which they do a lot of business.

Germany of course has changed a great deal since Dahrendorf wrote his classic study. Three generations have grown up since the 1960s and at least one new generation in the former East Germany has been socialized in a democratic republic. As noted, the Greens in particular, have been in favor both of a more open and participatory Germany and therefore have desired a Russia on similar lines. However the Europeanization of Europe and especially of Germany have also reinforced a bureaucratic approach to governing. The famous "democratic deficit" of the European Union has not fostered a democratic revolution in Europe against the French style technocracy of Brussels. Thus Germans can live with a "guided democracy" in Russia just as they can successfully live with Communist China and with technocratic European authorities imposting conditions on national governments like in Italy and Greece. The disillusionment with Europe, which is emerging in Germany as one consequence of the European debt crisis, has also weakened German confidence in the European model and confidence in the "Anglo-American" liberal model, which was never terribly strong to begin with has all but vanished.

The idea of democracy promotion in the American sense is also not really in the German lexicon. There is no German exceptionalism along the lines of American Wilsonianism and no sense of being "a city on the hill." The long, complicated and extensive history of the German–Russian relationship creates a different context for the approach of German foundations. Of the six German political foundations operating in Russia, only the Heinrich Boell Foundation, which is close to the Green party, and the Friedrich Naumann Foundation, which is close to the FDP, focuses on human rights and working with NGOs. The Friedrich Ebert Foundation, which is close to the SPD, tends to concentrate more on social democratic concerns such as social policy and security issues and works with state related players on the grounds that "the state in Russia decides, like it or not."[57] Again the legacy of the Brandt *Ostpolitik* is pervasive here. The German foundation approach differs from those of American NGOs such as Freedom House, or the Republican and Democratic Institutes in that the Germans don't want to convince Russians to be Germans while there is a sense that the US groups are trying to Americanize Russians. "We see the Russians as partners with whom we must work and take a long term approach which features continuous dialogues and bringing younger Russians to Germany."[58]

In the German case, therefore, it is not so much that economics trumps democracy as that the German version of democracy is open to living with light versions of authoritarian systems, particularly if they remain as open as Krastev contends. Particularly if these systems allow some form of market economy and reward foreign investment there will be little incentive for democratic crusades, especially from geo-economic or trading states that are not in military competition. To quote Krastev,

> The new authoritarian regimes' lack of any ideology also partly explains why the democratic world is reluctant to confront them. They do not seek to export their political models, and hence they are not threatening. The new authoritarian regimes do not want to transform the world or to impose their system on other countries. So the axis of conflict is no longer the free world versus the world of authoritarianism- it is more the free world versus the world of free riding.[59]

This is the source of tension between the United States and Germany as the American economic stake in Russia is minimal while a geopolitical competition continues. While the theory of democratic peace originated with a German thinker, Immanuel Kant, and has wide acceptance among German international relations theorists and with Guido Westerwelle, who stated in his Tutzing comments that, "peace is best guaranteed between democracies," there is no alternative concern that Russia poses a realist threat to German security. Russia is more of a problem to be managed than a threat to be confronted. While a public perception of Russia as a great power continues in Germany, it remains seen as a defensive and insecure power rather than an expansionist one.

The real challenge facing German policy is that the Ostpolitik paradigm is no longer seen to be promoting democracy in Russia. Handel is not producing Wandel. German business remains content to deal with an authoritarian state so long as it offers a stable and reliable investment environment. The public is more negative but still has a realist view about the need to live with a big Russia and remains skeptical that it can be changed from the outside. Yet the gap between values and interests is widening and the easy optimism expressed by Westerwelle that the two are compatible is becoming less sustainable in the face of the Putin state.

Who Makes Russia Policy?

The key players in the German policy process on Russia are the German government, the major political parties, and German business. Russia policy is what might be called "intermestic," a combination of domestic and international policies given the interweaving of the Russian and German economies. This means that not only are a number of ministries that deal with foreign and security policy involved in policy formulation, but also a number that are considered domestic ministries. The German private sector is especially important in this policy area as well.

The political parties and the Bundestag

While there is a broad consensus in Germany that Russia must be engaged rather than merely contained, there are some differences between the two main parties and these are reflected in differences between the Chancellor's Office and the Foreign Office. The parties and the Bundestag play a role in Russia policy and foreign policy in general, although less significant than that played by the government. Most politicians see their careers in domestic policies and view foreign policy as a specialization with few prospects for career advancement. Foreign policy has been the domain of the Government (i.e. the executive branch) not the parliament. Given the nature of the parliamentary system in Germany, Members of the German Bundestag (MdBs) tend to specialize in a policy area and stay within that policy area throughout their careers, serving on the relevant committees and acting as spokespersons for their party groups, or *Fraktionen* on their policy areas. Their positions are coordinated with the parliamentary party leadership and, if their party is in the Government, with the relevant ministry. A number of parliamentarians serve as State Secretaries in the ministries and serve as links between the party, parliament, and Government.

On Russia policy there are few Russia specialists in the parties or in the Bundestag. Andreas Schockenhoff, a CDU MdB served as Coordinator for German–Russian Inter-societal Cooperation and Markus Löhning, FDP, was Federal Government Commissioner for Human Rights Policy and Humanitarian Aid in the Black–Yellow coalition, and have been influential on the civil society aspects of German–Russian relations. The Foreign Affairs Committee tends to have jurisdiction on most aspects of Russia policy and has a few members who have been more active on Russia including Marieluise Beck of the Greens, Ralf Mützenich of the SPD, and Philipp Missfelder of the CDU. Gernot Erlor, who was Deputy Floor Leader of the SPD group and returned to the Foreign Office in the second Steinmeier term, has also been a major figure in the party on Russia policy. Three of the most senior figures, Ruprecht Polenz, CDU, Rainer Stinner, FDP, and Hans Ulrich Klose, SPD, have been influential voices but left the Bundestag after the 2013 elections. Their departure left a major void not only on Russia but on foreign policy in general with few immediately visible successors.

In general, there are two broad views in the German policy debate on Russia. There is the human rights and values faction, which focuses on the democratic and human rights situation in Russia. The second main grouping emphasizes a realist or economic approach and advocates a strategic economic partnership with Russia.[1] The Greens and some of the CDU are in the former group as well as many NGOs and civil society organizations while the latter is dominated by the SPD and German business groups. The Free Democrats have been divided between a pragmatic faction and a human rights faction. Their departure from the Bundestag following the 2013 election has removed them as players in foreign policy for at least the next four-year term of the parliament.

The SPD, both the leadership and the base, are more likely to lean closer to Russia than is the CDU. This is due not only to the legacy of Gerhard Schröder and his appointed successor, Frank Walter Steinmeier, but also to a cultural and political affinity to Russia and a distancing from America, which can be traced back as far as the first postwar SPD leader, Kurt Schumacher, who preferred a neutral and unified Germany to an Atlanticist and divided one. This was followed by Brandt's Ostpolitik that left a deep détente culture in the party. The SPD in the 1980s had an intensive dialogue on values with the East German Communist (SED) party and attributed the end of the German division largely to Gorbachev and Soviet policy.[2] The closeness of the Social Democrats to Russia reached its apogee under the Chancellorship of Gerhard Schröder, when the

SPD accelerated a shift toward Moscow and away from Washington, a shift that was ameliorated by the Presidency of Barack Obama.

Schröder came into office critical of the overly personalized "sauna diplomacy" of Helmut Kohl with Boris Yeltsin. The Russian financial crisis of 1998 and Yeltsin's physical deterioration had brought the Russian image to a low point in Germany. The arrival of Putin on the scene in June 2000 and the first get acquainted meeting with Schröder gradually warmed into a close political and personal relationship between the leaders. As one of Schröder's former aides in the Chancellor's Office put it, "They came from similar backgrounds and both fought their way up." They were both from poor families and worked their way up the political ladder by intelligence, guile, charisma, and ambition. Both studied law and were cynics about power. They both liked wealth and the good life, having been deprived of it as youths. Schröder was an "Armani Socialist," part of the so-called Tuscany wing of the left (the German equivalent of American limousine liberals), and someone who liked his association with industrial bosses from his time on the Volkswagen board. Putin made himself one of the wealthiest men in Russia through his use of protection arrangements with the oligarchs.

The recovery of the Russian economy under Putin opened up new opportunities for the German economy while the alliance between Putin and Schöder against the Iraq war solidified the relationship. The break between the Schröder government and the Bush administration over Iraq pushed Germany into a coalition with France and Russia against the United States for the first time since the formation of the Federal Republic in 1949 and marked a major turning point in German foreign policy.[3] Russia policy had been a *Chefsache* or Chancellor's policy, already under Kohl, and this became even more the case with Schröder.[4] As one former German diplomat and former ambassador to Russia put it, "In Putin's Russia, nothing happens unless you talk to the president. Schröder was perfect for that."[5]

After Schröder lost the Bundestag election of 2005, his chief aide, Frank Walter Steinmeier, who had played a key role in developing this relationship in the Chancellor's Office, continued Schröder's policies when he became Foreign Minister under the first Merkel government. It was Steinmeier and his top aide, Gernot Erler, who developed the policy of "Modernization through Interdependence" in dealing with Russia. Schröder also made an infamous statement labeling Putin in 2004 as a "flawless democrat" and reaffirming in 2012 after the Russian parliamentary elections that he did not take back this assessment, but he did tell one aide later that he regretted saying this with the comment, "what does it really mean?"[6] Schröder played on the realist tendency in the SPD that regards Russia as the Big Neighbor, one that must be accommodated. Even the Atlanticist former Chancellor, Helmut Schmidt, was quoted in 2003 as saying, "Russia poses far less of a threat to world peace today, than for example, the United States." Schmidt went on to describe Putin as "an enlightened potentate."[7] Add to this the importance of German energy companies in the heartland of SPD political power, North Rhine Westphalia, and there remains a powerful Russia realist group within the party.

There is also a smaller democracy promotion faction within the party. Frank Walter Steinmeier has characterized the larger debate on Russia as follows: *Principle Free Realpoliticians*, who don't worry about human rights but limit Russia policy to economics and energy or, if they are older, to security policy. *Incorrigible Do Gooders* who ignore all reality and believe that Russia can be changed only through the force of their outrage. He set these up as straw men and as clever and relatively dumb clichés and urged a more open and less fundamentalist debate, arguing that this is not over who is a better democrat but what is the best way to promote change.[8] The clear affinity for Obama within the Social Democrats and the reset policy of his administration toward Russia in his first term substantially narrowed the gap with the United States, or at least with the Democrats, on Russia policy. The return of tensions to the United States–Russian relationship in Obama's second term could open up old fault lines with the SPD.

The Christian Democrats under Kohl had moved from his early characterization of Gorbachev as Goebbels in 1986 to his close relationship with the last Soviet leader who had enabled German unification. Kohl put a lot of stake in personal relationships throughout his political career, and practiced sauna diplomacy with Boris Yeltstin. He did all he could to ensure that Russia would not be isolated over NATO enlargement and was central to the creation of what later became the NATO-Russia Council. After Kohl left office in 1998, the CDU was as critical of Schröder's Russia policies as Schröder was of Kohl's while in opposition. It pledged that if it won the 2005 election there would no longer be a Berlin–Paris–Moscow axis and called for "clear words" from the German Chancellor on the suppression of human rights in Russia.

Following the return of the CDU to power in 2005 in the Grand Coalition government, despite a tension between the realist "Silence for Gas" policy and the value-based "Speaking and Gas" policy,[9] Russia policy remained fully economized under the modernization partnership led by Steinmeier and the Foreign Office planning staff. As one of Germany's most experienced Russia watchers, Hannes

Adomeit, wrote of this concept, "Divested of its rhetoric, it's central idea is to help Russia overcome the perennial lopsidedness of its economy—preponderance of raw materials, notably oil and gas, and lags in technological innovation and global competitiveness—and at the same time increase the export and investment opportunities of German industry in Russia."[10]

The values faction of the CDU remained concerned about this tendency and pressed for more emphasis on the human rights dimension in German policy and for more concern for the views of the Central European partners in NATO and the EU, especially Poland.[11] This view found some support within the Chancellor's Office both with the Chancellor herself and with one of her key advisors, Eckhard von Klaeden. Von Klaeden, a leading Russia critic, estimated that 60 percent of his party supported his view, implying that close to a majority did not.[12] The geo-economic realist part of the party had formed an informal alliance with the SPD on Russia policy using the concept of a modernization partnership as a means of bridging the values and interests approach by tying economic modernization to advances in human rights and thus appeasing both factions. The short life of the concept is proof that the linkage did not work.[13]

Chancellor Merkel, as she has done on so many issues, straddled both sides. While seeing the need for a stable and constructive relationship with Russia, her formative years in East Germany left her with a strong concern for freedom and democratic rights. Her realist side was shared by her top foreign policy advisor, Christoph Heusgen, who in a meeting on November 22, 2006 with Deputy Assistant Secretary, David Kramer, said about the relationship with Russia that it is a "frustrating one," but "we have to work with these guys, we need them on Iran and other things."[14]

Russia policy remained relatively unchanged during the Grand Coalition, with Merkel emphasizing the importance of Russia and Russian energy. As one observer noted at the time, "with Angela Merkel, sobriety replaced the personal relationship that had existed between Boris Yelstin and Helmut Kohl, as well as the one between Gerhard Schröder and Vladimir Putin," yet although she was critical of Schröder's policy, "she never developed alternative concepts of her own."[15] The *Spiegel* observed, "Cronyism is gone but the cooperation continues."[16] The relationship with Russia began to deteriorate during the last year of the Grand Coalition. The short Georgia–Russia war and the energy crisis brought on by the confrontation between Russia and Ukraine and then with Belarus forced Steinmeier to stop talking about a modernization partnership.[17]

In its 2009 electoral manifesto, the CDU stated that "We want relations with Russia to be as close as possible, but that the depth and breadth of relations depend on Russia's behavior and willingness to meet its international obligations and play by the rules."[18] The 2009 elections resulted in the replacement of the Grand Coalition with a Black–Yellow one of CDU/CSU and FDP. This was followed by the return of Putin to the Presidency in 2012 and the growing suppression of human rights and democracy activists, including German NGOs. As a result of both developments, members of the CDU fraction in the Bundestag became more vocal in their criticism of developments in Russia.

Leading the way was Andreas Schockenhoff, the German Special Envoy for Russia and the Civil Society representative at the Petersburg Dialogue meeting. Schockenhoff was placed in this position by Merkel, who believed that the Petersburg Dialogue was one with too many Soviet holdovers and resembled the old Soviet tactic of transmission of the party line rather than dialogue. She wanted to change this by bringing in civil society and wanted Schockenhoff to play this role. He prepared a motion on Russia in the Bundestag in November 2012 stating, "The German Bundestag seriously worries that Russia will be facing stagnation instead of progress on its path toward building an open and modern society due to the deficit of rule of law, investments and innovation."[19] The Foreign Ministry rewrote this to read that Russia is "the key and essential partner of Germany and Europe . . . the largest state in the world that stretches through two continents . . . and is the crucial energy supplier in Europe." They added that global problems could only be solved with Russian participation.

Within the FDP, both the former party leader and Foreign Minister, Guido Westerwelle, and the chief foreign policy spokesman, Werner Hoyer, in opposition had been critical of the SPD's Russia approach and had favored nuclear power as a way of easing German energy dependence on Russia.[20] However, the legacy of long-time leader and Foreign Minister, Hans Dietrich Genscher, remained with the party, a legacy that would engage Russia and seek to ensnare it in a web of dependency.

The Greens have been the most critical of Russia on human rights grounds. They are also deeply suspicious of the collaboration between Russian and German energy companies, which they see as blocking the move toward renewable energy sources. One of the most prominent critics is Marieluise Beck, a member of the Bundestag and of the Foreign Affairs Committee. She received applause during the debate on the Schockenhoff motion when she referred to bribes paid by Siemens and Daimler in Russia and stating that they were not able to raise their voice in defense of the foundations of the rule of law. The Greens have the best contacts of all the German parties to Russian civil society. Although they accepted Schröder's Russia policy when they were in coalition with the SPD, they have less hope that Russia will modernize.

The SPD has not had the intensive debate over Russia, which the CDU and Greens have experienced. There is no Social Democratic Schockenhoff. The party faction abstained on the Bundestag resolution of November 2012 and in the words of one party insider, has been "stunned by the new moral approach which forgets the interest based policy."[21] Steinmeier continues to hold the view that engagement with Russia remains the most viable policy as there is more to the German–Russian relationship than just the human rights dimension, but has open questions on whether this should be discussed and is still valid.[22]

He confirmed this upon his return to the Foreign Ministry in the renewed Grand Coalition government at the end of 2013. He replaced Schockenhoff with Gernor Erler as the Parliamentary State Secretary in charge of German–Russian relations. Steinmeier in his first visit to Moscow after returning to the Foreign Office stating, "It is important to me at the beginning of my second term to offer a confidence full and constructive cooperation with Moscow." He had also written in an article in a German magazine that, "We need Russia for the practical solution for all security policy crises and conflicts of our time."[23]

While the passage of a compromise version of the Bundestag resolution passed in 2012, it indicated that, "the German political establishment across the political spectrum is increasingly worried about the direction in which Putin is taking Russia."[24] Despite this critique, there remains a broad German consensus on an approach of hedged cooperation and integration.[25] But this is accompanied by a growing sense in German policy and opinion-shaping circles that the hopes invested in the Medvedev era that Russia was moving in the direction of democracy have been crushed and that the engagement paradigm has failed. Yet it is unlikely that this represents the beginning of a paradigm shift in German policy as there remains no real alternative to some form of continued engagement.

Inside the German government

Chancellor's office and foreign ministry

As a leading expert in the study of German foreign policy, William Paterson, has noted, "A foreign minister has the advantage of inheriting a huge specialist ministry with embassies around the globe while a chancellor has to build up a specialist foreign policy staff in the Chancellor's Office. A foreign minister unlike a chancellor can devote almost all his/her time to foreign affairs while a chancellor has a quite different and hectic schedule (Helmut Schmidt calculated that no chancellor could devote more than ten percent of time to foreign affairs.)"[26] When Steinmeier and the SPD were part of her coalition, Merkel tended to defer to the Foreign Office on Russia policy, or at least to take it into account. Steinmeier brought his experience from running the Chancellor's Office for Gerhard Schröder to the Auswärtiges Amt (AA) and was the major architect of Russia policy during his term. The Chancellery was restrained in its support of Steinmeier's concept of "Rapprochement through closer ties" (*Annährung durch Verflechtung*), expressed in a policy paper produced by the AA while he was Foreign Minister. There was always a certain tension and rivalry between the two bureaucracies during this period, heighted by the fact that both parties were practically equal in their parliamentary representation and were temporary partners soon to be electoral rivals.

After her victory in the 2009 election and the creation of a CDU–FDP coalition resulted in Guido Westerwelle becoming Foreign Minister, Russia policy decisively shifted to the Chancellor's Office. The FDP was a much smaller partner in terms of seats in the Bundestag and its leader, Westerwelle was a relative neophyte in foreign policy. He took the post out of a combination of habit (all previous FDP leaders had been Foreign Minister in coalition governments) and politics (all Foreign Ministers had always been the most popular politicians in public opinion surveys). In doing so he followed the advice of Hans Dietrich Genscher, a former FDP Foreign Minister, who had urged him to take the job.

Westerwelle, however, proved to be a weak foreign minister and was discounted by the Russians as a serious interlocutor. He tried to make a mark with trips to Central European nations and developed a special relationship with Poland and its Foreign Minister, Radek Siroski, but was unable to develop his own Russia policy. While he and his top aide, Werner Hoyer, had criticized the use of the term strategic partnership in dealing with a Russia that does not share Germany's values, he used the phrase on his first official visit to Russia in 2009. Given that Merkel had already had four years' experience in foreign policy as chancellor, she felt more confident in dealing with key foreign policy issues than she did as a foreign policy ingenue in 2005. In addition, once Westerwelle was forced to step down by his party as chairman of the FDP and vice chancellor in May 2011 following a series of electoral defeats at the regional level, his political weight and that of his ministry further diminished.[27] Yet the Foreign Office continued to list the relationship with Russia as a strategic partnership on its website and Westerwelle used the term in his Tutzing speech of June 2013.

The chancellor's office is organized into six Directorate Generals plus a Protocol section with the key advisors on foreign and security policy located in the Foreign, Security, and Development Policy division (referred to as *Abteilung 2*), which was headed by Merkel's long-time chief foreign policy advisor, Christoph Heusgen. One of the CDU's top foreign policy parliamentarians, Eckart von Klaeden, was a Minister of State (*Staatsminister*) in the chancellery, but in this role was responsible for the reorganization and reduction of the federal bureaucracy. The chancellery staff remained small and preoccupied by the Eurozone crisis, while Russia policy was not a high priority for the chancellor. This had the effect of slowing any change or producing any initiatives in Russia policy.

The chancellery has taken a skeptical and geopolitical line on Putin's Russia, looking for ways to work with it in such areas as the issue of Moldova's breakaway region, Transnistria. The assessment has grown during Putin's second presidency that he is weakening the country and is increasingly isolated, yet there is no alternative partner with whom to deal. The assessment is that Putin sees Germany as a provider of hard cash, technologies and investment. Putin, always the cynic, believes that material interests will prevail, a view reinforced by the time he has spent with German CEOs, and thus ignores advice or criticism from the German government. His view gains credence from German business groups, which continue to view the Chancellor's criticisms of the Putin system as not conducive to good relations and openly miss the Schröder policy. Merkel has become increasingly skeptical about doing business with Putin, and, like Obama, sees little payoff in working with him and expects little change from the new Putin government. As a rational scientist and a woman who has used male egotism to play her rivals off against each other, she has been put off by Putin's displays of über-masculinity and his crude attempts to intimidate her. As one of her former aides put it, "She is super rational and not impressed by dogs," referring to Putin's attempt to intimidate her with his dog Koni. Her meetings with Putin have been cold and businesslike. As previously noted, one of her key advisors reportedly has described her reaction to Putin speaking to her in German as reminiscent of the style of a Stasi interrogator.[28] Her appointment of Schockenhoff was part of her attempt to rebalance the Russia relationship with a greater regard for the interests of eastern EU states, especially Poland, as part of a larger Europeanization of her approach. On the other hand she got solidly behind the rescue of the American car maker, Opel, by Sberbank, Russia's largest bank in the election year of 2009 and she supported the completion of the Nord Stream pipeline.

This approach has been characterized by Susan Stewart of the Stiftung Wissenschaft und Politik as: "On the whole under Merkel parallel tracks are visible: In the economic and energy realms Germany's approach toward Russia has been guided primarily by German business interests, even when these ran counter to broader EU goals. However, with regard to security, rule-of-law and other spheres, Germany's Russia policy has tended to be more in line with EU aims and has been able to 'upload' certain ideas to the Brussels level."[29]

The Foreign Office is engaged in Russia policy across a number of Political Directorates, especially Political Directorate 2 headed during the FDP/CDU/CSU government by Hans Dieter Lucas, an experienced East Europe and Russia hand, which covers most of the key security policy areas including NATO and Russia, Eastern Europe, and North America. Also important is The Directorate General for Disarmament and Arms Control 2A directed by Rolf Nikel, who worked for both Schröder and Merkel in Abteilung 2 of the Chancellery; and the Planning Staff headed by Thomas Bagger. A new actor is the department for Economic Affairs and Sustainable Development. This section deals with economic aspects of foreign policy and export promotion and has been gaining weight as Germany has become more of a global geo-economic power, reflecting the declining role of traditional diplomacy.

As the earlier look at statements made by both the Foreign Office and the Chancellor on Russia over the Christian-Liberal years shows, there is a good deal of similarity between the two in their comments on Russia and the German strategic partnership with its big neighbor to the east. While the weight of the Foreign Office on Russia policy declined under Westerwelle, he improved German relations with the smaller EU member states in East Central Europe, especially with Poland but the professional Foreign Service continued to argue that Russia cannot be changed from the outside and should be attached to as many Western networks as possible.

The other Ministry playing a role is the Ministry for Economics and Technology. It was headed during the Christian-Liberal coalition by the young chairman of the FDP, Philip Rösler, who replaced Westerwelle as party chairman in the spring of 2011 following a devastating electoral loss for the party in Baden Würtemberg. This massive ministry has interest in energy and raw material policy, foreign trade promotion, and promotion of activities of German Trade and Invest (GTAI), the economic development agency of Germany; as well as the Foreign Trade Chamber (*Aussenhandelskammer* or AHK) of the German Confederation of Industry (BDI). The AHK lobbies for and supports companies that want to expand into Russia.

Georgia: A case study in Germany's Russia Policy

The case of Georgia's candidacy for the NATO Membership Action Plan (MAP) and the German reaction to the Georgia–Russia war illustrates the tensions in Germany's approach toward Russia and the actors who shape that policy. Angela Merkel's split with the Bush administration at the NATO Bucharest Summit in April 2008 found her taking a realist approach toward Russia. Merkel went to the meeting with the understanding that the Bush Administration would not push for any further NATO enlargement. Condoleezza Rice offers a different interpretation in her memoirs, stating that the United States came to the summit without an agreement with the Germans and "no agreement in hand" but noting that President Bush had come down on the side of MAP for Georgia and Ukraine.[30] At that summit, much to Merkel's surprise, Bush, with no prior notice, proposed inviting Albania, Croatia, and Macedonia to join the alliance and for offering a MAP, to Georgia and Ukraine. Merkel and French President Sarkozy resisted the strong American pressure to admit Georgia and Ukraine to the MAP, the first step toward NATO membership. She was reported to be upset and even angry over the way Bush raised the issue at the last minute after she believed a compromise was in the works in which Washington would welcome the interest of Ukraine and Georgia in NATO and encourage them to work toward the MAP. As one American report described it at the time,

"Germany and France have said they believe that since neither Ukraine nor Georgia is stable enough to enter the program now, a membership plan would be an unnecessary offense to Russia, which firmly opposes the move. . . . Mrs. Merkel visited Moscow on March 8 and met Mr. Putin and his successor, Dmitry A. Medvedev. She told them that Russia would not be allowed a veto over NATO membership. But a senior German diplomat, Wolfgang Ischinger, said that offering membership to a divided Ukraine could destabilize the new government there, and that not enough diplomacy had taken place beforehand with Russia."[31]

Merkel stated at the time that, "We came to the conclusion that it is too soon for these two ex-soviet countries to be awarded NATO MAP candidate status . . . Countries that are directly involved in regional conflicts cannot, in my opinion, become members of NATO." However she went along in the end with a statement by NATO Secretary-General Jaap de Hoop Scheffer that "We agreed today that these countries will become members of NATO," a statement a German Russia watcher called "not necessarily reassuring (to Russia) as it had a temporary smell to it."[32] Merkel's opposition, shared by Steinmeier, was based on her concern that this would unnecessarily disrupt German and European relations with Russia over countries that were not worth the cost and did not meet NATO membership criteria.[33]

She, like most German leaders and commentators, had a deep distrust of Georgian President Mikhail Saakashvili for his intemperate ways and feared that MAP status would send the signal to Georgia that it would receive military assistance against Russia and to Russia that NATO was prepared to take aggressive anti-Russian positions. However the Russian–Georgian war of August 2008, seemed to change her view. The Spiegel reported this change as follows:

> Her attitude changed. It was no longer dominated by annoyance over Saakashvili. Now she was enraged at the highhandedness of the Russians. It seemed to her that they wanted to oust the Georgian president from office. Merkel is extremely sensitive to the issue of regime change. She knows how long and difficult it was to bring democracy to eastern Europe. Merkel sees Saakashvili, for all his faults, as a democratically elected, legitimate president. Georgia became for the chancellor a country that has to be helped.

> Nevertheless, she remained skeptical when she flew to Tbilisi. She spoke with Saakashvili, and something must have happened during their two-hour meeting because, afterwards, Merkel gave a press conference that made headlines around the world. She stood next to the president and said, "I think that a clear political statement is once again very important in this situation: Georgia is a free and independent country, and every free and independent country can decide together with the members of NATO when and how it joins NATO. In December, there will be an initial assessment of the situation, and we are clearly on track for a NATO membership."

> A new Eastern policy appears to be taking shape in the chancellery in Berlin. Merkel wants —in agreement with Foreign Minister Steinmeier—to support Georgia, but without driving Russia into a corner.[34]

The reaction of Steinmeier was more non-committal. "We face the danger of a dangerous conflagration," he said, without identifying a culprit in the conflict. Deputy Foreign Minister, Gernot Erler commented that the Georgians had breached a 1992 ceasefire agreement struck with Russia over South Ossetia, monitored essentially by Russian peacekeepers. "In this sense, it is also a question of a violation of international law as soon as you start to go down the road of military action." He acknowledged prior provocation of the Georgian leadership from Russian-backed South Ossetia's separatists, but said he understood Russia's reaction.[35] Gerhard Schröder was more sympathetic to the Russians, observing that, "I assume that no one in the Moscow leadership has an interest in military conflicts. There are enough internal problems in Russia that need to be solved . . . In my view, there have indeed been serious mistakes made by the West in its policy toward Russia. . . . There is a perception of Russia in the West that has very little to do with reality."[36] Steinmeier was reported to be unsettled by Merkel's strong stance on Georgia and worried that she might be backing away from their common position on MAP status. He remained deeply skeptical over any speeding up of the MAP process and hoped that Merkel continued to see it this way.

On the other side of the aisle, Merkel's own party was divided with CDU Russia critic, Eckhard von Klaeden declaring "It would be good if Moscow would stop adding oil to the fire," and that the Kremlin had intentionally brought about the conflict by issuing Russian passports to a majority of South Ossetians. Andreas Schokenhoff took a more Georgia critical stance, strictly rejecting awarding candidate status to Georgia, on the grounds that First, acceptance into MAP would now amount to "rewarding Georgia's rather dubious behavior." Second, it would be tantamount to "breaking with the enlargement strategy" of NATO, because this enlargement should not be directed against Russia. "In this situation, it would be interpreted as anti-Russian," Third, "What can and will NATO actually do if Russia launches another military campaign against Georgia as a calculated reaction to MAP? Are we prepared to escalate?"[37]

At the end both Merkel and Steinmeier's approaches were designed to support Georgia without pushing Russia into a corner. They allowed Sarkozy to take the lead in creating a neighbors conference to deal with the issue and helped with reconstruction aid, sending a message of solidarity with Georgia while keeping the lines open to Russia. This was a classic case of what analysts in the German Foreign Office labeled as Merkel's mastery of double meanings.[38]

German business

German business remains the key driver of German policy toward Russia. It is not the exclusive force but the most important one. German business, especially manufacturing and the energy sector, are influential in this broad area of what is considered public policy. It is in the private sector where Germany encounters and engages with the world and is the reason why Germany has become the most successful economy in the West. This is especially the case regarding Germany's relationship with Russia. During the Cold War, German business was limited primarily to the European and American markets. The end of the division of Germany meant the end of the division of Europe and the opening of markets in east and central Europe to German business.

These economic interests foster a mutual recognition of interdependence between the two countries. More importantly, they encourage German industry to lobby for good relations with Russia. This factor was almost completely absent during the Cold War, when German business was focused almost exclusively on European and especially U.S. markets; Germany's conservative foreign policy was oriented accordingly. Now, the Christian Democratic and Liberal parties, the parties with the closest ties to German industry, are evolving from Cold War anti-communist sceptics into pragmatic Russophiles who see the former Soviet Union as a promising target for capitalist expansion.[39]

The growing role of the private sector in international relations is not limited to Germany. As Steve Coll notes in the American case:

> The Gates Foundation, The Open Society Foundation, Google, Facebook, Apple and (alas) even the Walt Disney Company have arguably projected more influence in the Middle East and North Africa in recent years—including on the course of the Arab Spring- than the Department of State. These corporate and philanthropic actors have sometimes bigger budgets but also strategies that are better attuned to changes in technology, demography, and culture that are weakening states and empowering people and small groups worldwide.[40]

On Russia, German manufacturing and energy companies are the main players with the large multinationals leading the way and the small-to-medium-size firms, the Mittelstand, following in their wake. The German–Russian trade and economic relationship is well supported institutionally. Thus, the annual German–Russian Regierungskonsultationen, that is, the meetings of the German cabinet and the Russian executive, regularly include discussion of economic issues. Since 2000, a German–Russian Working Group for Strategic Questions of German–Russian Economic and Financial Relations (SAG) at high levels of the government and economics has been "linking politics and business" and is "providing impulses for joint pilot projects," with "discretion being at a high premium." At governmental level, on the basis of a previous declaration and an agreement on German–Russian Strategic Partnership in Education, Research and Innovation, the corresponding ministries are implemented the German–Russian Year of Education, Research and Innovation. Economic working groups with high-ranking members of the German and Russian business community meet in the context of the Petersburg Dialogue held in conjunction with the annual meetings of the cabinets. In 2009, the German–Russian Energy Agency (RUDEA) was founded, a joint venture linking the German Energy Agency on one side and Gazprombank and the Russian Energy Carbon Fund on the other, with the goal of "developing energy efficient markets in Russia . . . and opening new markets for German enterprises for energy efficiency technology."[41] The list of projects includes natural gas, energy efficiency, design, and construction of aircraft, automobiles, and railway transport.[42]

Given these interests, it is not surprising that German business will make extensive lobbying efforts to support a relationship where the German state must play a large role, given the role of the Russian state in the economic relationship. As one experienced German Bundestag staffer put it, "The companies are the door openers while the German political class is standoffish. There is no real Russophile caucus in political circles as no one wants to be branded as Putin's friend. Companies will not say we have had enough and have developed person-to-person chemistry with Russians."[43]

Lobbying in Germany is quite different than in the United States. In the latter, corporations give direct contributions to campaigns and use this as an effective lever to get what they want. American politicians are quite vulnerable to this form of inducement and pressure as the political parties have only a small role to play in providing campaign finance, leaving candidates to be political entrepreneurs. The Citizens United decision of the US Supreme Court in 2010 dramatically expanded the role of money in American politics leaving both candidates and politicians even more vulnerable to the pressure of money.

In the German case, public financing and the strong role of political parties in recruiting and selecting political candidates have limited the role of outside money in politics. In the 2013 parliamentary election campaign, for example, all the parties together spent $93 million compared to the $1.2 billion spent in the 2012 US presidential campaign.[44] However, interest group representation is both explicit and legitimate in German politics with candidates being both recruited and selected as representatives of a variety of interests including both business and labor. In recent years there has been a tendency away from large confederations of business and labor groups toward smaller more professional lobbying offices. One report estimated that there are up to 6,000 lobbyists based in Berlin.[45] The exact number is not known as lobbyists in Germany do not have to register.

In addition politicians can make substantial outside income and land lucrative jobs after leaving politics. The case of Gerhard Schröder is the most prominent example but Peer Steinbruck, the SPD Chancellor candidate in the 2013 election brought public attention to this source of outside influence on politics. Joschka Fischer became a consultant to the Nabucco gas pipeline project and Hans Dietrich Genscher formed a consulting group which promoted the interests of Ajerbaijan among other foreign clients. It was reported that Steinbruck, after he left the post of finance minister in 2009 earned €1.25 million in fees for outside-speaking from 2009 to 2012. His complaint at the start of the 2013 election campaign that the Chancellor was underpaid made matters worse.[46] Eckhard von

Klaeden of the CDU left politics after the 2013 election to join Daimler, another example of the role of outside incentives in political careers. The Russia lobby in Germany has collected a large number of former diplomats and business people with a stake in the Russian market.

A number of members of the Bundestag on key committees dealing with energy policy and Russia represent the interests of German business. In addition to this mode of lobbying, German business has a number of lobbying organizations who use the media, public conferences and meetings, like the Petersburg Forum, to get out their message. The exhibition on Germany and Russia sponsored by Germany's largest crude oil and natural gas producer, Wintershall, is one example of this type of public relations effort.

The most influential Russia lobbies of German business have been, the Ost-Auschuss der Deutschen Wirtschaft (OA), or the Committee on Eastern European Economic Relations, the German Russian Forum and the Confederation of German Industry (BDI). The most significant of these has been the Ost-Auschuss, which was founded in 1952 and is the oldest regional business initiative in Germany. It has both provided support to companies investing in Russia and other post Soviet countries, (but significantly not Poland, the Baltic States, or countries of East Central Europe) and served as a mediator between German business leaders and policymakers. The Ost-Auschuss has been extremely successful and influential when it comes to lobbying the German government on its policy toward the East, most importantly Russia. One obvious reason for this is the fact that the OA's membership encompasses a wide range of companies with substantial investments in Russia. It is a joint organization of the Federation of German Industries, the Association of German Banks, the German Insurance Association, the Foreign Trade Association of the German Retail Trade, and the German Confederation of Skilled Crafts, and all together it has almost 200-member companies.

Prior to 1989, the main objective of the OA was to overcome the economic division of the Western and the Eastern parts of Europe. Even as the Federal Republic of Germany was gradually granted some freedom in managing its economic relations with the outside world, West German–Russian business relations remained limited due to the so-called CoCom list, based on an export embargo agreed upon by the Western countries toward the Warsaw Pact countries. CoCom was designed to prevent the leakage of sensitive technology into the hands of the Soviet Union including so-called dual purpose technology that could serve both commercial and military uses.

Despite the export restrictions and other practical constraints, such as the nonconvertibility of the Deutsche Mark and the Ruble, the OA had already started negotiations with the Soviet Union in the early 1950s. In the following years, it secured the closing of trade agreements with Romania (1954), China (1957), and the Soviet Union (1958). Soon after an embargo on steel pipes had been lifted, the OA facilitated the negotiations about the first German–Russian pipeline. Starting in 1970, Mannessmann AG supplied pipes to the Soviet Union, which in turn agreed to supply gas to Ruhrgas AG once the pipeline was built, and to pay for the pipes from the money it was to get for the gas. Later the Deutsche Bank also entered this arrangement and supported below market interest rate credits to the Russian side.

During the 20 years of postwar CDU chancellorships, business representatives were continuously at odds with CDU leaders over the extent of restrictions applying to Germany in its trade relations with the East. The OA's motto of change through trade (*Wandel durch Handel*) became a forerunner to Willy Brandt's *Ostpolitik*. It is no coincidence that the 1963 Tutzing speech of Egon Bahr, the architect of the Ostpolitik, was titled "change through rapprochement" (*Wandel durch Annaherung*) and Foreign Minister Westerwelle used the *Wandel durch Handel* phrase in his June 2013 Tutzing speech. In the 1980s, business tensions with political leaders focused more on the credits the West provided to ailing Eastern economies. While the Ost-Auschuss welcomed the increased economic activity between the blocs, it did not find the strings attached satisfactory. When Germany was in the midst of Gorbymania in the late 1980s, the Ost-Auschuss leaders were questioning the Soviet leader's commitment to substantive economic reforms. Since the fall of the Berlin Wall it has supported the transformation process in the young democracies of Eastern Europe and is the voice of German business in many bilateral economic bodies. The OA was headed for many years by Klaus Mangold, a former member of the Daimler Chrysler board of management who was also on the E.ON and Metro boards and serves as honorary consul of the Russian Federation for Baden Württemburg. He was instrumental in creating the Petersburg Dialogue, increasingly a "business *über alles*" meeting, which avoided issues that the Russians would find sensitive, like human rights. With his retirement in 2010 the OA lost a very forceful and effective leader and his departure has weakened its influence.

The Dialogue avoided discussion or criticism of Putin's growing repression of opposition within Russia and Mangold's successor, Eckhard Cordes, wished Putin success in the presidential election and said his candidacy was encouraging news. Cordes is also prone to lecturing the German media for their insufficient knowledge of Russia.[47] The committee published a strategic paper in 2011, which advocated abolishing visas between the EU and Russia and other East European countries, a proposal taken up by Foreign Minister Westerwelle in 2013. Its executive director, Rainer Lindner, called the December 2011 parliamentary election, "the most free and democratic" since the end of the Soviet Union.[48] This was too much for Angela Merkel who made it clear to the Petersburg Dialogue's organizer, that if changes were not made, she would delink the consultations between German and Russian government officials from the meeting. As noted earlier, she also had her close confident and Deputy Floor Leader in the Bundestag, Andreas Schockenhoff, appointed to head the civil society working group of the Dialogue.[49]

The German–Russian Forum is a nonprofit organization founded in 1993 with offices in Berlin and Moscow. It organizes conferences, workshops, seminars, career fairs, and exchange programs to enhance the cooperation between Germany and Russia. The Forum derives its significance from its high-profile membership. Half of its 300 members are representatives of the business world, including Germany's largest companies.[50] The others are politicians, political parties affiliated think tanks, leaders of media concerns, journalists, and academics. The Forum's Chairman since 2003 has been Ernst-Jörg von Studnitz, a former German ambassador to Russia. Its Kuratorium includes Eckhard Cordes and Klaus Mangold, Gernot Erler of the SPD, Manfred Stolpe and Lothar de Maziere, former leaders in eastern Germany after unification and Hans Joachim Gorning, a managing director of Gazprom Germania and someone suspected of former ties with the Stasi. The Forum's is best known as a co-organizer of the Petersburg Dialogue.

Unsurprisingly the German business community has a much more positive view of Russia than the rest of German society. An annual poll of German business assessment of the business climate in Russia commissioned by the OA found that in December 2011 about two-thirds of those polled assessed the business climate in Russia as very good and that 64 percent expected positive shifts in economic development. The Eastern Committee concluded, that German business likes stability and link it to Putin's return.[51] However Boris Nemzov, a Russian opposition figure warns that "Europe must decide between gas and values" as it has in dealings with Iran and Venezuela. While Putin may be seen in the West as a strong man, he is destroying the institutions of the state and provoking future unrest.[52]

The issue is not so much what German business should do but how its interests should be reflected in broader German policies. Businesses have different interests, missions, and constituencies than governments. They are in business to make money and to increase shareholder value. They are not humanitarian organizations and while they can do much to promote decent work conditions for those who they employ, and should be pressured to do so, they should not be expected to risk their profits by alienating foreign political authorities by mixing business with politics. Political leaders, in contrast, have an obligation to balance and weigh economic interests into a broader spectrum of values and interests and should do this in pursuit of the public or national interest. This is the distinction between the private and public sector. The question, then, is to what degree political leaders allow economic and private interests to dominate large policies.[53] In a geo-economic state such as Germany the boundaries between public and private have become blurred.

Visa liberalization: A case study in German policy making

The Ost-Auschuss membership and its leaders have focused on a number of issues regarding Russia, including greater support for both the German *Mittelstand's* efforts in Russian and the development of a Russian *Mittelstand* as partners, improvement in Russian infrastructure and workforce training and rule of law effort. Visa liberalization has been a key policy priority and provides an informative case study in how Russia policy is made in Germany and to some extent in Brussels.

The question of visa liberalization between Russia and the European Union has been on the agenda of their bilateral talks since 2003. After Russia's WTO accession had become more or less a done deal, the visa question became the most important issue for that country in its relations with the European Union. A mismatch between Russian and European expectations had been evident for a long time. In 2011, while Dmitry Medvedev was still president, he tried to speed up the process and secure that negotiations would progress automatically once Russia met certain technical requirements. At that time the head of the European Commission, Jose Manuel Barroso, said that the lifting of visa requirements was still years away. After Putin's reelection, the Magnitsky scandal and Russia's demand for a visa waiver for those holding so-called service passports (i.e. civil servants), negotiations stalled for more than a year. In response, Russia changed strategy and threatened to introduce retaliatory measures, such as requiring visas from the crews of European airlines. In the meantime, Russia also managed to secure an agreement on the introduction of three-year, multiple-entry visas to the United States, which further increased its confidence to put pressure on the EU.

The idea of visa liberalization has also been highly contested within the EU. While Germany did not oppose the deal as staunchly as Britain or the Baltic states did, it also did not come forward with its support. However, this position changed in early 2013 when Westerwelle was joined by the Minister of Interior in supporting the liberalization. This in turn led to an acceleration of the negotiations between Russia and the EU as well. The currently discussed arrangement would grant multiple-entry visas to students, journalists, businesspeople and those holding service passports *with* biometric identification. When a German government spokesman was asked the government's response to Russian opponents of Putin who will not be given visa free travel while Russian officials will, he responded, "Our relations with Russia are broad and they include these groups of persons you mentioned. Any rapprochement with Russia will benefit all the people in Russia and in the EU." [54] However the economic motive was clear to many observers. Critics noted that opponents to Russian President Vladimir Putin—be it businessmen like Mikhail Khodorkovsky or punk singers like Pussy Riot—are still being jailed and say the judiciary serves as a political arm of the government . . . . They also suggest that economic interests—Russia is Europe's largest gas supplier and German companies have set up several joint ventures with Russian businesses—play a stronger role than they should.[55]

This refers to the major reason for the change in German policy, the tenacious lobbying by the Ost-Auschuss which had been publishing studies about the visa issue's adverse effects on business relations and polls showing that the liberalization is a priority for an overwhelming majority of German companies doing business in Russia. The OA noted that while Finland was issuing 800,000 visas annually to Russians, the German number was just 300,000. The organization had hired private companies to assist in outsourcing applications.

German resistance to visa liberalization, especially in the Foreign Office, goes back to the attempt of then Foreign Minister Fischer to liberalize visas with Ukraine in 2005 as a way of opening Europe up to the east. The political reaction in Germany was severe as he was charged by the CDU of opening the door to prostitutes and criminals with inadequate screening procedures. The affair almost cost him his job and since then German diplomats have been sensitive to blanket visa liberalization to eastern neighbors.

This decision to liberalize the visa regime is acceptable to otherwise opposing sides in Germany. Those arguing for a more lenient approach would support an even wider ranging scheme, while those worried about Russia's human rights abuses see it as an opportunity to support the most open, pro-Western elements in Russian society, although Germany's neighbors, with the exception of Poland, do not view it this way. The decision was in direct contrast to the decision of the United States to limit visas to certain Russian officials under the Magnitsky Act and in the face of opposition in the European Parliament. This policy stands in marked contrast to the Magnitsky sanctions passed by the US Congress banning visas to Russian officials associated with the imprisonment and murder of Magnitsky. In fact German authorities refused to grant safe passage to Magnitsky's employer, William Browder, to attend a conference in May 2013 in Berlin on the case in Germany, citing concerns that Russia would request his extradition.[56] In an earlier discussion Westerwelle told the press in Berlin, "Some of their [Russia's] decisions I cannot comprehend. But we have to keep up discussions with Russia in a spirit of mutual respect. They are our strategic partners." He added: "If the visa liberalization for service passports happens, it would be a nice, welcomed progress. It is a very important topic to them. Putin brings it up all the time, so it is important for us too."[57]

The role of German think tanks, political foundations, and academia

The German strategic community remains small given the growing weight of Germany in the world and its growing independence from both American and European foreign policy. The Stiftung Wissenschaft und Politik (SWP), the German Council on Foreign Relations (DGAP), and a few academic centers are the principle places for nongovernmental interest in Russia. Although Germany is the leading Western power in developing Russia policy, German expertise on that contrary is generally believed to be declining. As Hannes Adomeit characterizes opinion in this community: . . . "the overwhelming majority of German academic specialists on Russia, Moscow based correspondents of the major German newspapers and television channels, the heads of German political foundations working in Russia, the Russia desk in the foreign office and the (few) members of parliament knowledgeable about Russia and Eastern Europe hold a negative view of the direction the country has taken under Putin."[58]

While the evaluation of the direction of the Russian economy, politics, and society remains largely negative, on foreign policy, the general sense of the German expert community of the Russian world view, as summarized in a survey taken in 2009, is one of a nineteenth-century zero-sum power politics. While Russia is seen as having an inflated view of itself as a great power, in reality it is more of a regional power. "Russia thinks geostrategically and follows national interests."[59] This view is characterized by the following commentary by a journalist for the *Frankfurter Allgemeine Zeitung*:

It is Russia's tendency to see relations with the West as a zero-sum game—in which a gain of one side always corresponds to a loss of the other—that makes closer cooperation difficult and that turns natural conflicts of interest into serious conflicts. The fact that the Kremlin defines its interests as part of a power game and not factually makes it difficult for the West to formulate a policy that takes into account the legitimate interests of Russia (and not only its rulers). The West cannot respond to the destructiveness of Putin's foreign policy in kind, but it should stick to its firm principles.[60]

Given its energy and other natural resources and its role in Germany's immediate neighborhood, Russia remains an indispensable partner for Germany in the view of these elites. Russia is not seen as a military threat although it can play the role of spoiler in its immediate region. It relies on its energy resources as a major instrument of its foreign policy. When it comes to the future relationship, German specialists remain divided. Even in 2009 during the Medvedev presidency, there was no consensus on where the relationship was headed with views ranging from no change and a continuation of a case-by-case pragmatic approach to a sense that Russian modernization would hang on the 2012 elections. Most believed full modernization was a long way off. The division between the value oriented and economic realists within the parties also characterized broader elite opinion. German policy is seen being driven largely by economic interests and change would likely come from the private sector. If the cost of doing business with Russia becomes too high then a change in German policies would follow.

> Germany's strong pursuit of its economic interests in its relationship with Russia will likely remain constant, leaving it vulnerable to criticism within the EU. If, though, as appears increasingly possible, Russia becomes weaker internally due to its failure to modernize on a variety of fronts, it may grow less attractive as an economic partner for Germany. This could bring other aspects of Germany's Russia policy to the fore, ones that are more compatible with adherence to principle and broader EU interests.[61]

At the DGAP, Alexander Rahr served as the think tank's top Russia specialist until his departure for Wintershall in 2012. He was Program Director of the Berthold Beitz Center at the DGAP and a Senior Advisor at the Wintershall Holding GmbH before joining the company full time in 2012. From 1977 to 1985 he was visiting research fellow in the Soviet leaders research project at the Federal Institute of Eastern Europe and International Research, Cologne. The Institute was the top policy center on the USSR and was merged into the SWP after the end of the Cold War. Rahr served as a research fellow at the Research Institute of the DGAP and Director for Russia and CIS Programs from 1994 and is emeritus professor of the Moscow State University of Foreign Affairs. The Beitz Center, created in 2004 is named after Berthold Beitz who held a leading position in Krupp and then in Thyssen Krupp and had been a major force in the expansion of business between then West Germany and Russia in the 1970s.[62] Rahr is the leading German academic advocate of close German–Russian cooperation and his ties to the Ost-Auschuss and to Wintershall reflects the influence of German business as well as Russian interests on the Russia policy debate. Here is part of his commentary after the November 2012 Petersburg Dialogue meeting.

> The majority of people in Germany are happy that over the past twenty years we have developed normal strategic and allied relations with such a major world power as Russia. Bilateral trade has exceeded $80 billion a year. But the trouble is that there are traditional groups in the West, above all in Germany and France, groups of intellectuals who could venture too deeply into the realm of philosophizing, which may lead to the rejection of modern Russia for a number of reasons. They view Russia as an undemocratic country that is infringing on human rights and freedom of speech. They have gone so far as to question the need for partnership. . . . I was impressed by how well Chancellor Angela Merkel maneuvered between the pragmatic line and the advocates of a policy of [European] values. Of course, burning problems, such as the verdict against the punk group Pussy Riot, attract public attention. But it is important that despite any misunderstandings and differences in world outlook, the most important of our joint projects have not been curtailed, but are continuing and have even been expanded. At the same time, we must not forget about our ideological differences, which has survived following the collapse of communist beliefs, and is hindering our progress. The Cold War legacy is still hanging over our head.[63]

Rahr became increasingly critical of Merkel and Germany's Russia policy in 2013, accusing German Ostpolitik of "having lost its balance" and arguing that "When we speak today of Russia only democracy and human rights are mentioned, but never is it discussed what Europe and Russia can gain as partners."[64] At the same time, one of Rahr's colleagues at DGAP, Stefan Meister, was a leading critic of Germany's Russia policy, labeling it too accommodating.[65] He has been critical of the concept and execution on the modernization partnership with Russia, calling it a false approach based on false assumptions. The Germans want a political modernization while the Russia elite is only interested in technology transfers. The Germans want the rule of law while the Russians want to hinder it in order to protect their power and privileges. He argues for a more critical German approach, given the dependence of the Russians on the European market. The current German approach undermines the credibility of Germany with a growing critical Russian public and hinders modernization. Meister left the DGAP to join the European Council on Foreign Relations Berlin office in 2013.

Rahr was succeed by Ewald Böhlke as head of the Beitz Center. Böhlke served from 1995 to 2012, as a scholar for futurology at Daimler AG, focusing on regional research in Eastern Europe and the Middle East, the implementation of scenario workshops for the air and space industry, and strategic analysis and consulting on cooperation projects between European and Russian businesses.

A more critical assessment or Putin's Russia can be found in the analysis of the Russia Research Group in the Stiftung Wissenschaft und Politik, the leading foreign policy think tank of the German government. Its former top Russia analyst, Hannes Adomeit, has been critical of the German approach to Russia, denying that it is a strategic partnership or that the modernization partnership has modernized Russia.

> Official Berlin's portrayal of Germany and Russia as being "united by a strategic partnership" is wide of the mark. In reality, a common strategy does not exist. There is no agreed-upon plan of action with corresponding means allocated and a set time frame. Objectives diverge, and so do values. Officially, the "partners" convey the notion that, some disagreements notwithstanding, the relationship is one of friendship and trust. However, since 2000, diverging perceptions and differences of interest have combined to undermine confidence. Even propagandists for Moscow's point of view in Berlin acknowledge that the "friendship" is essentially "cold," and serious analysts characterize the state of affairs as an "alienated partnership . . . in private, German government officials and—openly—German non-governmental actors, including business leaders, are disillusioned and disappointed about the course Russia has taken under Putin."[66]

Similarly, Susan Stewart, an analyst in the Russia Research group at SWP is critical of the impact of Germany's economics driven policy on its relationship with Poland and other EU member states.[67]

Finally the European Council on Foreign Relations has an office in Berlin but tends to focus more on Germany within the EU has not looked at German–Russian relations in a systematic way. Its addition of Stefan Meister will improve this capability and one of the leading advocates of understanding Germany as a geo-economic power is Hans Kundnani, who is the editorial director of ECFR in London and has written a number of influential pieces on Germany's geo-economic approach.[68]

What all this portends for German policy is difficult to say. There remains a sharp divide between the worlds of academia and of policy with think tanks in a netherworld. Most of these analysts believe that Germany's Russia policy is largely driven by economics and business.[69] Russia policy is largely determined by German economic interests and is driven by the private sector. As Timothy Garton Ash observed, "While German business has globalized itself spectacularly over the last quarter century, with companies holding board meetings in English, and managers being as much at home in Sao Paulo as in Stuttgart, the political class has become even more provincial than it was before."[70] In fact some of the best and brightest of the German foreign policy elite have moved to the private sector including, Wolfgang Ischinger to Allianz, the aforementioned Eckhard von Klaeden to Daimler and Thomas Mattusek to Deutsche Bank. The next chapter examines the role of business in the German–Russian relationship.

4

Doing Business with Russia Inc.

Economics is the driving factor in the German–Russian relationship.[1] Almost all of Germany's Russia watchers see this as the constant factor and one that favors a geo-economic approach over a value-oriented one. Whatever the ups and downs in the broader relationship, the economic one remains a success story from the German perspective and remains its anchor. This relationship preceded unification. During the Cold War, the West German government resisted extraterritorial attempts by the Reagan administration to block the construction of the Trans-Siberian gas pipeline and the head of Deutsche Bank, Wilhelm Christians Friedrichs, was a major and influential advocate for Russia–German trade at that time.[2] Major energy deals followed in the 1980s. Unification itself was a German–Russian economic deal with Germany paying over $52 billion in aid to the USSR up to the time of its collapse in 1991, and then to Russia, in order to get Soviet/Russian troops out of eastern Germany. As the director of the Center for Eurasian, Russian, and East European Studies at Georgetown University, Angela Stent pointed out, "One major legacy of unification was that a united Germany was as central to Soviet foreign policy as a divided Germany had been . . . United Germany was the USSR's major economic partner, key to its economic health."[3] As she goes on to observe, the asymmetries in the relationship shifted after the end of the Cold War from a German dependence on Russia for inter-German relations to a Russian dependence on unified Germany for its post-communist transition.[4]

The economic relationship in the first decade after German unification did not greatly change from what it was in the Gorbachev years. The collapse of East German–Russian trade, which resulted from the radical restructuring of the former East German economy, resulted in a major decline in the economy of the former East Germany. United Germany continued to be Russia's most important trading partner, but the pattern of trade remained unchanged with Germany importing Russian raw materials, especially oil and gas, and exporting manufactured goods.

Energy trade remained the most important aspect in the relationship although there were changes in the players with Ruhrgas, which had a monopoly of the German–Soviet gas deals, now in competition with Wintershall.[5] In the 1990s German firms became more active in the Russia telecommunications, truck and auto markets, but remained frustrated by the delays, administrative confusion and absence of an enforceable commercial legal system.[6]

The relationship remained stagnant through the 1990s, reaching a low point during the Russian financial crisis in August 1998. The Red–Green coalition came to power in the wake of this crisis and was facing the impact of major losses by German investors as a result of asset striping and defaults on bond payments in Russia. Yet this bad start was soon followed by a period where "Russia was transformed from an unreliable boarder to a market of unlimited possibilities."[7] Schröder and Putin created a partnership between an energy-dependent German trading state and a modernizing Russia. Schröder became the major advocate for German investment in Russia and for an energy policy dialogue, arguing in 2004 that the confidence of Western investors in Russia had been fundamentally renewed and reestablished.[8] By 2011, German–Russian trade resulted in a turnover of about €75 billion, with German exports to Russia totaling €35.4 and imports at €40.8 billion. Russia ranked twelfth in exports and eleventh in imports for Germany with a total turnover equal to that of German trade with Poland.[9] Germany has an embassy and a number of consulates in Russia, but the representation of German business is much more intense with over six thousand German firms on the ground and an investment of over $19.5 billion in Russia.[10] German companies created 226,000 jobs in Russia in 2011.[11] In contrast, only about 950 Russian firms employ about 4,600 people in Germany. Add to this the major energy relationship in which over a third of German energy imports come from Russia[12] and the constraints on German public policy are obvious. This relationship will deepen in the wake of the Merkel decision to shut down Germany's nuclear capacity, as nuclear energy accounts for a quarter of German electricity, a gap that cannot be filled by renewable sources alone. To the extent that German elections are about the economy and jobs, the relationship with Russia is an important, if indirect, electoral factor.

Dealing with the devil: German business in Russia

Gazprom's monopoly-seeking activities cannot be explained by economic motives alone. It is difficult to distinguish where the Russian Government ends and where Gazprom begins. Clearly Gazprom has sacrificed profits and needed domestic infrastructure investments to achieve Russian foreign policy goals.

Senator Richard Lugar, Hearing of the Senate Foreign Relations Committee, June 13, 2008

As Senator Lugar has noted, dealing with Putin's Russia Inc. is hardly a purely commercial relationship, especially in energy. Fiona Hill and Clifford Gaddy have described the Putin system in their book, *Mr. Putin: Operative in the Kremlin*, as a tiered system or a series of concentric circles, with Putin at the center acting as a CEO of the corporation that is Russia. Putin rules as a CEO, or at least his version of CEO. It is a one-man operation, which avoids overlapping spheres of authority, with all power emanating from Putin. It is a new version of the old Soviet democratic centralism with individuals in the inner circle allowed to differ on policy until Putin decides, then absolute loyalty is required. As Hill and Gaddy note, "it is a highly centralized decision-making system that is based on trust only among a few inner circle confidants and with distrust of everyone else and is backed up by threats . . . it is not money that guarantees loyalty or holds the top level together. Instead it is the fact that the money derives from activity that is or could be illegal. Participants are not bought off in the classic sense of that term. They are compromised; they are made vulnerable to threats.. . . Loyalty is ensured through blackmail."[13] Corruption, they note, "is the glue that helps keep Putin's informal system together."[14]

The system of concentric circles emanate out from the President with links to outer circles through key individuals who play the role of ombudsmen. The Russian economy is structured around the exploitation of its natural resources and paying for imports with exports of energy and raw materials. The economy of Russia Inc. is distinctive in its heavy reliance on this single sector and on a very few value-creating companies. Ten companies provide for 90 percent of Russia's oil output with Gazprom producing nearly 80 percent of its natural gas. These resources provide "a built in reserve for surviving crises."[15] This structure allows the ruling elite to gain income without undergoing structural reform of the wider economy.[16]

This model also gives a major role to the state requiring foreign companies to work with it. Many have done this despite the major obstacles including massive corruption, because returns on capital have been worth the cost. Beyond these "strategic sectors" Western businesses have had a more mixed record, "but with the right local political and economic connections there is money to be made. Without them, foreign firms can fall prey to powerful and better-connected competitors or rapacious officials."[17] When Putin was prime minister foreign energy companies worked with Igor Sechin, who served as Putin's ombudsman on energy through a commission known as TEK. When he returned from being prime minister to being president in 2012 he was intensively lobbied by foreign energy companies to create a TEK in the Presidential office, which he finally did much to their satisfaction.[18]

The costs of corruption

While corruption is endemic to the Putin system and is the oil on which it runs, there are different types of corruption, most importantly the corruption of the state and its companies and the corruption of organized crime. The Wikileaks release of American diplomatic cables revealed that one leading Spanish prosecutor, Jose Ginda Gonzales, labeled Russia, Belarus, and Chechnya as mafia states in which "one cannot differentiate between the activities of the government and OC (organized crime) groups." The US embassy in Moscow also filed numerous cables alleging close connections among criminal gangs, top political leaders, and the security services.[19]

The emergence of mafia states are a new threat, which are the product of the end of the Cold War and globalization. As Moises Naim of the Carnegie Endowment has observed, "Across the globe, criminals have penetrated governments to an unprecedented degree. The reverse is also happening: rather than stamping out powerful gangs, some governments have instead taken over their illegal operations. In mafia states, government officials enrich themselves and their families and friends while exploiting the money, muscle political influence and global connections of criminal syndicates to cement and expand their own power."[20] Given this intermeshing of crime and politics, in mafia states, "the national interest and the interests of organized crime are now inextricably linked."[21] While organized crime is hardly a new phenomenon, what is new in today's world is that criminals no longer stay underground and with the end of the east–west division and the opening of the world economy in its wake, the opportunities for organized crime through immigration, money laundering, narcotics, and human trafficking combined with weak states have resulted in a merger or take over of states by these new types of nongovernmental organizations. Developments in Bulgaria, the Czech Republic, and other new democracies in Europe have provided evidence of the political impact of the Russian mafia on political stability.

If Russia is a mafia state it is a different kind of mafia state because the mafia is under state control and does not control the state as it does in weak states. Many members of Russian OC come from pasts in the Russian intelligence and police services and it is unclear to what extent their activities are directed by the state or simply tolerated. Russia ranks near the bottom on Transparency International's Rating of Perceived Corruption and the return of Putin to a third term as president cemented the fusion of crime, corruption, and politics for at least the medium term. This Russian variant of a broader phenomena is the most dangerous given its size and proximity to major European countries and the fact that Russia has nuclear weapons and a permanent seat on the UN Security Council.

Germany faces a number of major challenges in dealing with this Russian combination of state and organized crime. On the criminal level, Germany has become in the words of one German state interior minister, "a paradise for the mafia."[22]. The head of the Berlin Criminal Office reported already in 2008 that Berlin had 68 organized crime cases with more than a thousand individual crimes. These range from the booming car theft market through extortion and protection rackets up to high-end money laundering. Influencing of politicians has also become a major concern of the police, one they feel is not adequately shared by German politicians.[23] In addition Russian criminal elements have often linked up with former East German Stasi agents.

The bigger issue is the problem of business corruption. Given the major role of German business in the Russian economy, the challenges and risks are great. Dealing with Russia Inc. poses real dangers for a liberal democracy. Western and German business practices can have a beneficial effect on Russian business and legal cultures, and the view of German business in general is that they will reduce corruption and introduce a *Rechtstaat*, that is a state of law. As the former British ambassador to Russia, Sir Andrew Wood points out, Germany "has a highly developed system of cooperation between its firms abroad, and between those firms and its foreign ministry. One result is to give prominence to those who argue that restraint in criticizing Russia is necessary for engagement and longer term progress towards the integration of Russia into a Europe based on common values."[24] This is a main point of the OA as well. As its managing director, Rainer Lindner pointed out:

> The often cited conflict between business interests and democratic values does not stand up to closer examination: through their economic activity, new production plants, and the creation of jobs, German companies contribute a great

deal to the stabilization and development of societies in all of Eastern Europe. German companies and plants employ millions of people in these countries. Through their business practices they export values and rules that change these societies. Even if they are not immediately visible, these are lasting changes.[25]

While Germany has a well-deserved reputation for honesty, reliability, and efficiency in government and business, there have been a number of high profile corruption scandals in both the public and private sector, including the resignation of the President, Christian Wulff, over an influence buying scandal in 2012. An article in a German business publication has even labeled Germany a "banana republic," arguing that it has become a systemic problem.[26] Statistics indicate a rise in cases of corruption reported by German police forces from 2009 to 2010 of 148 percent totaling 15,746 cases.[27] One estimate puts the cost of corruption to Germany at €250 billion in 2012, up from €220 billion in 2005.[28] German criminal law prohibits the private sector from both offering and accepting bribes, but only individuals, not corporations or other legal entities, are criminally liable. However, corporations are subject to fines. Until the late 1990s, bribes paid by German companies to foreign officials were tax deductible.[29] Legislation passed in 1999 has made foreign bribes illegal.

After years of weak regulation and enforcement, German authorities are now stepping up the investigation and prosecution of anticorruption laws. This is done at the state (*Land*) level rather than the federal level. While many of these cases involve American and West European countries, entry into the Russia market has caused great opportunities for both profit and corruption. Major German companies such as Siemens, Commerzbank, and Mercedes as well as German subsidiaries of global companies such as Hewlett Packard, have been involved in bribery cases in Russia.

The case of Siemens AG

Perhaps the most notorious case involved the electrical and engineering giant, Siemens AG. Siemens has developed a large stake in the Russian market in the area of renewable energy, especially wind turbines, and other high-tech sectors. The experience of Siemens in Russia illustrates both the potential and the pitfalls for the German role in Russia. Siemens was welcomed to Russia by both Medvedev and Putin as Peter the Great had welcomed artisans and manufacturers from Germany to modernize Russia. The company has taken the lead in modernizing Russia's train network getting a contract for almost €2 billion for the Moscow-

Petersburg line and Sochi Olympics trains. All in all Siemens made €1.3 billion in
Russia in 2009, and its profits there have been rising, with the number of Siemens
employees planned to double from 3,000 to 6,000 over the next three years.

In this new endeavor, Siemens joined with Russian billionaire Dmitri
Pumpjanski to form a new company, Sinara. The exclusive entrée to the inner
Russian power center paid off. Siemens is more deeply connected than anyone
else. As its CEO, Peter Löscher said, "Russia is a very important market for us."
In order to compete in this market, he needed the Kremlin given the Russian
state is the most important contractor. Putin and Medvedev had to be persuaded
to invest in certain projects of national significance as would any private
entrepreneur.[30] The other side of this coin is corruption. As *The New York Times*
reported in 2008:

> The company pleaded guilty in federal court in Washington to charges that it
> violated a 1977 law banning the use of corrupt practices in foreign business
> dealings. The fines that the company agreed to pay on the American side of the
> case—$450 million to the Justice Department and $350 million to the Securities
> and Exchange Commission—dwarf the previous high for a foreign corruption
> case brought by Washington. . . . Officials said that Siemens, beginning in the
> mid-1990s, used bribes and kickbacks to foreign officials to secure government
> contracts for projects like a national identity card project in Argentina, mass
> transit work in Venezuela, a nationwide cellphone network in Bangladesh
> and a United Nations oil-for-food program in Iraq under Saddam Hussein.
> "Their actions were not an anomaly," said Joseph Persichini Jr., the head of the
> Washington office of the FBI. "They were standard operating procedures for
> corporate executives who viewed bribery as a business strategy."[31]

Siemens was sanctioned by the World Bank in 2009 for corrupt practices of its
subsidiary, Siemens Russia, for paying $3 million in bribes for its transportation
project in 2005 and 2006. The settlement included a commitment by Siemens
to pay $100 million over the next 15 years to support anticorruption work, an
agreement of up to a four-year debarment for Siemens' Russian subsidiary, and a
voluntary two-year shut-out from bidding on World Bank business for Siemens
AG and all of its consolidated subsidiaries and affiliates. Siemens had also agreed
to co-operate to change industry practices, clean up procurement practices,
and engage in collective action with the World Bank group to fight fraud and
corruption.

> "This settlement provides significant consequences for past wrongdoing by
> Siemens. At the same time, Siemens ongoing extensive cooperation could

help the World Bank hold more corrupt firms and individuals accountable for
diverting precious development resources away from the people who need them,"
said Leonard McCarthy, Integrity Vice President at the World Bank.. . . "We look
forward to continuing to work with the Bank to eliminate fraud and corruption
in our markets and we see this as confirmation of our work to establish a robust
compliance program and to pursue collective action together with the Bank in
those markets," said Andreas Pohlmann, Siemens Chief Compliance Officer.[32]

Siemens's use of bribery and other forms of corruption was worldwide, but
its dealings with Russia have led to charges that it sold parts to a Russian firm,
Atomstroyexport, which were destined for or ended up in the Bushehr nuclear
power plant in Iran. Siemens claimed that it did not know that the parts were headed
for Iran via Russia when they were intercepted at Frankfurt airport in 2010.

Other companies, most prominently Daimler and the German subsidiary
of Hewlett Packard have been involved in corruption as well. Daimler's Russia
related corruption was on a much smaller scale than that of Siemens, involving
about $4 million in bribes to encourage Russian representatives to buy €65 million
worth of Daimler vehicles.[33] However, its global operations resulted in a fine of
$185 million from the US Securities and Exchange Commission for bribes it
paid in over 20 countries. Hewlett Packard's fully owned German subsidiary was
under investigation for allegedly paying about €8 million as bribes for a contract
worth €35 million to provide a computer system to the Russian Prosecutor
General's Office.[34]

These and other cases have raised questions about this seamy side of the
German export success story.[35] The Russian side of this is part of this larger picture
and for some companies a small part of larger corporate practice. Both Siemens
and Daimler as part of their SEC fine agreements have pledged not to pay bribes
in the future, although Daimler and a number of other German companies have
also decided to no longer be listed on the US stock exchange in order to avoid this
type of SEC scrutiny in the future.[36] In order to combat this pervasive Russian
culture of corruption, over 50 international firms, the majority being German
firms including Siemens, Deutsche Bank, and Daimler's Mercedes Benz Russia
undertook an initiative to combat corruption. They pledged not to give bribes
to officials or to give payments to political parties in an initiative developed by
the Berlin-based Transparency International.[37] However, if Russian firms do not
also comply, these foreign firms will be at a disadvantage.

This series of cases raises the question of who is changing whom and whether
immersion in the Russian market is leading to reforms in Russia or is rather
deepening corruption. Under the Medvedev Presidency there were at least

some attempts to reign in corruption, but the return of Putin to the Presidency resolidified the "Putin system" and has undermined these inadequate reforms. How will German business react to this continuing climate of corruption and crime? As Marieluise Beck of the Alliance '90/The Greens and a critic of Germany's approach to Russia put it, the German approach to corruption in Russia has been bolstered by Germany's unwillingness to criticize it: "Our logic is we must be nice, good friends with the Kremlin because we want their oil and gas. But the Putin show would be over if he couldn't sell them to his Western partners."[38] Corruption has hindered even further foreign investment in Russia and is costing Russia at least $300 billion annually.

As one former Canadian corporate executive warns, "penalties in US courts certainly should help remind German corporations of their own global vulnerabilities. But even this is simply outside pressure. There is a cultural challenge here. Corporations rot, like all systems, once they are touched by corruption. Their long term profitability or even survival is put at risk by placing too much reliance on unreliable partners. Complicity is a short term strategy."[39]

Gazprom in Germany

As already noted, most of the recent growth in German exports is now coming from the East—Russia, Eastern Europe, the Gulf states and Asia, while United States–German trade with the United States remains robust with a total trade in 2010 of $130 billion, with exports ranging from $71 to $94 billion since 2007 with an average net balance for Germany of plus $37 billion.[40] This compares to total trade with Russia of $63 billion in 2010. German trade with China in contrast stood at $140 billion in 2010.[41] While trade with Russia is roughly in balance, Germany is running about a $14 billion dollar deficit with China, yet almost all of the growth in German exports over the past two years has come from China. The economic crisis in the eurozone has seen a further relative diminishment of the role of the EU market in German exports and the rise of exports to non-EU countries.[42]

The energy link with Russia puts it on a different level than the one with Poland and other Central European markets. In addition, the scare over the availability of rare earth metals, which arose when China halted its exports of these metals, has Germany looking to Russia for access to these vital metals.[43] Add to this the major energy relationship in which over a third of German energy imports come from Russia and the constraints on German public policy are obvious.[44] This relationship deepened in the wake of the Merkel decision to shut down Germany's nuclear capacity, as nuclear energy accounts for a quarter of German electricity. However, as Senator Lugar's comments illustrate, Gazprom is not a normal multinational energy company. Rather than a simple profit-oriented company it is rather an organization that serves the interests and the agenda of the Russian state. It emerged from the privatizations of the 1990s to become Russia's largest company, following Putin's policy of supporting national champion companies in strategic sectors of the Russian economy. Putin has used it as a tool of his foreign policy, cutting supplies to Ukraine, Georgia, Belarus, and Moldova and using its resources to buy up television stations and newspapers, which then become supportive of his policies.[45]

In order to gain control of the energy sector, Putin has used Igor Sechin, his deputy prime minister, as his enforcer. Upon returning to the presidency, Putin made him the president of Rosneft and the secretary of his Commission for the Strategic Development of Fuel and Energy and Environmental Safety, which has exclusive competence over the oil and gas sectors. Sechin, who has been described as Darth Vader in the Russian press and as "the scariest person on Earth," oversees the country's abundant natural resources, reigns over the storied Kremlin faction known as the "siloviki"—roughly, "powerful ones"—which includes the military and intelligence services. These men believe that the state should control access to natural resources, and were against the appointment of Dmitry Medvedev to the presidency. An increasingly vocal cadre of Medvedev appointees, some reform-minded, made moves to quell the influence of the siloviki, but Sechin kept his grip on power.

There is little solid information about the man. Like many of Putin's inner circle, Sechin is a St Petersburg native. In the 1990s he worked in city government. Before that, it's widely believed that he was a spy; Moscow sources confirm that he was a member of the GRU, the KGB's foreign-intelligence arm. His duties may have included working in Angola and Mozambique, probably as a translator. An American who worked directly with Sechin in the 1990s said Sechin showed utter loyalty to Putin—a fact that is key to his current standing.[46]

After assuming the presidency for the first time, Putin replaced the leadership of Gazprom with his own team, including Medvedev, and they all profited as a result. Putin himself is reported to own 4.5 percent of the company.[47] Gazprom is a vertically integrated company, which controls all aspects of gas production from extraction through delivery, including the ownership and laying of pipelines. This has opened up multiple opportunities for skimming and bribery for a wide variety of those close to Putin and to organized crime.[48] Gazprom's reach extends beyond energy to include the media company Gazprom Media that controls the five most important television stations in Russia, and two-thirds of all Russian media.[49]

Gazprom's European strategy is part of its larger international expansion strategy that has been centered around the goal articulated by Alexander Medvedev, director general of Gazprom Export, "to become the largest energy company in the world." Within Europe its strategy is to diversify its structure to control the distribution and sale of the gas to the European consumer. It has, consequently, diversified into the transportation, distribution, and power-generation industries, including acquiring storage facilities and distribution hubs. It does this through ownership of foreign subsidiaries or shell companies to invest overseas.[50] The liberalization of energy markets in the EU offered an opportunity for Gazprom to expand in Europe, but EU legislation also requires notification of non-EU companies operating in European gas networks, a policy directed against an overdependence on Russian energy.[51] In September 2011, European Commission investigators raided a number of Gazprom's European offices, including Gazprom Germania in Berlin, with the purpose of investigating allegations that the companies had colluded to divide markets, hindered access to distribution networks and blocked efforts to widen sources of supply. This was part of a wider effort to liberalize European energy markets by making it easier for companies without distribution networks to gain market access through unbundling supply and infrastructure operations.[52]

Gazprom has tried to increase European energy dependence by attempting to work arrangements with Algeria to establish a cartel to limit Europe's gas alternatives and to push the South Stream pipeline over Nabucco, which was designed to limit European dependence on Russian energy. The decision to construct the Trans Adriatic Pipeline (TAP) effectively killed the Nabucco project in 2013. The Nord Stream pipeline is an important component of this strategy. Gazprom does all that it can to prevent a common EU energy policy and prefers bilateral relations and special deals with countries such as Germany and Italy. A common EU policy would foster diversification of sources and unbundle national utilities, in the process cutting profit margins and reducing Gazprom's incentives to buy European companies. It would also weaken bilateral special relationships with Russia.[53]

Gazprom operates in Germany through its fully owned subsidiary, Gazprom Germania. About half the jobs created by Russian firms in Germany are due to

Gazprom. Its reach within Germany includes owning shares in the following companies:

- Wingas (50%), with about 18 percent share of the gas market in Germany, a joint venture between GAZPROM Germania GmbH and and *Wintershall*, the largest crude oil and natural gas producer in Germany.
- VNG—*Verbundnetz Gas AG* (10.5%), the third largest natural gas company in Germany (after *E.ON Ruhrgas* and *Wintershall*).
- Wintershall Erdgas Handelshaus Zug AG (WIEE) (50%).

These holdings give Gazprom control of 38 percent of the German gas market. The Nord Stream Pipeline is a joint venture in which Gazprom owns 51 percent and Wintershall Holding and E.ON Ruhrgas AG each with 15 percent. The key German companies in this sector are E.ON, Vattenfall Europe, RWE, and EnBW. Gazprom has a joint venture with Wintershall through Wingas, which is a subsidiary of BASF, the chemical giant. Its main Nord Stream collaborators are E.ON and BASF. Merkel's hasty decision to end German reliance on nuclear energy went against previous CDU policies and concerns about the implications of such a shut down for German dependence on Russian energy. The initial commercial reaction was the decision of RWE to sign an MOU with Gazprom, which opened the door to the latter's expansion into Germany and Europe. RWE, unlike E.ON and Wintershall, had avoided dependence on Gazprom prior to the nuclear phase-out decision.[54] However, it now faces major losses in the German market and is carrying heavy debts, opening it up to foreign ownership.

To this point the German government has blocked Russians from investing in aerospace and defense corporation EADS, Deutsche Telekom, or the semiconductor manufacturer Infineon—all companies with high tech or national security assets. If Gazprom becomes a part owner of RWE it will get into the business of downstream delivery of energy, a lucrative business. Gazprom now sees the decision to get out of nuclear power by 2022 as increasing annual German demand for gas by 20 billion cubic meters (bcm) from its current level of 36 bcms. As one analyst argues, "Moscow seeks to extend into Germany (and into Europe via German partners) a business model whereby commercial supply of gas is linked with acquisition of industrial assets through joint ventures."[55] Gazprom's activities have raised some concerns in Germany including those of Elmar Brok, Member of the European Parliament and a leading CDU politician, who already warned in 2006 that the Russian energy concern was pursuing a strategy, which would result in "without Gazprom nothing can happen."[56]

The Gazprom German team

Gerhard Fritz Kurt Schröder (1944)

- Chancellor of Germany from 1998 to 2005.
- chairman of the board of Nord Stream AG.
- Close friend to Putin.

Vladimir Kotenev

- 2004-2010 Russian ambassador to Germany.
- Director of Gazprom Germany since 2010.

Hans-Joachim Gornig

- Former Managing Director of GAZPROM Germania GmbH.
- Former deputy chief executive of the gas and oil industry in East Germany

GAZPROM Germania GmbH (Berlin)

- Engagement in the production, trade, and storage of natural gas, liquefied gas, and gas condensate in Europe and Asia.
- Exploration and production of refined gas, liquefied petroleum gas, liquefied natural gas, and gas condensate.
- Trading of natural gas from Russia and Central Asia in Germany and Western Europe.
- Formerly Zarubezhgaz-Erdgashandel-GesellschaftmbH-founded in 1990.

Vladimir Vladimirovich Putin (1952)

- Prime Minister of Russia.
- From 1985 to 1990 KGB agent stationed in Dresden, East Germany.

Felix Strehober (1963)

- Financial Director of GAZPROM Germania GmbH.
- Studied in Moscow from 1978 to 1982 and worked for the Stasi between 1985 and 1989.

Matthias Warnig (1955)

- Managing Director/CEO of the Nord Stream AG and former intelligence operative for the East German Stasi.
- Furthered by KGB Lieutenant-Colonel Vladimir Putin in Dresden.

Hans-Uve Kreher

- Director on personnel and organizational matters of GAZPROM Germania GmbH.
- Former Stasi agent under operative names "Roland Schröder" and "Hartmann".

That this is far more than a commercial operation is clear from the key personnel employed by Gazprom Germania. It employs a number of former East Germans reputed or suspected of being Stasi agents who had worked with Vladimir Putin when he was a KGB agent in East Germany in the 1980s. Putin was deeply shaped by his time in Dresden and when he has returned on his trips there as the leader of Russia has referred to it as "returning home." He arrived there in 1985 when he was 32 and just beginning his intelligence career. The KGB office was located at No. 4 Angelikastrasse across the street from the city's main Stasi headquarters.

> There is little information about Putin's specific tasks in Dresden, but specialists and documents point to several assignments, including recruiting and preparing agents. The work likely involved Robotron, a Dresden-based electronics conglomerate, which was the Eastern Bloc's largest mainframe computer maker and a microchip research center. At the time, a major KGB effort was underway to steal Western technology. The Soviet Bloc was so far behind, according to a German specialist, that agents at Stasi headquarters often preferred to work on a Western-made Commodore personal computer rather than on their office mainframe. The presence of Robotron may have provided Putin with legends (covers) for sending technicians to the West, or for recruiting Westerners who came to East Germany from such large electronics companies as Siemens or IBM. Putin may also have been interested in military electronics and intelligence about NATO from informers in the West.[57]

Putins's current Gazprom networks includes the following key figures:

Matthias Warnig, managing director of Nord Stream AG, who is reported by the *Wall Street Journal* and Moscow's Kommersant business daily to have been a former Captain in the foreign intelligence directorate of the Stasi and allegedly cooperated with Putin in the 1980s in recruiting West Germans citizens for the KGB.[58] According to an extensive report in the *Wall Street Journal*, Warnig received numerous medals in recognition for his service, which seems to have focused on industrial espionage, including the energy business in the West.[59] After German unification, Warnig became head of the Russian division of Dresdner Bank and during his tenure there the Moscow office enjoyed a lucrative business relationship with Gazprom and Rosneft.[60] Dresdner played a role in the state takeover of Khodorkovsky's Yukos oil company in 2004 facilitating its acquisition by Rosneft. Warnig plays an important role for Putin as an ombudsman and a crucial intermediary between Russian and Western energy companies and is on the board of directors of Rosneft.[61]

Hans Joachim Gornig, vice director for Oil and Gas, was responsible in the GDR for gas lines linked to the USSR and convinced the then head of Gazprom, Viktor Chernomyrdin, to establish Gazprom Germania. He is also the manager of ZMB GmbH, a subsidiary of Gazprom Germania since 1993. In 2008 the German media reported that Gornig arranged contracts between ZMB GmbH, with the company Gasconsult GmbH in which he was the co-owner. According to the conditions of the contracts, amounting to €1 million, Gasconsult GmbH was to provide communication and PR services to the ordering party. However, in reality these services were provided by the employees of Gazprom Germania and Gazprom. Gazprom Germania refused to comment on the allegations within the German media.[62]

Felix Strehober, finance director and reputedly a former high ranking Stasi member, who denies he worked for the Stasi, a denial contradicted by a file found in the Office of the Federal Commissioner dealing with former Stasi files. These records indicate Strehober served as an elite officer in the Stasi and worked for a time in the company run by the infamous currency trader and Stasi officer, Alexander Schalk-Golodkowski.[63] As one report notes:

> He came under investigation in May 2008 for allegedly lying about his past as a former East German spy, according to Cologne chief prosecutor Guenther Feld. More than a hundred documents from the Stasi archives were uncovered accusing him of working with state security, while he was a student in East Berlin. Strehober, who studied in Moscow from 1978 to 1982, joined the Stasi in 1985 and worked for the feared East German secret police until 1989. Strehober was fined for hiding his past, but no verdict was reached and his case was suspended.[64]

Hans-Uve Kreher, Gazprom Germania's director for personnel and organizational matters was an informal employee of the Stasi, "and collaborated with the organization under the operative pseudonyms of Roland Schroeder and Hartmann. Kreher himself does not deny that he had worked with the Stasi. A company spokesman declared that they knew about his past, however, he added that 'we are not an enterprise penetrated by Stasi agents.'"[65]

Finally, there is the connection to former Chancellor Gerhard Schröder, who accepted a position as chairman of the supervisory committee of the North

European Gas Pipeline Company (NEGPC), which had overall responsibility for the building of the Nord Stream pipeline. The majority shareholder in NEGPC is Gazprom, with 51 percent, while the German energy companies E.ON and BASF each own 24.5 percent. Schröder receives a salary of upward of €250,000 in his new post. As one website reported at the time:

It has now emerged that shortly before stepping down from office, Schröder proposed that the German government underwrite a loan of one billion euros to Gazprom from two German banks for the construction of part of the pipeline. In the event that Gazprom was unable to repay the loan, Schröder's government agreed to pay much of the Russian company's debt. Gazprom recently declared it would not take up the offer. On December 9, just weeks after the formation of a new grand coalition (Christian Democratic Union-Social Democratic Party) government in Germany, the new economics minister, Michael Glos, and the head of Gazprom, Alexei Miller, publicly celebrated the launching of the pipeline project. On the same day, ex-chancellor Schröder accepted an offer from his friend Putin to take up the post of chairman of the supervisory committee.[66]

The Washington Post reacted sharply to Schröder's move:

It's one thing for a legislator to resign his job, leave his committee chairmanship and go to work for a company over whose industry he once had jurisdiction. It's quite another thing when the chancellor of Germany—one of the world's largest economies—leaves his job and goes to work for a company controlled by the Russian government that is helping to build a Baltic Sea gas pipeline that he championed while in office. To make the decision even more unpalatable, it turns out that the chief executive of the pipeline consortium is none other than a former East German secret police officer who was friendly with Vladimir Putin, the Russian president, back when Mr. Putin was a KGB agent in East Germany. If nothing else, Mr. Schroeder deserves opprobrium for his bad taste.[67]

The comments of the then Chair of the House Foreign Affairs Committee, Tom Lantos, were even more searing, referring to Schroeder as a "political prostitute." Lantos said, "I referred to him as a political prostitute, now that he's taking big checks from (Russian President Vladimir) Putin. But the sex workers in my district objected, so I will no longer use that phrase."[68]

It is hardly surprising that former Stasi agents would be employed by Russia. They had limited job prospects after unification and their only comparative advantage was their networks in the former Warsaw Pact and their Russian language capabilities. Dresdner Bank alone hired over three thousand people from the former East Germany, all of whom had to sign a questionnaire in which they denied connections to the Stasi. As the investigative reporter, Jürgen Roth commented, although most Germans don't suspect it, the old Stasi connections still exist, "Gazprom couldn't have been as successful without them."[69] It is not surprising that Putin would use his old network to create a new one in the country, most important to Russia's energy and other economic and strategic interests. He himself was quoted telling the German consul in St Petersburg, "I understand you've got a campaign going against former employees of state security, they're being caught and persecuted for political reasons, but these are my friends, and I will not renounce them."[70] As the *Wall Street Journal* noted, "It isn't surprising that Mr. Putin would turn to veterans of the KGB and friendly intelligence services to get things done. In the eyes of many Russians, the agency's former operatives still have an aura of cool efficiency and patriotic self-sacrifice. Men who risked their lives as spies during the Cold War developed special bonds of loyalty that carry over into post-communist times. Mr Putin has openly celebrated his KGB résumé. Former Stasi officials, by contrast, were often stigmatized in post-unification Germany because people saw them as representatives of a hated police state. East Germans believed that the Stasi spied on people in schools, at work and in church."[71]

Today Saxony, Putin's old base of operations, remains a main base for Russian business. Using Schröder's wide network, Putin expanded this base and helped legitimize what the Russians are doing in Germany and provided a lobby to promote not just Gazprom's interests but those more broadly of Putin's regime. As Marieluise Beck, the Green parliamentarian put it, "With the Nord Stream deal, Schröder gave the Russians the first real possibility of dividing and conquering." A report on her comments went on to note, "She is convinced Gazprom is different from Western firms because beyond the usual merging of politics and business, it actually helps execute Moscow's foreign policy by offering very lucrative contracts to European energy companies. Their executives then act as lobbyists for the Kremlin, leaning on their governments to put their national interests above a unified European energy strategy."[72]

Gazprom lobbying is especially strong in North Rhine Westphalia, where RWE and E.ON Ruhrgas are located. Gazprom sponsors the Schalke soccer club, and spends lavishly on public relations including amusement parks, and Russia language lessons in schools. Its reach and overreach was exemplified by the awarding of the Quadriga Prize in October 2011 to Putin, which in the past went to Gerhard Schröder, Vaclav Havel, and Mikhail Gorbachev. He was to be awarded the prize for his "service to the dependability and stability of

German-Russian relations." The public outcry that followed a report in the *Sueddeutsche Zeitung* and the threat to return his prize from Vaclav Havel forced the foundation, which had funds from a number of German companies, to withdraw the offer.[73]

Doing business in Russia involves the continuing risk of corruption but beyond what might be called "normal" corruption, there is the problem of corruption as an instrument of state policy. Here Anne Applebaum's observations on the Russian role in the West is especially relevant:

> ... the members of the Russian elite may no longer aspire to launch international Communist revolution, as they did in the 1930s. But they do aspire to change the Western norms and behavior that they see as standing in their way: they want to make Americans and Europeans less interested in human rights, more accepting of corruption, and perhaps more amenable to Russian investment and Russian oligarchs. To some degree they can do so openly. Their money buys them the services of retired Western officials, including a former German Chancellor, as well as access to public relations firms, advertising agencies, and lawyers.[74]

The German investigative reporter, Jürgen Roth has noted that this factor is downplayed in Germany.

> In Germany, with a few exceptions, politicians and publicists persistently sustain the foolish opinion that the mafias are a quantité negligeable, a parasite in an otherwise virginal society, a kind of octopus of the Mediterranean and East. This stubborn refusal to face reality on the part of politicians along with a condescending attitude towards citizens is based on a dominant, politically fragile way of speaking, by which the concept of mafia describes a method of exercising power socially and culturally linked to the south of Italy.[75]

This Russian strategy is most apparent in the states of eastern and southern Europe. While Russia is not openly promoting an alternative model to that of liberal democracy outside of its borders, as a Bulgarian commentator has noted, "The clash between the Russian oligarchic model of economic and political control and a Western style democratic system produces structural instability in the Eastern part of Europe, which may prove a strategic challenge for the EU and the transatlantic security system. The Russian strategy of energy monopolization is aimed, first, at charging extraordinarily high prices and, second, at undermining the Western strategic periphery in Eastern Europe."[76] The use of both energy companies and shell companies, which disguise Russian control of business interests has become a major security threat in eastern and southern Europe.[77]

A complicating factor in the Russia first approach of many German businesses has been the return of the markets of east Central Europe to significance for German exports and investment. German trade with the Czech Republic, Poland, and other former Warsaw Pact countries is booming and eclipsing business with Russia. Imports from the region total over €40 billion a year compared to the €15 billion from Russia. However the OA membership does not include these markets and thus does not effect its lobbying for business in Russia.

Implications of the energy revolution

The Russian share of the German and European energy markets has been declining since 2009 following the gas crisis with Ukraine. Its share of the EU gas market fell from 47 percent in 2003 to 34 percent in 2011. The role of the European Commission in restricting Gazprom's activities in the EU as well as the growing role of the European Parliament has created increased resistance to dependence on Russia energy.[78] The potential shale gas revolution in the United States and the prospect of Liquified Natural Gas exports to Europe promises to be a game changer. Even Wintershall is diversifying with Norway and is promoting shale gas and E.ON has negotiated lower gas prices with Gazprom.[79] Statoil of Norway and Qatar have emerged as rivals as well as its Gazprom's Russian competitors, Rosneft, and Novatek. The Russians face the irony of another American technological revolution, this time shale gas, undermining its strategic position, just as the Strategic Defense Initiative (SDI) of the 1980s did. It appears that Russian energy influence on Europe peaked in 2008 and that these changing market conditions mean that its energy exports to the EU are not likely to remain a major source of leverage, and in fact the EU may now have gained the upper hand in its dealing over energy with Russia.[80]

The *Energiewende*, the new energy policy of the Merkel government, which includes the planned closure of nuclear power by 2022, also offers a long-term challenge to Gazprom. Key factors influencing demand include the promotion of biofuels and alternative fuels, renewable energy, energy taxation levels, and efficiency standards for buildings and cars. Gazprom's gasfields are aging and in decline. The precipitous drop in gas prices makes the link to oil prices unsustainable. Its revenues have fallen and its net worth in 2013 was estimated at about a third of its value in 2008. Production has been stagnant since 2001.[81]

The implications for Russian policy in general and for German–Russian relations may be profound. Russia Inc. under CEO Vladimir Putin, having based its entire business model on energy and other natural resources (with the energy sector providing 40 percent of state revenue) and using Gazprom to finance its entire system has meant that Russia missed the chance to use its revenues to diversify and modernize its economy. The political authorities will have less cash to buy off a restive public and will have fewer resources to finance its foreign policy. As Anders Aslund of the Peterson Institute concludes, this may provide a silver lining in that Russia may become less of a corrupt petro state in the future, but this is only a hope.[82]

These developments also pose choices for Germany over the coming years on where to go with Russia. As a report from Radio Free Europe concludes: "With the changing gas market offering Germans their best opportunity to tack toward a strong, unified EU position, the debate about relations with Russia is growing increasingly serious. But whether it leads Berlin to pursue energy security by looking beyond its immediate national energy interests—enriching the energy industry through a "privileged" relationship with Russia—before it's too late to decide otherwise remains to be seen. How the struggle over energy plays out will affect other serious matters, including the advocacy of democracy in former Soviet republics, which Russia sees as part of its sphere of influence."[83]

What will this all mean for a geo-economic strategy? Will it shift the balance of power in the relationship more toward Germany and weaken the Russian position? Whatever the results, the deep German economic stake in Russia will continue to limit its options. Germany will continue to depend on Russian energy but the economic stake is deeper than just energy and the role of German business is likely to keep German companies engaged in Russia well beyond the Putin era. Germans will face the reality that Russia will not develop into a *Rechtstaat*, given the extensive corruption and linkages between criminal groups and the state. The German private sector will face the growing threat of contamination by Russian practices as Anne Applebaum and others have warned.[84] German companies may reach the point where the costs of corruption and the lack of a reliable legal and investment climate may become too high and they may begin to exert concerted pressure on Russian authorities to reform, but given the extensiveness of the problem this may not be a realistic option. Given the imperative of exports for the German economic and political system, German business will continue to lead on Russia policy.

However Russia Inc. poses a geopolitical problem for the German government. The penetration of Russian crime and oligarchs into eastern and southern Europe poses a real threat to democracy and to NATO. Here the debate of interests versus values make a return in a way in which values will redefine interests. The return of Putin and his increasingly authoritarian system led the Obama administration to the conclusion that the reset had reached its limits and that there was not much left it could accomplish with Putin. Both German policymakers and private sector leaders were facing the exhaustion of their paradigms of engagement and *Wandel durch Handel* without having any viable alternatives. This will be the challenge facing them in the remainder of this decade.

Security and Geo-Economics

Free trade routes and a secure supply of raw materials are crucial for the future of Germany and Europe. Around the globe, changes are taking place in markets, channels of distribution, and the ways in which natural resources are developed, secured, and accessed. The scarcity of energy sources and other commodities required for high technology products will have implications for the international community. Restricted access can trigger conflicts. Disruptions of transport routes and the flow of raw materials and commodities, e.g. by piracy or the sabotage of air transport, pose a threat to security and prosperity. This is why transport and energy security and related issues will play an increasingly important role for our security.

German Ministry of Defence, Defence Policy Guidelines, 2011

The geopolitics of geo-economics

Edward Luttwak and a few other strategists began to recognize at the beginning of the 1990s, that geo-economics was replacing geopolitics at the core or center of the globalizing international system.[1] While military power and traditional security concerns still dominated the peripheral areas of the world, the globalizing core states in the central arena of world affairs had entered what Robert Cooper later labeled the postmodern world.[2] In this system the global core traditionally included Europe, North America, and Japan, but has since expanded with globalization. "War between them has become almost unthinkable . . . Hence military power and classic diplomacy have lost their traditional importance in this central arena of world affairs."[3] As James J. Sheehan observes in his study of the demilitarization of Europe, there has been, "a subtle but definite shift in the meaning of international security, which had increasingly become a problem of maintaining order and stability rather than defending territory against aggression."[4] In Europe this has been especially the case as the European states that had been shaped by war before World War II were now made by peace.[5] Although interstate war has diminished, the international system still rests on individual territorially defined states that continue in an adversarial competition for power and influence, however this competition is now channeled chiefly by economic means. Unlike mercantilism, which left open the option of war as an instrument of state policy, "today developed states compete in the marketplace not on the battleground."[6]

As Luttwak points out, state policies are determined at the micro-level by a variety of actors, so a geo-economic strategy is shaped by the political and bureaucratic system of the state. He notes, ". . . there can be no successful geo-economic action without ambitious industrialists and effective economic bureaucrats."[7] In France the state and its bureaucracy continue to play a major, if diminished, role given its highly centralized state while in Germany the private sector is much more influential given the diffusion of power in the German system and the relatively weak central bureaucracy. Again Luttwak, the state "must allow mere commerce alone to reign on the main stage of international life, under the undisputed control of business people and corporations. By embracing it state bureaucrats can assert their authority anew."[8] The French analyst, Pascal Lorot, writes, "Nations are engaged—alongside their national companies—in offensive policies to conquer external markets and to take control of sectors of activity considered to be strategic. For nations today the quest for power and assertion of their rank on the world stage depends more on their economic health, the competitiveness of their companies and the place they occupy in world trade."[9] Even beyond this is the contention of Rawi Abdelal of the Harvard Buisness School, that commercial *realpolitik* has replaced traditional *realpolitik* as great power politics is now based on the profit motives of and shared ideas of firms.[10] Yet as Joseph S. Nye has observed, economic power is "largely local or ephemeral or both. It is difficult to wield on a global scale. The basic reason is that the locus for most decision-making is households and firms, and is thus highly diffuse."[11]

Globalization has only accelerated these tendencies from what Gideon Rachman has called a zero-sum future into a zero-sum present.[12] The increasing porousness of borders, the growing role of multinational corporations with global strategies and the decline of the national security state have led to a switch from the territorial state to the trading state. The key concern of political leaders is now with prosperity and competitiveness, not with security in the central global core. Security remains a problem in what Robert Cooper calls the premodern and modern world and the post 9/11 focus on terrorism is an example of the threats emanating from the periphery, but the American response with its exaggeration of military power and the security nature of threats has led it to fall behind in the real competition of the twenty-first century. Germany, in contrast, has forged ahead as one of the most successful contemporary geo-economic states.

Today, as the defense policy guidelines makes clear, the security of its supply of raw materials, especially energy and minerals, is the most pressing rationale for German defense strategy, in short the defense policy of a geo-economic power. This has a number of implications. It means that German security interests will be defined largely by its economic interests. Germany's strength lies in its prowess as an export power, but this is also a potential vulnerability given the role of factors outside of Germany's control. This means first and foremost that German planners must place safeguarding access to the raw materials and the international production chain needed to run the German export economy at the top of their defense priority list. It also implies giving priority to its relationships with those states that are either major German markets or providers of key natural resources, as well as promoting the German defense industrial base and German defense jobs and becoming a major arms exporter.

Military force: *Nein Danke*

Germany has seen itself as a civilian power since it reemerged from the ashes of World War II, first as West Germany of the Bonn Republic and then later as the united Germany of the Berlin Republic. The once fiercely military nation of Prussia has been a post-national postmodern power for over 60 years. Unification did not make any significant alteration in this self-perception. However, Germany is not a pacifist nation. It has substantial armed forces and a defense budget of $46 billion in absolute terms, which makes it the tenth largest in the world, although this comprises only 1.3 percent of GDP.

With the new strategic conditions of the post-Cold War world, German defense policy needed to develop a new rationale for the development of its force structure and procurement of equipment. German defense planners have undergone a number of strategic shocks since the end of the Cold War. First there were the series of conflicts in the Balkans, followed by the attacks of 9/11 and more recently the Libyan intervention of NATO.[13] The German aversion to the use of force has been tempered by what its former Green Foreign Minister, Joschka Fischer, once termed the lessons of the Third Reich: "Never Again War and Never Again Auschwitz." To which a third, "Never Again Alone" needs to be added. When these imperatives collided in Kosovo, Germany chose to use force to avoid genocide but it did so together with its NATO partners. Similarly, in Afghanistan it chose to intervene because of its NATO obligations. However it opposed the American war in Iraq, an opposition the overwhelming majority of Germans think then and now was justified. This was followed by the case of Libya in 2011, in which Germany abstained from intervention and in doing so chose the never again war option over the never again genocide imperative and the never again alone principle. At the same time it sided with two of its most important trading partners, China and Russia, against its NATO allies as it sided with France and Russia against the United States in the Iraq War.

Germans have consistently ranked near the bottom of Western nations in their belief that military force can bring justice. The Transatlantic Trends surveys have found that while Americans tend to be the most willing to see force linked to justice, the Germans are lower in comparison to Americans with only 27 percent in 2013 agreeing with the proposition that "under some conditions war is necessary to obtain justice," compared to 68 percent in the United States. However Germans are close to where other Europeans polled came out on this issue, with the exception of the United Kingdom.[14] Here again, German political culture meshes nicely with its interests as a geo-economic power. In this same poll a full 89 percent agreed that economic power is more important in world affairs than military power.[15] The use, or the threat of the use, of military force threatens trading relationships not only in terms of export markets but also in terms of access to raw materials, and is very dysfunctional for a geo-economic power.

During most of its existence, the United States provided for West Germany's security, including secure sea lines of communication. This has allowed Germany to maintain its position as a consumer of security provided by the United States. This condition is now changing given the shift of American strategic interests from Europe to the Pacific and the Indian Ocean. European security is now being left increasingly to Europeans at a time when all European nations, including the two major military powers, France and Britain, are cutting back on their defense budgets. Germany as well, already at the low end of defense spending, is further cutting its defense budget. As an analysis on the state of European security policy put it, "EU governments are increasingly turning inwards and defense budgets are being cut across the board. Little attention is devoted to strategic thinking on Europe's hard security position in the world."[16]

Germany has become *Die Nein Nation*, the country that feels its lack of participation in the Iraq war and its participation in the Afghan conflict has justified non intervention. The slow move away from a strategic culture of reticence, which culminated in the Afghan commitment, has now become undone. While over half of the German public supported the German military intervention in Kosovo and early on in the Afghan action, by the time of the Libyan conflict, almost two-thirds opposed German military intervention while at the same time two-thirds favored the NATO military intervention. In other words, Germans expressed the view that others should take on the risks for something that they thought should be done.[17] The ability to say no to America and the growth of a sense of sovereignty has also contributed to a policy of nonintervention.[18]

Defending Germany Inc.

While some contend that this is a return to pacifist roots, in fact Germany is pursuing the grand strategy of a geo-economic power. As outlined in the opening chapter, this means that it sees its power as being defined by prosperity and success in the growing competition of global economic market place. Hard security is not a priority in the world in which Germany operates. It was pulled into Afghanistan out of its NATO commitments, a legacy of an era when hard security was a priority in a divided Europe and a divided Germany. It operates in Cooper's postmodern world and leaves the conflicts of the periphery to the United States. The lessons of Afghanistan that are likely to be learned in Germany will be to not allow Germany to be drawn into conflicts in the periphery but to concentrate on succeeding in the new competition of economics. This is also linked to domestic politics, where politicians are measured by their economic performance not their military successes. It also means that export success promotes an aversion to involvement and the use of force. As an expert of German and EU foreign policy, Ulrich Speck notes:

> The relationship between an economic success that is driven by exports and the reluctance to interfere in other countries affairs is the big "unknown" in the analysis of German's role on the international stage. It could be argued that by staying neutral or by staying in the EU mainstream, German politics manages to avoid confrontations and clashes that might end with interference of its business relations. But how a relative abstinence from foreign policy and a global network of economic relations are related to each other over the longer term is subject to speculation. Foreign policy experts rarely look at the economic aspects, and economists tend to ignore foreign policy.[19]

In other words, this is not pacifism but rather noninterventionism, which often becomes acquiescence. It can also result in what the German journalist, Jörg Lau, has labeled "the German love for dictators."[20]

Defense and defense spending are subordinated to these larger strategic objectives. Terrorism remains a top threat, but is viewed as one of an internal and criminal nature to be dealt with by the traditional means of law enforcement and intelligence at home. German strategists prefer a defensive strategy of dealing with the problem in Europe as opposed to the offensive, proactive strategy of going to the external sources of terrorism in the lands from which they emanate in contrast to the approaches taken by the Americans, Israelis, French, and British. Germans spent over a decade dealing with domestic terrorism in the 1970s and 1980s in the form of the Baader Meinhof group and were unsparing and often ruthless in their responses to it. But they learned the lessons of not overreaching at an excessive cost to civil liberties and understanding the political nature of terrorism. The attacks of 9/11 were hatched in Hamburg and the German government has been aggressive in tracking and eliminating terror groups based in Germany and has closely cooperated with its partners, including the United States on a variety of levels, but it has concluded that the military instrument is not very effective in dealing with this threat. German security officials are more worried about the threat at home with German- and European-based Jihadists than with going after them outside of Europe.

The resource and markets imperative

The greatest security challenges for geo-economic Germany are maintaining the sea lines of communication (SLOCs) to insure the economic system operates unhindered, protection against cyber attacks and especially industrial espionage including data protection, maintaining access to raw materials, and maintaining a secure defense industrial base. Unchecked immigration and movements of displaced persons, preventing the proliferation of weapons of mass destruction and dealing with the problems of organized crime will also be security imperatives. In regard to Russia, specifically, dealing with the effects of Russian corruption and organized crime, Russian cyber attacks and the geopolitical competition in eastern and southern Europe will be the primary security threats for German security policy, displacing the Cold War security concerns about a Russian military threat to the German homeland.

The German export machine is extremely vulnerable to disruptions in its supply chains and export markets. The expansion of its markets with the end of the division of Europe in 1990 and with the globalization that followed has meant that over €85 billion of its economy depends on maritime links. Ninety percent of its foreign trade volume and 60 percent of its value depends on maritime transport.[21] The dependence of the EU as a whole is also substantial with 90 percent of its foreign trade and 40 percent of the internal market dependent on maritime routes. These dependencies are as existential as the threat of nuclear war was during the bi-polar era.

Access to raw materials is likely to become a major factor in the security policies of all nations, especially Germany. The US National Intelligence Council in its *Global Trends 2030: Alternative Worlds* report concludes that an increase in the global population from today's 7.1 billion to 8.3 billion by 2030 along with an expanding middle class and swelling urban populations will increase pressures on natural resources.[22] The report of the Transatlantic Academy on global resource competition examined the strategic side of this competition and noted that for a country like Germany, which is highly dependent on the import of raw materials, not only access but the spill-over effects of interstate conflicts over resources, especially in Asia, will have direct effects on both the German economy and German security.[23]

German public and private sector leaders are growing increasingly concerned about the security of access to the minerals and energy needed to fuel the German economy. Germany imported over €84 billion of resources in 2009, €62 billion for energy and €22 billion for minerals. Given its almost total dependence on imported raw materials, it has taken a number of steps to develop a raw materials strategy including the creation of a resources agency. A number of government related think tanks including the SWP and the Bundeswehr Transformation

Center have undertaken studies into the implications of a raw materials deficit for Germany. As one analyst put it:

> In the next decade the policy of the German government, including foreign policy, will be affected by the consequences of the decreasing availability of natural resources. It can be expected that the mission of the Bundeswehr will be redefined, and the importance of African states and current exporter countries such as Russia and China for German policies will increase. At the same time, Germany will seek to strengthen cooperation among importer countries, which should make pressure on resource-exporting states more effective. In this context, it can be expected that the efforts taken to develop an EU resource strategy or even a "comprehensive resource policy" will be intensified; or at least, the EU's energy policy will permanently include the issue of sourcing raw materials.[24]

The team of authors of the Future Analysis department of the Bundeswehr Transformation Center focused on the consequences of an irreversible depletion of raw materials and on the consequences of the world reaching the peak oil threshold in 2010.[25] They warned of shifts in the global balance of power, of the formation of new relationships based on interdependency, of a decline in importance of the Western industrial nations, of the "total collapse of the markets," and of serious political and economic crises. The *Spiegel* report on the Bundeswehr study focused on the implications for Germany's relationship with Russia:

> The scenarios outlined by the Bundeswehr Transformation Center are drastic. Even more explosive politically are recommendations to the government that the energy experts have put forward based on these scenarios. They argue that "states dependent on oil imports" will be forced to "show more pragmatism toward oil-producing states in their foreign policy." Political priorities will have to be somewhat subordinated, they claim, to the overriding concern of securing energy supplies. . . . The relationship with Russia, in particular, is of fundamental importance for German access to oil and gas, the study says. "For Germany, this involves a balancing act between stable and privileged relations with Russia and the sensitivities of (Germany's) eastern neighbors." In other words, Germany, if it wants to guarantee its own energy security, should be accommodating in relation to Moscow's foreign policy objectives, even if it means risking damage to its relations with Poland and other Eastern European states.[26]

The Bundeswehr study was written just before the emergence of the shale gas revolution in the United States and its emphasis upon the centrality of oil to future scenarios now appears overwrought. While the time lines may be pushed back further into the future, the essential problem of resource scarcity remains and the conclusions drawn for German security policy remain valid. The report highlights the fundamental tension between an interest- and values-based foreign policy for Germany, which is heightened by resource dependence:

> ... new selectivity in supply relationships may lead to some countries appearing to be more convenient partners; that is, those whose foreign policy is deeply rooted in the principle of non-interference in other countries affairs, and thus in the absence of political conditionality. . . . value—based concepts of foreign, security and development policy may increasingly become subject to pressure to conform to more pragmatic rival models, like those already pursued by China and India.[27]

The report warns of the need for short-term cooperation with authoritarian regimes in the fields of energy and security conflicting with long-term goals of bringing about change in these regimes. It concludes that, "the integration of economic interests and aspects of supply security into security policy and interministerial cooperation in this field is likely to be the central issue of security discourse in the years to come."[28]

In addition to the energy dependence already discussed, there is a concern for access to rare earth minerals, which are vital to many of the high-tech applications of German industry. German business under the leadership of Federation of German Industry, the BDI, raised concerns at this time as well about German dependence on resources, especially rare earth minerals. The OA produced a paper on China's expansion into Africa and Central Asia including its restrictions on rare earth exports. It concluded that Germany and the EU have vital interests in gaining access to raw materials and that China is making a major effort to secure natural resources, especially in rare earth minerals. The paper noted that these resources are vital to the high-tech sector and that they exist in Russia and Central Asia. The OA has proposed a natural resource strategy with Kazakhstan and is working with the German federal government to develop a strategy based on the model of the natural gas cooperation developed by the OA with the Soviet Union in 1970.[29]

This resource imperative will further temper the *Moralpolitik* side of German foreign policy as evidenced by Merkel's signing a rare earth accord with Nursultan

Nazarbayev in February of 2012, which gave German companies better access to rare earths. Merkel raised the issue of human rights with the Central Asian dictator, but was rebuffed.[30]

Resource vulnerability and dependence has direct security implications for the German private sector, especially the resource extraction industries. Western companies face the problem of providing security for operations in areas where states are weak or nonexistent. Steve Coll's study of the role of Exxon Mobil in dealing with security for its fields in Africa and Asia is one example of a larger issue, writing, "Exxon's sway over local politics and security was greater than that of the United States embassy."[31] Coll describes how the company had to provide for its own security in the oil-rich Ache region of Indonesia, which had been experiencing a successionist guerrilla war.[32] German firms face similar security challenges. The Bundeswehr study on peak oil discussed the challenges facing private companies in areas with fragile statehood, which provide a vacuum of government functions and in which there is a need for "corporate counterinsurgency."[33] As German interests in these resource-rich but government-poor regions in Africa, the Middle East, and Asia grow, so do these security challenges.

German defense planners will have to be concerned over the issue of sea lines of communication (SLOCs) insuring delivery of raw materials and industrial components as well as for export of German goods. The United States Navy has been the major provider of this public good for the world, including Germany, but it is likely to be challenged in the future by China as the latter extends its maritime reach to feed its expanding resource-dependent economy. India is also expanding its maritime role in the Indian Ocean region, further diluting the American maritime presence. The German navy took part in antipiracy operations off the coast of Somalia and is likely to see this as an important future mission. As one German report citing the great American maritime strategist, Alfred Thayer Mahan observed, "... control of the sea determines a state's economic welfare. Globalization without container ships is not conceivable."[34] Given that Germany thinks of itself as a land power and given the severe constraints on the defense budget, it is likely that it will have to rely on the EU, NATO, and the United States to protect its SLOCs, and it is likely to be pulled into more missions dealing with this priority. Given the decline also in the military budgets of Europe's primary maritime powers, Britain and France, Germany will have to actively shape NATO and European alternatives for dealing with these threats.

The Merkel doctrine and arms exports

Cover used with the permission of Der Spiegel

On the defense industrial side, German policymakers have given a priority to maintaining a defense industrial base for jobs, exports, and the technological expertise it produces. The major cuts in German defense spending have put great pressure on the German arms industry to find markets outside of Germany. German arms exports started to rise in the mid-1960s and by 1981 reached an annual value of $2 billion. After some fluctuations in the early 2000s, the arms business began to rise again. In the past decade German arms exports have more than tripled and now comprise 11 percent of the global market. On the basis of the annual value of exports, the 2006–10 period all made it to the top ten years of the German arms industry of the post-war era. In these years, Germany became the third biggest arms exporter in the world after the United States and Russia. The German government has approved arms exports to Saudi Arabia, Bahrain, Yemen, Syria, and Libya. In 2009 alone, Germany made over €1 billion in arms sales to the Middle East, including tear gas, pepper spray, electric shock gear, shackles, and water cannons.[35] Arms exports totaled over €10 billion in 2011, with 42 percent headed for non-NATO or the NATO equivalent of EU countries, a jump from just 29 percent in 2010. Given Germany's special responsibilities to Israel and the special nature of that relationship, these arms sales raise another especially poignant choice between "Moralpolitik" and geo-economics and the trend is clearly, but not exclusively, in the direction of the latter.

This shift has been conceptualized as the Merkel Doctrine, based on the chancellor's decision to only send troops to conflict zones in emergency situations and instead to sell "partner countries" weapons so that they can defend themselves. This is in part a response to the German experience in Afghanistan and the public revulsion against German involvement there. Under this approach, the government has a rationale for not getting involved in conflicts beyond Europe. As the Spiegel noted, "The chancellor points out that her foreign policy is 'committed to values' of democracy and human rights. And yet she permits weapons shipments—in the name of stability— to unsavory regimes whose human rights records are often appalling."[36] This doctrine is a reversal of many years of policy in the Bonn Republic of limiting or prohibiting exports of weapons to "areas of tension." This was one legacy of the Holocaust and Germany's determination not to provide weapons that could be used against Israel, with "areas of tension" being a code word largely for the Middle East. German leaders also did not want to be involved in providing weapons to autocratic regimes that would use them to suppress dissent. It was for this reason that the then Chancellor Helmut Schmidt denied the sale of Leopard tanks to Saudi Arabia in the 1970s, despite pressure from the arms industry.

Table 5.1 World's largest arms exporters 2001–10

2001–10 Rank	Supplier	2001	2002	2003	2004	2005	2006	2007	2008	2009	2010
1	United States	5908	5229	5698	6866	6700	7453	8003	6288	6658	8641
2	Russia	5896	5705	5236	6178	5134	5095	5426	5953	5575	6039
3	Germany	850	916	1713	1105	2080	2567	3194	2500	2432	2340
4	France	1297	1368	1345	2219	1724	1643	2432	1994	1865	1834
5	United Kingdom	1368	1068	741	1316	1039	855	1018	982	1022	1054
6	China	499	509	665	292	303	597	430	586	1000	1423
7	Netherlands	203	239	342	209	583	1187	1326	530	545	503
8	Sweden	880	191	526	314	538	432	366	454	383	806
9	Italy	216	426	341	212	774	502	684	417	514	627
10	Israel	407	436	368	628	368	299	438	281	807	472

Source: Stockholm Peace Research Institute: the totals are in euros

Tank exports To Saudi Arabia: A case study in the Merkel Doctrine

On June 27, 2012 in the small cabinet room in the German Chancellery, a paradigm shift in German foreign policy occurred.[37] There a meeting of the Federal Security Council took place chaired by Chancellor Angela Merkel in which a decision was made to deliver more than two hundred of Germany's top of the line Leopard 2A7+ model to the Kingdom of Saudi Arabia.

> This would be the first time Germany supplied heavy arms to an Arab government that has declared its intentions to fight its opponents "with an iron fist," a country that deployed tanks against demonstrators in a neighboring country and ranks 160th on the Economist's Democracy Index, just a few spots above North Korea, which holds the very bottom spot.[38]

Merkel, on this day, broke with the long-standing German policy, from Helmut Schmidt through Gerhard Schröder, not to export weapons of war to crisis regions. Merkel "determined it to be acceptable to deliver weapons wherever doing so best serves Germany's geopolitical and economic interests."[39] The first phase, which began in 2010, was initiated by Frank Haun, the chairman of the board at Krauss-Maffei Wegmann:

> "As chairman of the board at Krauss-Maffei Wegmann, a Munich-based arms manufacturer with 3,500 employees, Haun was looking to tap new markets. Krauss-Maffei Wegmann had been hit hard by the Greek crisis as well as by budget cuts at the Bundeswehr, Germany's armed forces. The number of orders the company received was dropping and annual sales looked likely to slip beneath the billion-euro threshold by the end of the year. Haun also liked to complain about the 'enormous competitive disadvantages' his company faced, because 'in no other country in the world' did the defense industry face 'more severe export limitations' than in Germany. Given all these factors, Saudi Arabia fit quite nicely as a new market for the Leopard tank."

Haun addressed the Defense Ministry, the Chancellery and the Foreign Ministry, relaying the considerable interest from Riyadh to buy Leopards. Riyadh indicated that Saudi Arabia was interested in buying 200 tanks, making the deal worth up to €5 billion. Haun met with Foreign Minister Westerwelle and was able to get the Foreign Ministry to go along with the deal, a break with its usual reticence to do these type of deals. Both Merkel and Westerwelle agreed not to block the deal, but with one caveat: "No German government sells heavy-duty 'made in Germany' military equipment to an Arab country that stands in opposition to Israel's security interests."

The Spiegel account of the meeting relates that the Foreign Ministry staff noted that the possibility of these weapons being used against demonstrators in the Arab Spring weighed against the deal while the Saudi's role in the region as a security guarantor in the region was an argument in favor. The foreign minister did not take a position in the meeting while the economics minister spoke in favor and the justice minister argued against it on the grounds that it went against German policy going back to Hans Dietrich Genscher's time as foreign minister. Interestingly, all three ministers were members of the FDP. In the end Westerwelle went along with the decision to sell the arms to the Saudis as he knew that Merkel had made up her mind to do so. Merkel cited Israael's approval of the deal and the need to have Saudi Arabia act as a counterbalance to Iran. "Another argument put forth in the chancellery that day was that the deal would be a complete package, not a one-time delivery, with Germans providing technical support, logistics, and training as part of the agreement. This would give Germany long-term influence in the country, the tanks providing a point of access to Saudi leaders. . . . The session minutes, classified as confidential, show the various arms deals discussed that day in table form. Beside the agenda item Saudi Arabia, just one word is noted: "Approved." At around 5:25 p.m., the chancellor brought the session to a close. The ministers had taken less than an hour to make history."

In a speech in September given to a group assembled by the Körber Foundation, Merkel elaborated on her decision stating that it was right to arm countries in order to act in Germany's interest: "If Germany shies away from military intervention," the chancellor suggested, "then it's generally not enough to send other countries and organizations words of encouragement. We must also provide the necessary means to those nations that are prepared to get involved. I'll say it clearly: This includes arms exports." In her second key point, the chancellor outlined a new, internationally networked arms policy. "But we should try to go a step further," Merkel continued. "If we in NATO agree that the organization is not capable of solving all conflicts and that emerging, newly industrialized countries and regional organizations should take on more responsibility, then we in NATO also need to take steps toward a common policy when it comes to arms exports." The speech was the formulation of the Merkel Doctrine and its new defense guidelines.

In a position paper delivered to the European Commission on October 27, 2011, the German government argued that when it comes to export controls, "The effort to prevent proliferation and destabilizing arms accumulations should not unreasonably hinder or impede legal trade, particularly when it comes to economic relations with new regional powers." The document focused on so-called dual-use goods, which have both military and civilian applications. Both "foreign and security policy considerations" as well as "economic interests" should be "adequately considered."[40] This marked a clear shift in the direction of a geo-economic security policy, one that serves both strategic and economic interests and supports a German defense industrial complex, albeit of a different nature and scale than the American one.

The German arms industry remains a significant political force in Germany and is able to lobby effectively for both preferential awarding of defense contracts by the German Ministry of Defense as well as for a free hand in exporting arms. As one report on lobbyists in Germany notes, "Who and to what extent lobbies for the export and production of weapons is completely non transparent—both from the side of the arms firms as well as from interested buyers."[41] Small compared to its British and French counterparts, German defense companies tend to be regionally concentrated in Baden Wuertemberg and Bavaria, giving them clout within the chancellor's party, the CDU and its Bavarian sister party, the CSU. The arms industry directly employs about 98,000 people and indirectly another 218,640 people in Germany. The Table 5.2 lists the top five German arms industries and their ranking among the top one hundred in the world, including EADS, which is a joint venture European venture with a large German ownership stake.

As the Spiegel article noted, "Either it shrinks with declining demand, or it develops new markets. But those markets happen to be regions of the world where dictators are at war with one another, religious regimes are funding terrorists or autocrats use violence to suppress their own people. The biggest growth markets are in the Middle East and in the emerging economies of Southeast Asia and South America."[42]

This is also the conclusion of the SIPRI annual report in 2013, which states, "One of the consequences of the financial crisis in the USA and Europe has been additional pressure to seek new export markets. This has led the USA and European states to streamline bureaucratic procedures and to be more willing to engage in licensed production, technology transfer and cooperative production arrangements."[43] In the wake of the Merkel Doctrine, German exports have continued to climb.

As noted above, decisions on arms exports are made in secret by the Federal Security Council, which consists of the chancellor and the eight permanent members of the Cabinet. Journalistic reports indicate that the Justice Ministry and the Development Ministry have been the major skeptics on loosening controls on arms exports, while Finance, Defense, and Economics (the core geo-economic ministries) have been in favor. The foreign minister is reported to take public positions opposing these sales, but privately has promoted arms sales in a number of cases, including to Russia and Egypt.[44]

One consideration behind this strategy is that it serves business interests and saves or even creates jobs. Germany has continuously lowered its military

Table 5.2 German firms in the SIPRI top 100 arms-producing and military services companies in the world excluding China, 2011. (Figures for arms sales, total sales and total profit are in millions of US dollars)

Rank [b] 2011	Rank [b] 2010	Company [c]	Country	Sector	Arms sales (US$ m.) 2011	Arms sales (US$ m.) 2010	Total sales, 2011 (US$ m.)	Arms sales as share of total sales, 2011 (%)	Total profit, 2011 (US$ m.)	Total employ-ment, 2011
7	7	EADS		Aircraft, Electronics, Missiles, Space	16 390	16 360	68 295	24	1 442	133 120
26	32	Rheinmetall		Artillery, Electronics, Military vehicles, Small arms/ammunition	2 980	2 660	6 192	48	313	21 520
49	57	ThyssenKrupp		Ships	2 080	1 340	68 244	3	−2 479	180 050
54	54	Krauss-Maffei Wegmann[i]		Military vehicles	1 740	1 590	1 807	96	..	..
60	63	Diehl		Missiles, Small arms/ammunition	1 380	1 210	4 072	34	71	13 970

Source: Stockholm International Peace Research Institute
http://www.sipri.org/research/armaments/production/Top100

expenditure since the end of the cold war and has stayed below NATO's 2 percent of GDP prescription over the last 20 years. Although Germany is the third largest contributor to the NATO mission in Afghanistan, its opposition to the invasion of Iraq and the intervention in Libya confirm the country's traditionally skeptical stance toward foreign interventions. With little appetite for participating in missions abroad and shrinking military budgets, the tens of thousands of jobs provided by the arms industry in Germany can only be upheld by the expansion of foreign markets.

These are the jobs that the proposed merger of Europe's two defense giants, the British BAE and the Franco-German EADS might have endangered. The idea of the merger was based on sound business considerations and would have created the world's largest aerospace company and the perspective of a long-needed deepening of the EU's defense industries. However, the deal collapsed when Angela Merkel unexpectedly blocked it. Although the exact reasons for withdrawing her support are unclear, fears of a lack of German influence in the future firm, the transfer of the headquarters to Toulouse and London and as a result the outflow of high-tech jobs from Germany lay behind the decision.[45] Chancellor Merkel clearly put German interests ahead of interests in creating a more credible European defense industry and capabilities in making this decision. Given the declining defense market in Europe EADS will have to expand into emerging markets in China, India, Brazil, and the Middle East.[46]

Germany has a clear interest in consolidating the European defense market. Only by consolidating its defense industries on a European scale can German firms remain competitive against American firms and they can do so in markets that are not politically sensitive. The case of Airbus is a good example as a purely German firm would not have the capabilities or capacity on its own to compete with Boeing. In addition only by defense consolidation can these firms have a European and global market large enough to sustain themselves. This will require the German government to decide which defense industries it can support and how it can promote European consolidation.

The NATO Libya operation revealed significant deficiencies in European defense capabilities, deficiencies that will only grow with the cuts to defense budget around Europe, including in both Britain and France. The Libya campaign saw a shortage of reconnaissance means and aircraft as well as the lack of a global electronic interface to coordinate weapons systems. The Libya case was also an indication of the long-range strategic consequences of the US shift toward Asia in its strategic priorities, leaving the Europeans to fill in the gap in their region.

The long-term result of these trends is "a Europe that is incapable of defending its strategic interests outside its borders."[47] The German government will have to make some tough decisions on the defense industrial division of labor within Europe and will need to draw a line between industry and strategy, including deciding, "What role does national and international arms industry play in German security policy and vice versa."[48]

Drones and German security

The development of drone technology is a major development in military technology with important implications for security policy and the ability to keep up with competition in the high-tech sector. Drones now pose a central question for the future of security policy as they now promise a casualty free (for the attacker) means of using force and after the Afghanistan experience this means minimizing "boots on the ground." Given the aversion of all Western democracies in the wake of the wars in South Asia and the Middle East to deploy forces for substantial periods of time, drones are a tempting low cost alternative for politicians and military planners. This is a concern for many Germans who fear that drones will make it easier to turn to the use of force and would elevate its role in a world in which they would like to see the contrary occur. Regarding the use of drones, the German public was by far the most opposed of all the Western publics polled with 61 percent opposing and 38 percent approving their use compared to an average of the 11 EU publics surveyed of 53 percent disapproving and 41 percent approving. In the United States approval was overwhelming by 71 percent to 25 percent disapproving.[49] The discussion in Germany has tended to blur the differences between combat and surveillance drones, and what each should be used for.

The drone issue became a major concern for Defense Minister Thomas de Maziere in 2013 when it was revealed that the Ministry of Defense (MoD) had spent €600 billion on developing a European version of the American drone known as Eurohawk only to discover that it was not safe to fly in European skies. De Maziere had to cancel the program in May 2013 and almost lost his job over this project due to the way he handled it once it was revealed, seeming not to take responsibility for knowing about the issues involved and seeming to tolerate an attempt by the Ministry to prevent the information from being revealed. The project was a joint venture between EADS and Northrup Grumman. Nortrhrup manufactured the Global Hawk while an EADS subsidiary developed its reconnaissance system.

"The problems, which ultimately led to the Euro Hawk failure, arose out of this business arrangement. The American airspace permit for the Euro Hawk— the prototype was built in the US—was not valid in Germany and could not be obtained, because German regulators had no experience with the new drone technology. And according to the German defense ministry, the American side withheld documents detailing the technical specifications of the Euro Hawk. As a consequence, it could not be proven beyond doubt that the Euro Hawk would not pose a danger to civilian air traffic.

The Euro Hawk company claimed that the drone system functioned flawlessly, while promising that it would lay out an 'affordable and doable' plan to address the safety concerns. In other words, the project could be completed if money kept coming from the defense budget. But the defense ministry cancelled the program in May and is now searching for a new platform. The reconnaissance system designed by EADS should, if possible, be used in an alternative drone project."[50]

Like a number of other attempts by German firms to collaborate with American defense contractors, Euro Hawk was a failure.

Beyond the issue of management competency and responsibility, there is also the technological aspect and prospect that, as Markus Kaim of SWP put it, "Germany is being left behind. Apart from the United States and Israel, many countries have or are developing armed drones, such as Britain, China and India." A technological gap is opening between most NATO countries that do not have drones, and the United States, which will widen even further, adding more strains to the alliance.[51] Here again there will be a conflict between the geo-economic imperatives of technological competition and a strategic culture that remains deeply suspicious of the development of military capabilities.

The Merkel Doctrine became an issue of contention not only with a number of influential civil society groups, including the churches and human rights organizations, but also within her own party. Roderich Kiesewetter, an arms expert within the CDU parliamentary group, urged that the Bundestag be given a veto right on arms exports, but his motion was rejected by his party. The chair of the CDU's working group on defense, Ernst-Reindhard Beck forcefully defended German arms exports, stating in June 2013, "We who are proud of export nation Germany should also be so regarding arms exports."[52] The dark side of this approach became apparent after the use of chemical weapons by the Syrian government in August 2013. Just days before the Bundestag elections of 2013, it was revealed that German firms, along with other Western companies, had contributed to Bashar El Assad's stockpile of chemical weapons.

Also despite German criticism of America's gun culture German firms ranked third in small arms exports to the United States behind Brazil and Austria, selling 313,528 firearms in the US market in 2011 according to the US Bureau of Alcohol, Tobacco, and Firearms.[53] This is part of a larger market for German small arms exports as Germany is the third largest exporter of small arms in the world, trailing only the United States and Italy.[54]

The German approach to viewing arms sales as primarily driven by economic considerations carries with it a number of strategic implications. Arms exports have an impact on regional military balances making Germany responsible for both change and stability in a region. In addition, Germany carries a responsibility to provide spare parts so that in the case of conflict it becomes a de facto ally of the nation or nations it supplied. As one commentator notes, "If Saudi Arabia goes into a war with German tanks, providing spare parts to Riad and thus support to its campaign and could raise the terrorism danger in Germany."[55] In addition, customers are demanding not only the weapons systems but the technological know-how as well, creating tomorrows competitors. The more international German firms become the less dependent they will be on German policy and German interests.

Germany faces some important choices regarding the future of its arms export policy. To what extent should it be driven by industrial priorities as opposed to a security-policy-based rationale? How transparent should these policies be? Currently these are very nontransparent decisions made in secret by the Federal Security Council with the Bundestag being informed after the fact. Finally how European should defense industrial consolidation be and how can German policies support this needed Europeanization?[56]

Cyber security and industrial espionage

Cyber security is another key security concern for Germany. As one study on cyber security policy in Europe observes, "The old threat scenario involving tank divisions from the East has been replaced by the challenge posed by invisible adversaries whose geographical source can often not be determined. Virtual attacks, threatening critical infrastructure, government institutions and personal data form one of the key challenges to security policy in the 21st century."[57] The United States has created a Cyber Command and NATO has recognized in its 2012 Strategic Concept that defending against cyber attacks is an urgent security challenge.

In Germany a number of steps have been taken to shape its response to this new security threat, including the adoption of a national cyber security strategy in 2011, the consolidation of cyber security competences in the hands of the Federal Government Commissioner for Information Technology and the creations of the National Cyber Defense Center that integrates the capabilities of the intelligence and security services.[58] A National Cyber Security Council was also established in 2011 involving the chancellery, various ministries, the states, and industry representatives as associate members to decide wider cybersecurity policy and to strengthen cooperation between government and business. However funding and personnel for these initiatives remains small.

German security planners have to be primarily concerned with combating *cyberwar* by states against the military and civilian populations of other states as was the case of Russian cyberattacks on Estonia and Georgia or the Stutznetz attacks on Iran; this category would also include *cyberterrorism* such as the hacking into cybersystems to create nuclear power plant meltdowns and *cyberespionage* involving breaches into governmental or nonstate enterprises by foreign government agencies. For example, the German Minister of the Interior told the 2011 Munich Security Conference that the German government experiences four to five attacks every day on its cybernetwork. It is also estimated that the German government has infiltrated over 90 computers in Afghanistan and Congo.[59]

The emergence of cyberpower in the twenty-first century is a major example of power diffusion and creates a challenge for states as "more things are happening outside the control of even the most powerful states."[60] This diffusion also blurs the lines between domestic and international and spills over into the competencies of almost all government agencies and the private sector. It also blurs the lines between governments and criminal elements as is the case with the Russian Business Network, which has inherited some capabilities and personnel from the former Soviet state and maintain connections with the government.[61] The Bundeswehr acknowledged that it has a Computer Network Operations Team capable of offensive action. It is part of the Strategic Reconnaissance Command stationed in Rheinbach, near Bonn. Press reports suggest the unit started training a few years ago and reached initial operational capability in 2012. However, actual offensive operations would require the approval of the German parliament, as all German military actions do.[62] In the view of a German defense analyst and former planner, Germany needs to do more on the offensive capability side:

> Cyber is a particular important issue addressing in particular "prosperity." Germany is well regarded by experts as among the leading nations in the world. Yet the government is not too well prepared. The best expertise is in private

groups and the military. There is a lack of a governmental capability. The official position is: focus on cyber defense, which is ridiculous with regard to the cyber environment that clearly favors the attacker. There will be several interagency and multinational initiatives to come to include participation of countries such as Brazil and Japan but the capability for offensive action remains more theoretical than practical. Our CERT teams are excellent, but neither the legal situation nor equipment, training and organization allow for offensive action.[63]

Cybercrime, including theft of intellectual property, extortion, fraud, and identity theft, is not a security threat in this sense although it is a major problem for law enforcement and for the private sector.[64] The competitive edge of German industry is centered around its ability to apply sophisticated and precision technology to industrial products. German dependence on high-tech exports and patents has made this an especially important concern, given that German companies face the rise of major competitors, especially China, where the issue of stolen intellectual property from German firms is a growing concern.[65] A prime example is the field of solar technology where Chinese firms have used German technology to produce solar panels at the same levels of quality but for much lower cost, in effect driving German firms out of many markets. For a geo-economic state, this is like having hundreds of Pearl Harbor attacks daily. A July 2013 survey of 400 German businesses conducted by Ernst and Young revealed that German companies were increasingly concerned about industrial espionage, with 76 percent expecting it to increase in the future, although 82 percent felt their firms were adequately protected. When asked which countries or regions posed the greatest risks for industrial espionage, China was listed by 28 percent, the United States by 26 percent, and Russia by 12 percent.[66]

The survey was taken in the immediate wake of the revelations by Anthony Snowden of the US National Security Agency's Prism program, which dealt with activities focused on combating terrorism. However the continuing revelations of the linkage between eavesdropping for terrorism and individual data protection blurred the lines among counter terrorism, industrial espionage, and civil liberties. When the same question was asked two years prior only 6 percent of German companies listed the United States as a high risk center for industrial espionage and data theft. Concerns about Russian attacks also had increased, doubling from 6 percent in 2011 to 12 percent in 2013. The main concrete results of cyber attacks were the violation of patents (24%), counterfeiting of products (24%), and poaching employees to gain inside information (21%) and the main motives attributed for these activities was to gain a competitive advantage (48%).

The governmental threat assessment has centered on mafia style private actors operating on the demand of the Russian government as well as for international organized crime groups. The website http://www.sicherheitstacho.eu/ hosted by the Bundesamt für Sicherheit in der Informationstechnik (BSI), which updates cyber attacks monthly revealed that Russia ranks high as a source. However, Germany itself ranks relatively high as a source of cyberattacks, with about a half a million a month emanating from German-based sites.

The Snowden leaks set off a firestorm in Germany over the issue of data privacy. Snowden revealed that 500 million pieces of personal data were intercepted each month in Germany with the collaboration of the BND, the German Intelligence Agency. Not only was German business confidence in the US damaged, but public pressure on the Merkel government to take action was substantial. This was ratcheted up with revelations in October 2013 that the NSA tapped into Merkel's personal cell phone. Given the German past, which included eavesdropping and spying on citizens by Hitler's Gestapo and the East German Stasi, Germans are more sensitive to this than most Europeans. The sharing of information between Western intelligence services is one thing, but American spying on the offices of the EU representatives in New York and Washington and on the German chancellor indicated a much more comprehensive and uncontrolled program, which had little to do with counter-terrorism. Distrust of American motives spilled over to such American companies as Google and Apple when they reported that they had turned over records of individual Europeans to the American government.

The cyber world is central to geo-economic powers. It has the potential of shifting perceptions of partners and adversaries or more likely blending the two so that Germany's key partners, like the United States and China, can also become it key adversaries at the same time. Following the disclosure that the Americans had tapped into Merkel's phone and had done a massive search of French phone and internet data, the commercial dimension came out into the open. The United States has engaged in a major effort to deal with what the White House called an unprecedented level of theft of trade secrets by China and American intelligence officials have pointed to efforts not only by China but by EU nations to steal commercial secrets. The French have been considered by American officials as "one of the most talented powers at stealing industrial secrets and intellectual property . . . although in recent years they has been pushed to the sidelines by the Chinese."[67]

To German private sector executives, the Americans provide both an important market and an important competitor. Nostalgia about the Berlin

Airlift and the fall of the Berlin Wall is being replaced with images of America as Big Brother and of a country that spies on its friends and allies. It undermines confidence in American companies and gives an opening to German ones.[68] Some early estimates put the losses to US cloud companies in Europe at between $22 and $35 billion and Prism has made the case for European cloud systems. Reinhard Clemens, CEO of Deutsche Telekom's T-systems group, already argued in 2011 that creating a German or European cloud computing certification could advantage domestic cloud computing providers. He stated, "The Americans say that no matter what happens I'll release the data to the government if I'm forced to do so, from anywhere in the world. Certain German companies don't want others to access their systems. That's why we're well-positioned if we can say we're a European provider in a European legal sphere and no American can get to them." And after the recent PRISM leaks, German Interior Minister Hans-Peter Friedrich declared publicly, "whoever fears their communication is being intercepted in any way should use services that don't go through American servers."[69] The French and German governments proposed stricter controls on data flows and data protection both within the EU and in the major free trade and investment talks with the United States.

Russia and German security

Russia is no longer a direct military threat to German security but rather an indirect one. Most German assessments of Russian military capabilities stress their weaknesses and problems rather than their capabilities to strike Germany. It remains a nuclear power but its conventional forces have outdated capabilities with only ten percent of its weapons systems judged to be up to date. It is especially deficient in the high-tech and information systems areas and remains an industrial army in an era of network centric warfare.[70] It needs to be reshaped into a smaller and more deployable force but the resistance of the military leadership combined with other spending priorities has undermined any serious reform. The short war with Georgia in August 2008 provided evidence of how incapable Russian forces were in network centric operations and how deficient they were in the areas of communications, tanks, aircraft, and helicopters. They were capable of defeating a small post-Soviet country but remain incapable of dealing with a larger conventional war.[71]

If military reforms were to succeed, Russia could pose a major factor in regional conflicts in its immediate region, but it will not pose a credible conventional threat to Germany and its NATO partners. The restructuring of German armed forces away from its old heavy conventional force structure aimed at preventing an invasion from the East toward smaller more mobile forces reflects this basic shift in the threat perception. Russian nuclear forces remain a threat and the Kremlin has used the threat of targeting these forces on Europe to counter the development of NATO anti-missile systems. German defense planners are interested in air and missile defense systems not to deal with a Russian threat but in regard to broader NATO responsibilities and threats from the south.[72] Missile defense systems will be needed to protect German and NATO forces deployed outside of the NATO region. There is also a geo-economic interest in missile defense systems, "From a military-technical point of view, Germany is aware that if it made no national contribution to the system, German companies would largely be excluded from air and missile defense development projects in Europe, and in the future Germany might become dependent on its allies in both the military and industrial dimensions."[73]

As detailed in the previous chapter, German concerns about Russia stem from the corruption it supports and fosters both within its borders and in Europe. Cyprus is an example of this new type of threat. The financial crisis that struck that island in 2012 brought a direct clash between Germany and Russia. As one journalist observed, "Kremlin anger over its losses in Cyprus could put the nail in the coffin of the 'special relationship' shared by Germany and Russia, German businessmen and advisers increasingly fear."[74] When Cyprus went to the EU to bail it out from its financial crisis, the terms set threatened to cause huge losses for Russian billionaires and state-run businesses, and possibly for Putin himself. Cyprus had become a Russian island, kept afloat by Russian money-laundering operations. As the German government deliberated over how it should respond to the request of Cyprus for an EU injection of €10 billion, (of which €2 billion would come from German taxpayers) the German Intelligence Service wrote a report pointing out that any bailout would benefit Russian oligarchs, businessmen, and Mafiosi. The report noted that the amount of Russian money in Cypriot banks totaled €26 billion, larger than the GDP of Cyprus.

> The BND officers didn't bring good news. Formally, the island nation sticks to all the rules on combating money laundering laid down by the EU and other international agreements, the agency said. The country had passed the necessary laws and set up the required organizations. But there were problems when it came to implementing those rules, it added. They weren't being applied properly. The Cypriots, the BND said, sign everything, pledge a lot, but keep few of those promises. Money laundering is facilitated by generous provisions for

rich Russians to gain Cypriot citizenship, according to the BND which found that some 80 oligarchs have gained access to the entire EU in this way.[75]

Cyprus is another case, like Bulgaria, Croatia, and the Czech Republic where Russian money and corruption are being used to control weak states and undermine both the EU and NATO. The geopolitical side is enhanced by the large gas reserves discovered off the coast of Cyprus and in which the Russians have an interest. Talk of a possible Russian naval base on the island was also in the air. In the end the troika of the EU Commission, the ECB, and the IMF provided a €10 billion package in return for central control of the banks and other restrictive measures. Russians depositors did take a haircut and the result further soured German–Russian relations and undercut those in Germany who would foster a closer relationship.

Despite these new security challenges, Germans remain committed to a form of cooperative security with Russia. They cannot change geography and must find ways of living with a nuclear power in its neighborhood. Germany also has to manage the region between Russia and itself, which has been the source of bloody competition during the twentieth century. It is to this region that we will now turn.

Germany's *Russlandpolitik*: Implications for the United States, Poland, and Europe

Russia as the centerpiece in the German–American relationship

Both Russia and Germany remain important to the American foreign policy agenda. Russia is a component in a wide array of policies central to any American administration, including dealing with Iran and the construction of a broader nonproliferation regime, energy security, nuclear arms reductions, and Afghanistan. Russia policy will also be central to American designs for European security, including how to deal with aspirants in the shared neighborhood between NATO and Russia. Finally the Russian role in helping to broker the Syrian regime's use of chemical weapons in 2013 helped bail the Obama administration out of a dangerous cul-de-sac and might result in the destruction of Syria's chemical arsenal.

Germany has become Washington's key European partner in all areas of European policy, and will be a key player in Europe on dealing with Russia. Berlin plays a decisive role in shaping a coherent and successful Russia policy and no unified European policy on Russia is possible without Germany. Yet while Germany is crucial to any Western policy consensus on Russia, there are real differences in interests, cultures, and approaches between Berlin and Washington, which could lead, and have led, to divisions if not handled well. There is a real prospect that without a common approach, Germany will increasingly play the role of mediator between Russia and the United States on issues that go beyond the bilateral policy agenda.

There has long been an undercurrent in American thinking of worry about Germany's reliability as a partner on Russia, dating back to Lenin's withdrawal of Russia from World War I, through the Rapallo complex of the 1920s, the

Molotov–Ribbentrop Pact of 1939 and then over divisions on détente policies in the 1980s. What then are the sources of both divergence and convergence of approaches between Berlin and Washington and how can the two develop a common strategy?

The legacy of 1989 in Germany and the United States

Part of German–American divergences on Russia lies in the lessons learned from the both World War II and the end of the Cold War. Germany conducted a war of annihilation against the Soviet Union designed to destroy and eliminate populations rather than secure limited objectives. A sense of guilt for these atrocities still remains in contemporary Germany and fosters an inclination to avoid policies that seem aggressive, including assertive rhetoric.[1] In addition, Germans tend to believe that the reason the Cold War ended peacefully and Germany was reunified was due to détente and engagement with the other side. The German public has consistently credited Gorbachev and former Foreign Minister Hans Dietrich Genscher for the peaceful ending of East–West hostilities. The lesson drawn for future policy was that dialogue, diplomacy, mutual trust, and multilateralism were the best approach for dealing with seemingly intractable opponents.

The American strategic culture is, in Cooper's terminology, a modern one.[2] It remains national rather than post-national and views the world in balance of power terms, although it has a stronger ideological component than that of a traditional realist state. It gives force and the threat of the use of force a higher priority than do most EU countries, especially Germany, and has a greater belief in the concept of just war. Its unparalleled military capabilities are both a product and reinforcement of this culture. Consequently, a major narrative in the United States on why the Cold war ended is a vindication of the more aggressive policies of Ronald Reagan, the Reagan of the military build up, the Strategic Defense Initiative, "the evil empire" and "tear down this wall Mr. Gorbachev." The alternative narrative that emphasizes the Reagan of Rekjavik and arms control agreements is less prominent than it is in Germany. The successful realist diplomacy of G. H. W. Bush and James Baker in ending the Cold War peacefully is often downplayed. This neoconservative Republican view of the world, one that emphasized the role of resolution and military strength in the defeat the Soviet Union, and which disparaged negotiations as appeasement, remains an important strand in American thinking about the world in general and Russia in particular.

In addition, the argument between the realists and the neoconservatives within the Republican party and realists and liberal interventionists among Democrats, was also one about the relevance, or lack thereof, of domestic political systems to foreign policy. Realists in America, as in Germany, tend to look primarily at external behavior of states and the implications of state behavior for the international political system while both neoconservatives and many idealist and interventionist Democrats stress the importance of democracy and the respect for human rights at home as fundamental to international behavior.[3] Realists view the struggle with Russia as simply a continuation of a struggle built into a state system, which is based on the competition for relative power advantage and security. Their approach toward Russia is one, however, which would recognize Russian interests and the limits of American power in a region close to Russia and in which American influence is less important than the dangers of over-extension and vulnerability. American realists also emphasize the American stake in a good working relationship with a power that has a permanent seat on the UN Security Council and a nuclear arsenal, which can still destroy the American homeland.

Thus the legacies of over 60 years of diplomatic experience have led policymakers in Washington and Berlin toward diverging strategic cultures, a divergence reinforced by American military capabilities and Germany's downgrading of military force as an instrument of statecraft. This divergence crosses party lines so that even a Democratic American president is more likely to see the need for a hard power component of a smart power approach to the world as compared to a Christian Democratic chancellor. That this legacy is still very much alive and well was evident during Foreign Minister Steinmeier's first visit with Secretary of State Hillary Clinton in February 2009. The correspondent from the *Sueddeutsche Zeitung* contrasted this cordial meeting with those between Steinmeier and Condoleezza Rice, in which they disagreed strongly over the causes of the fall of the Soviet Union, with Steinmeier declaring it the result of detente policies while Rice credited it as the fruit of Western strength.[4]

The German and American publics and Russia

When we look at the German and American public's views of Russia today, the differences are less dramatic than we would expect, given this background. As described in Chapter 2, the German public is quite critical of Putin's Russia on human rights and democracy grounds. The 2013 Transatlantic Trends survey, for example, found that Germans were more skeptical than Americans about the desirability of Russian leadership in the world. While Americans were almost evenly split over whether it would be desirable for Russia to exert strong leadership in world affairs, with 46 percent saying that this was undesirable to 40 percent holding it desirable, a full 69 percent of Germans felt that this was undesirable to 29 percent who felt the opposite.[5] Also on the favorability of opinion question the negative to positive responses where 74–21 percent on the negative side for Germans and 59–28 on the negative side in the United States.[6] In addition, Germans feel about as warmly toward Russia as other Europeans or Americans.[7]

Americans are like Germans in that they don't like Putin's Russia but know that they have to live with it. Already by 2008 a Chicago Council on Global Affairs survey found that Americans support talking with leaders of countries of hostile or unfriendly nations, with up to two-thirds of those surveyed supporting talks with North Korea, Cuba, and Iran.[8] This and other surveys indicate a resurgence of a more restrained approach to Russia and the world following the debacle of the Iraq war and the growing strains on the American economy. Even prior to the election of Barack Obama as president, polls were showing a growing American public fatigue and disenchantment with the Bush administration's approach and legacy in foreign policy, including skepticism about the ability of the United States to export democracy. The 2013 version of Transatlantic Trends confirmed this when it posed the following question. "Concerning recent developments in the Middle East and North Africa, some people say that stability is more important even if it means accepting nondemocratic governments. Others say that democracy is more important even if it leads to a period of instability. Which view is closer to your own?" Only 47 percent of Americans responded democracy to 43 percent for stability while in Germany 55 percent chose the democratic option to 41 percent stability.[9] If policy gaps develop between the United States and Germany over Russia policy there are to be found more at the elite level rather than with the general public in both nations. This divergence among elites is due not only to history and political culture but also to the nature of the stakeholders in Russia policy in both countries.

Assymetrical economic stakes

While the publics are not as far apart as conventional wisdom posits, there is a clear divide between the United States and Germany when it comes to the economic stakes involved. While German business has been the "anchor" of the German–Russian relationship for centuries and the energy relationship a key component of that anchor, the American economic stake in Russia is far smaller. Russian–American trade between the two countries was about $40 billion in 2012 with US exports totaling only $10.7 billion and imports at $29.3 billion. This is a major increase from the late Yeltsin years when total trade was around $10 billion or even over the past five years from 2007 when it stood at only $27 billion.[10] The United States was the thirteenth largest investor in Russia in 2011, with $1.3 billion in total investment, $88.2 million of which was Foreign Direct Investment or FDI.[11] America exports automobiles, machines, and tools, including tractors and agricultural goods while importing raw materials, largely petroleum products and minerals.[12] The entry of Russia into the World Trade Organization in August 2012 and the lifting of the Jackson–Vanik restrictions on trade with Russia to grant Russia Permanent Normal Trade Relations (PNTR) status opened up the prospect of increased US exports to Russia. Those promoting the granting of PNTR have argued that would open Russian markets for American firms in the areas of aerospace, agricultural machinery, and agriculture in general, automotives, chemicals, construction, and a wide variety of other areas.[13] There have even been arguments similar to those made by the Ost-Auschuss regarding how business can promote opening up society in Russia. Under Secretary of State William J. Burns told the annual meeting of the United States–Russia Business Council that:

> Nor is it just the John Deeres and Boeings who stand to benefit. A predictable, rules-based system with recourse to dispute resolution will also help small and medium-sized businesses that lack the reach and resources to compete in a more uncertain environment. Respect for WTO rules can unleash a new wave of business activity in Russia—not just from American businesses but from businesses around the world. . . .

> To tap into its remarkable pool of talent, and to attract the critical mass of investment needed to diversify its economy, Russia must also provide firms—both foreign and Russian—with a level playing field, including better legal protections and transparent, predictable rules. Russia's ratification of the OECD anti-bribery convention will be a step in the right direction and we welcome systemic reforms such as those proposed last spring that would protect whistleblowers who expose official corruption. These steps would send strong signals to investors about Russia's commitment to rule of law. Other tools like a Bilateral Investment Treaty should also be explored. The protections and

reassurance that Bilateral Investment Treaties bring would encourage Russians and Americans alike to invest in each other's economies.[14]

However the coupling of the granting of PNTR with the Magnitsky legislation banning the travel of officials associated with the death of the Russian lawyer, put a damper on these hopes and brought out the dangers of investing in Russia.

American investment in Russia remains low, although many American firms invest through European subsidiaries, and is part of a general trend in which investment in Russia comes from accounts held by Russians in Switzerland, Cyprus, and the United Kingdom to move money in and out of the country, with the outward flow increasing in 2012. There is no energy relationship to speak of and given the development of shale oil and gas this area is not likely to be a significant one in the future. The American Russia lobby is confined the US Chamber of Commerce and to groups like the Coalition for United States–Russia trade and the United States–Russia Business Council, which are small in comparison to their German counterparts.

In contrast to German interests, American interests in Russia are almost entirely strategic, starting with nuclear weapons and Russia's role in areas of key importance to the United States, especially in Central Asia and the Caucasus and to the security threats posed by Russia. As Samuel Charap has observed, "The (Russia and the United States) national security establishments continue to view each other as adversaries, almost twenty-five years after the Cold War ended."[15] The democracy agenda has been more important in the formulation of US policy than it has in Germany, but the Obama administration has downgraded this as a priority and now seems closer to the German approach. The contrast is striking between the second Obama inaugural speech when he stated, "We will support democracy from Asia to Africa, from the Americas to the Middle East," and his speech on September 24, 2013 to the UN General Assembly in which he, in the words of the Washington Post editorial board, "explicitly ruled out the promotion of liberty as a core interest of the United States."[16] In short there are more German stakeholders in the relationship with Russia on the economic side than there are in the United States while there are more American stakeholders in the strategic community than there are in Germany. The former benefit from engagement while the latter tend toward threat perceptions.

While there are substantial geopolitical, cultural, and economic differences between German and American views, interests, and policies toward Russia, the need for a common approach remains crucial to both countries. A major split over Russia policy could have important spill over effects on the broader United States–German relationship and on overall Western policy toward Russia.

The German–American strategic debate

The debate on how to deal with Russia depends on assumptions about what motivates Russian foreign policy and the linkage between domestic politics and external behavior. As described by Ellen Barry, there are two broad scenarios, concerning where Russia is headed: interdependence and cooperation or retrenchment and nationalism.[17] Under the first scenario, the financial and strategic pressures working on Russia will force it to pull back on its foreign ambitions and cooperate with the West. The second scenario takes the opposite conclusion, namely that tight economic times will foster nationalist behavior and policies. Russian leaders will try to play the nationalist card against an external enemy, especially against the United States, as Prime Minister Putin did in his scathing attack at the Munich Security conference in 2007 and at the Davos World Economic Forum in January 2009. As Barry notes, "to a Russia intent on reclaiming great power status, there may be something elemental about resisting America."[18] The economic crisis only accentuated the debate within Russia itself on the lessons it needs to draw from the collapse of energy prices and the severe financial crisis within Russia. As one commentator put it, "Will they conclude that the west has 'infected' Russia and retreat into isolationism? Or will they realize that Russia's fate is inextricably tied to the world economy and engage more fully?"[19] These considerations have been reinforced by the energy revolution of the past five years and its implications for the broader Russian economy.

The assumptions about the direction and sources of Russian policy lead to different strategic conclusions. Those tending toward what Peter Rudolf calls an "essentialist view of Russian foreign policy," see Russian foreign policy through a prism in which, "the authoritarian turn in the Russian polity and a strong-handed assertiveness in Russian foreign policy are two sides of the same coin."[20] The West, under this approach, "responds with a policy that in substance if not in name amounts to military containment,"[21] It will give up on the idea that Russia will be a partner and believes that Putin will use Russian alienation from the West to solidify the authoritarian system and defend it against domestic opposition. This seems to be the direction he has chosen since his re-election to the presidency in 2012 after which he increased his resistance against the West and his reliance on small town and rural Russian nationalism against the cosmopolitan urban centers of Moscow and St Petersburg.

While the neocontainment advocates tend to believe that Russia has given up on integration and partnership with the West, another approach, which Rudolf labels hedged cooperation and integration, is agnostic about the long-term intentions of Russia. It is based on an "interactionist" view of Russian foreign policy that accepts Russia as a great power with legitimate security interests and whose cooperation is needed for the management of key security and global issues. This school advocates an interest based, realist approach that sets priorities and avoids NATO overextension. It also holds out the hope that engagement and hedged cooperation will ensnare Russia in a web of interdependency and give it a large stake in cooperation over confrontation. In the American debate both Henry Kissinger and George Shultz are clearly in this school, and it is the one which the Obama administration has followed for the most part.[22]

President Obama came into office with very limited foreign policy experience and his formative view of Russia was shaped by his work with Senator Richard Lugar on the securing of Russian nuclear assets. Early in his first term he had Vice President Joseph Biden lay out the new approach in a speech to the Munich Security Conference in February 2009, where he spoke of pushing the reset button on relations with Russia, and was reinforced by the President's meeting with Medvedev in April 2009.[23] The term "reset" was an indication that the new administration believed that the policies of the Bush administration were not working and needed to be substantially revised. He believed that the Bush administration had overextended American commitments beyond what was within both the American national interests and capabilities. A self-described realist, the president saw Russia through the prism of American global interests and he made it clear that he favored a new, less confrontational approach toward Russia and other hostile powers like Iran.

The Obama administration regarded Russian cooperation as important to their top priority of stabilizing Afghanistan. They also sought a new START agreement and reductions in nuclear arsenals. They restructured and delayed deployment of anti-missile systems in Poland and the Czech Republic without any advance notification alienating Poland and other Central European allies, but pleasing Angela Merkel who had lobbied both Bush and Obama to stop the project. NATO membership for Ukraine and Georgia was put on the back burner as both countries had taken themselves out of serious contention for NATO membership, at least for the medium term and they looked to the EU for ways of bringing these two contentious states closer to the West. President Obama's realism was reinforced by the economic crisis the United States was undergoing. The new team in Washington wanted to cut back on their external commitments and avoid with Russia at a time of major domestic challenges thus aid in what Obama later called nation-building at home.

The reset accomplished some of its major goals. It succeeded in lowering the climate with Russia and achieved a new Strategic Arms Reduction Treaty, agreements on civilian nuclear cooperation, on Afghanistan transit, cooperation on Iran and other areas.[24] Entry of Russia into the WTO opened up the prospect of an enhanced United States–Russian economic relationship. However there were significant limits to the reset policy including little movement on Georgia and continued friction and competition in Europe's eastern neighborhood and little progress toward re energizing the United Nations.[25]

The reset also reset German–American relations both generally and in regard to Russia. The realist Obama approach fit well with that of the Grand Coalition. As noted, the Steinmeier–Clinton meeting early in the new Administration's term was a relief to the German government and public and signaled that Russia would be less of an obstacle in rebuilding the damaged German–American relationship. NATO enlargement and missile defense were defused as points of contention between Berlin and Washington and when the Merkel–Westerwelle coalition came to power at the end of 2009, the new German relationship with Poland and other nations in East-Central Europe also went down well in Washington. The START agreement was strongly supported by the Merkel government as was the accession of Russia to the WTO. Differences remained over the Magnitsky Act as German business was hardly interested in new impediments on doing business with Russia but tensions over Ukraine and Georgia eased. Chancellor Merkel came to be regarded as the most important European leader by Washington and the critical turn she made toward the new Putin regime paralleled a similar tone and assessment by the Obama team. The view on both sides was that there was little to be accomplished with a Putin government that saw the relationship with the West as a zero-sum game. When Obama canceled his meeting with Putin in scheduled for September 2013, the reaction in Berlin was supportive. As Samuel Charap described it, "Germany had a blame America first" posture when it came to troubles in NATO–Russian relations. The reset completely turned the tables on that logic, and the Germans began to be much more critical of the Russians on ballistic missile defense cooperation and other issues. In the words of one SPD foreign policy official, "if Obama can't make this work then no one can."[26]

Yet the options for Germany remained more limited than those for President Obama. Obama had taken the view that if the relationship stopped providing real benefits for the United States he would simply move on and ignore Russia. This was never really an option for Merkel or for any German leader. Even following her cold meeting with Putin in Berlin in April 2013, where she was openly critical of the human rights situation in Russia, both the general nonconfrontational style of German statecraft and economic ties kept her from disrupting the relationship any further. Unlike Obama, she did not feel that she could cancel a meeting she knew would not produce any real deliverables. As one reporter noted at the time, "Experts say that even if political relations cool a bit, the economic factor has simply become too important to sacrifice on the altar of human rights. They say Putin may face a few gentle, formal criticisms from Merkel this weekend, but nothing resembling the acrimonious dialogue that has thrown Russia's relationship with the US into full reverse in recent months."[27]

Strategic options for the United States

American administrations have a number of options in approaching the German–Russian relationship. They can choose a bilateral approach with Russia, an EU-centered one or one focused around Germany and Poland. The EU, under French leadership brokered a weak settlement of the Russia–Georgian conflict and the Russia–Ukraine gas dispute and should play a larger role. However this will require greater cohesion on developing a European-wide Russia strategy, a major task. There is no European consensus on Russia and Russia policy, although Europe is closer to one now that it was four years ago. Still European countries diverge in their interests, vulnerabilities, and strategic cultures as they relate to Russia.[28]

This leaves a number of bilateral options including France, the United Kingdom, and Poland. While it will work with the United States on a number of strategic issues, most recently Libya and Syria, France is not really a major player on Russia. France has the convenience of nuclear power that allows it to remain independent of Russia on energy and as a permanent member of the UN Security Council, it finds it useful to work with Russia on strategic issues as President Chirac did during the Iraq war when he formed a coalition with Berlin and Moscow against Washington as part of his effort to promote a multipolar world. This policy was later abandoned both due to Putin's intransigence and the impact it had of France's relationship with the new member states of East-Central Europe.[29] France also does not have the deep economic relationship with Russia that Germany has, although during the Sarkozy Presidency and in the wake of the financial crisis the French economic stake in Russia has grown. French investment in Russia rose to nearly €12bn in 2012 and military cooperation is intensifying with the two French-built Mistral-class helicopter carriers on contract with the first, the Vladivostok, to be delivered to Russia in 2014. However, under Francois Hollande, France has clashed with Putin over Syria and the Russian image in the country is quiet negative. France is less engaged in both Russia and Central Europe than the other potential partners and has no real Ostpolitik. It has ceded influence within the EU to Germany on Russia policy and remains focused on the Mediterrean.[30] Still every French government has an imperative to balance its relationship with Washington with that with Moscow and France will continue to have an interest in a good working relationship with Russia but it will not be a primary partner for Washington developing a Russia policy.

While the United Kingdom is home to many Russian oligarchs and their money, its relationship with Russia is the worst of any of the major European powers and it remains marginal to any European discussion on Russia. It still suffers over the poisoning of Russian émigré Alexandr Litvinenko in 2006 in London by Russian security services, subsequent harassment of the British Council and the British ambassador in Moscow as well as disputes with BP and Shell over oil and gas fields in Russia. The personal relationship between David Cameron and Vladmir Putin has been a frosty one as illustrated at the Petersburg G20 meeting in September 2013 when Putin referred to Britain as "a small island that no one listens to."[31] Yet the economic relationship has grown. As one Russian minister put it, "Paradoxically, the UK-Russia business relationship has never suffered due to politics and lots of UK businesses are in Russia. More and more Russians are going to Britain for the education and the financial services." In fact the volume of trade actually quadrupled over five years and reached $22.5 billion in 2008.[32] BP reentered the Russia market with a deal for Arctic oil with Rosneft and United Kingdom investment in Russia has grown, yet the United Kingdom remains isolated from Russia and is likely to be more of a supporting player for the United States in this policy area.

Poland's resets with Germany and Russia

Poland remains the other key partner for both the United States and Germany in developing a Russia policy. Germany would be in an awkward position regarding its smaller neighbors to the east if the United States made clear that Germany was acting as its sole partner in this area. Having Poland in support of a joint United States–German policy is therefore crucial. The Polish relationship with both Germany and Russia underwent a remarkable improvement with the replacement of the Kaczynski government (2005–7) by that led by Donald Tusk and his Foreign Minister Radek Sikorski. Characterized in 2007 by a European Council on Foreign Relations report as a "new cold warrior," that report observed of Poland at the time, "Motivated by Russian pressures, but also by unresolved historical grievances, they have missed few opportunities to criticize Russia in public."[33] The Schröder government helped bring Poland into the EU in 2004 but was regarded with suspicion in Warsaw given his clear priority for the Russian relationship and his neglect of the smaller member state's interests.

The relationship between Merkel and Kaczynski was a low point in the post-Cold War Polish–German relationship. The German chancellor maintained strategic patience during the Kaczynski years and moved ahead with improving the relationship once the Tusk–Sikorski team came in. The most dramatic example of this new attitude came in a remarkable speech in Berlin by Sikorski on November 28, 2011 when he stated, "I fear German power less than German inaction."[34] Although Sikorksi was referring to the euro crisis he was also making a broader point. The new Polish government realized that it could better defend its own interests when the whole EU stood behind it and that a poor relationship with both Berlin and Moscow only isolated Warsaw. As the former Polish ambassador to both Berlin and Washington, Janusz Reiter puts it, "A good relationship with Germany widens Poland's room for maneuver and makes it a more attractive partner for others. It also makes Poland more relaxed about Russia."[35] This view is seconded by long time East Europe watcher Edward Lucas who characterized the change in the following summary:

> The genius of the Tusk-Sikorski approach to Polish foreign policy is that the two men have stopped playing to the gallery and started thinking about the real Polish national interest. It cannot possibly be in Poland's interest to have bad relations with all its immediate neighbors (and arguably not with any of them). It is particularly perverse to pick fights with both your important neighbors, while relying on support from faraway countries such as the United States or even from Britain ("been there, done that," Poles might say bitterly to that idea). The quality and quantity of attention that Poland can expect in Washington is not commensurate with Poland's need for external support, especially if it is on icy terms with both Berlin and Moscow. That was the dead-end into which the previous government of Jarosław Kaczyński had backed the country.[36]

However the follow on Russian investigation and handling of the plane crash in Smolensk, which took the life of Polish President Lech Kaczynski and 95 high officials of the Polish political elite in April 2010 remains a festering wound in the relationship.

The Polish public was open to this shift as well and was never really comfortable with a confrontational approach toward Moscow. Polls show consistently that the Polish public is relaxed about Germany. Two-thirds believe that they have benefitted from German unification, largely due to the large trade and investment relationship. For two decades now, Germany has been Poland's most important trading partner, with a share of 26 percent in the export sector and 22 percent in imports. Since 2009, Poland has held tenth place in the ranking of Germany's trade partners ahead of Russia. In 2012, Poland attracted a total of €13.6 billion in foreign direct investment (an increase of 30 percent, compared to 2010) with, €3.6 billion due to German companies (2010: €1.8 billion). The value of FDI inward stock from Germany was €23 billion. In the same period, Polish companies invested approximately €1.0 billion in Germany.[37]

On their views of Russia, Poles in 2013 had a 59–30 percent unfavorable to favorable view of Russia compared to the German public's 74–21 percent unfavorable over favorable view.[38] On German views of their relationship with Poland, a 2013 Bertelsmann survey found that 70 percent believed it was good to only 18 percent poor while the German view of its relationship with Russia was divided with 47 percent hold it to be good compared to 42 percent bad. Fifty-nine percent thought that Germany's relationship with Poland should be based on cooperation and compromise while 32 percent felt that it should be based on strong defense of their own interests; the numbers for the relationship with Russia were 43 percent for cooperation and 48 percent for a strong defense of interests.[39]

The tougher line of Merkel and Schockenhoff on Russia since the end of 2012 has also bolstered Polish confidence in German policies in their region, as noted by one leading Polish analyst: "Looking east, Germany under Merkel has provided Poland with much-needed reassurances with respect to Russia and Eastern Europe. Germany and Poland are now much closer together in their assessments of Russia's tactics. They also coordinate closely and put out joint feelers toward Russia—as evidenced by more frequent trilateral meetings among foreign ministers and planning staffs. Poland would like that to continue after the German election."[40]

The relationship between Guido Westerwelle and Radek Sikorski was a close one as Westerwelle made the repair of German relations with the region a priority, making his first official visit to Warsaw and not Paris, as had been the tradition. They authored a joint letter on November 8, 2011 to the EU High Representative for Foreign Affairs and Security Policy, Catherine Ashton, urging the EU to revamp its relationship with Russia. The letter called for a mix of measures to support Russian modernization, including Russian entry into the WTO and a possible free trade zone with the EU and Russia and also urging a firm line on rule of law and human rights.[41]

This all has meant that Poland has now become an active player in any joint United States–German approach toward Russia. However as Lucas points out, while Germany now takes Poland seriously, "Germany is polite and friendly but it is not an ally for Poland in the sense that it sacrifices its own important interests to suit Poland."[42] Germany and Poland differ on a number or issues relating to Russia. Berlin is less supportive of the EU's Eastern Partnership and on Georgia, it remains more open to a common security approach to Russia, it is more hesitant on pulling Ukraine toward the EU, it went ahead with the North Stream pipeline over Polish objections and has complicated the development of a Polish Liquified Natural Gas terminal. As Polish analyst, Bartek Nowak points out, "Poland was forcing the Eastern Partnership while Germany was forcing Modernization Partnership with Russia. Both projects in both countries were considered as being in competition. In fact this reflected very different attitudes towards countries 'in-between' EU and Russia. Apart from this, Germany believed, that in Russia the bottom-up modernization is possible. Poland has never believed in this (only during a very short period after 2010 Smolensk tragedy)."[43]

There is agreement among Polish and German analysts that Russia pursues a zero-sum approach to foreign policy and is continuing the superpower politics of the Soviet Union. However German analysts have tended to see Russian foreign policy as motivated by a feeling of fear and lack of appreciation and acceptance as a great power while their Polish counterparts see a more consistent pursuit of national interest.[44] Germans see Russia as a partner due to its global role while Poles see it as a partner due to its geographic proximity and need to stabilize the region. While Germans do not see Russia as a direct threat they and Polish analysts understand why Ukraine, Belarus, and the Caucasus see it as a threat. The Poles are less sanguine than the Germans on threat perception. As one of Poland's leading foreign policy analysts, Pawel Sieboda, describes it, "the Polish leadership shudders when it observes Russian defense policy. Poland does not understand Nato's insouciance towards Russia's military potential. Russia's army has serious shortcomings, but Russia remains a nuclear power—and an unpredictable one at that. The 2008 Georgia war may have been forgotten in the west. Not in Poland."[45] Poland was a driving force in NATO's contingency planning for its region.

Polish analysts are more likely to regard Russia as a country that will use economic instruments and energy for broader foreign policy purposes than do their German counterparts. Germans are likely to believe that a partnership with Russia could stabilize Ukraine and the frozen conflicts in the region while Poles are more skeptical about Russian cooperation in solving international conflicts. Importantly, Poles want to link Russian modernization efforts with democratization of the country while the Germans are more divided on linking the two. There remains a greater tendency in Poland to push democracy promotion efforts in Russia than there is in Germany.[46]

Unlike Germany, the Polish–Russian economic relationship is insignificant. Trade remains centered around imports of Russian oil and gas with Poland exporting about $1.4 billion to Russia and importing $6.3 billion in 2011. Foreign direct investment is also minimal with Polish FDI in Russia totaling $597 million and Russian FDI only $32 million in 2010.[47] The entry of Russia into the WTO has not had much of an impact on this relationship to date. On the energy side, Poland is making a major effort to reduce energy dependence on Russia, constructing an LNG terminal and exploring shale gas options at home. Poland still imports about two-thirds of its gas from Russia and had been involved in price disputes with Gazprom, given that it is paying above market prices to it due to this dependence.

The German–Polish relationship regarding Russia will be tested in the coming years over policies relating to the Eastern Partnership and specifically to Ukraine, Georgia, and the area that lies between the EU and Russia. Poles will remain far more skeptical about Russia as a security partner and about bringing it inside the tent on dealing with European security. Germans took Medvedev's proposal for a pan European security treaty far more seriously than did the Poles, who saw this as another ploy to weaken NATO. While the Obama administration badly mishandled the missile defense issue, informing the Poles that they were changing the system on the anniversary of the Soviet invasion of Poland in 1939 and without any previous consultation,[48] Poles still regard the US security commitment as vital and have a view of NATO as an Article 5 defense alliance rather than a cooperative security organization.

Ukraine will be a real test of German–Polish cooperation on Russia policy. On Ukraine Janusz Reiter sees "Germany as the key and it is divided on the issue. Many Germans do not understand the historical importance of making Ukraine a part of Europe. However, Merkel would not sacrifice Ukraine for a better relationship with Russia. Germany remains the key player in the EU on Ukraine." Germans remain more skeptical about the prospects for reform in Ukraine. Merkel in 2012 compared Ukraine to Belarus and seemed to threaten a boycott of the EURO 2012 championships. Germans have been reluctant to do more with Ukraine until it shows substantial progress on democratic reforms and fear harming prospects for the long-term evolution of Russia democracy by pushing for Ukraine to opt for the West. Putin's pressures on Ukraine to join his new customs and Eurasia Union and not to move closer to the EU brought Poland and Germany initially closer together on this issue but may still serve as a long-term irritant in that relationship, given that the German relationship with Russia is far more important than its ties to Ukraine. From the Russian perspective keeping Ukraine out of the EU orbit allows it to maintain a neighboring state with a corrupt structure whose elite will remain dependent both on Russian energy and financial aid and also on the corruption of the Putin system.

The role of the European Union

The key question regarding where Poland and Germany go on Russia relates to the role of the European Union in dealing with Russia. Poland has a clear interest in Europeanizing Russia policy to the greatest extent possible. As Edward Lucas points out, "Compared to any individual country in the newish members of the EU, Russia indeed looks like a superpower; compared to the EU as a whole, Russia looks puny in everything except its nuclear arsenal. The Kremlin can cause great mischief in, say, Georgia, or in Ukraine, or in Latvia. But it is in no position to pick a fight with the EU as a whole. This does not mean that the former captive nations can rely on a united EU policy toward Russia. But it does mean that Russia approaches its relations with the EU from a position of fundamental weakness."[49]

Poland needs to be part of a larger European approach where Germany has been more likely to follow a bilateral relationship with Russia. "Germany as a big country, does not need to fear not being treated by Russia as an equal partner and therefore it is more willing to talk with Russia bilaterally."[50] This bilateral approach was especially clear in the energy policy area where Germany blocked any real consolidated EU energy policy for a variety of reasons and which remains a major obstacle to closer Polish–German cooperation on Russia policy, as Poles fear that Germans will go their own way in relations with Moscow. However Germany has an interest in also using the EU to give it greater weight in dealing with Russia and can at times hide behind the EU when it wants to pursue policies that will antagonize Russia. This may be the case regarding the commission's tough stance on Gazprom. The shale and renewal energy revolution also has the prospect of shifting the balance of interdependence back toward Europe and thereby reducing Russian leverage.

Russia has traditionally not taken the EU seriously as a foreign policy actor and has preferred to work bilateral deals instead. The prolonged European financial and economic crisis combined with Russia's own domestic uncertainty has reinforced the aversion in Moscow to dealing with Brussels. There are signs this is changing. The movement of the European Commission to liberalize energy markets and to take on Gazprom is a sign of a greater Europeanization of energy policy and even on Russia policy. The Eastern Partnership and the EU's moves to include Ukraine, Moldova, and Georgia in a Deep and Comprehensive Free Trade Agreement have raised the geopolitical stakes for both sides. The future of Ukraine, in particular, is a central issue for Putin. Putin's plan to create a Eurasian Economic Union is a clear attempt to shape a Russian sphere of influence to counter that of the EU and is a signal that the EU may become a far greater threat than NATO. Russia clearly sees the Eurasian Union as an alternative to the EU and as an instrument for "enhancing Russia's geopolitical standing in relation to its two biggest neighbors in Eurasia, the European Union to the west and China to the east. This is a far cry from Moscow's policies of the early 2000s, which prioritized Russia's integration into the European Union."[51]

There is little doubt that the European Union is the best way to leverage the power of its member states in their relationship with bigger powers like Russia, China, and the United States. But the member states will have to conclude that this advantage of size and scale outweighs parochial interests. Some like Greece and Cyprus are especially vulnerable to Russian pressure and could be used by Moscow to block actions on Ukraine. Angela Merkel seems to doubt what she has termed the community approach in favor of an intergovernmental one in foreign and security policy and the continuing European economic and political crisis has undermined confidence in the EU as a serious foreign policy actor. The disenchantment with Europe and with the European market that has been growing in Germany since the onset of the economic crisis in the eurozone and the pull of Germany Inc. to move beyond European markets in order to sustain German economic growth may continue to tilt Germany toward either more bilateral policies or toward a more intergovernmental approach within the EU.

From the American perspective, the United States would clearly favor a European approach to Russia as part of its own Russia policy. The increasing devolution of responsibility from Washington to Europe to deal with problems in its region has been a hallmark of the Obama foreign policy in such cases as Libya, Mali, and in dealing with Russia's role in Europe. The Pacific Pivot, war fatigue following Iraq and Afghanistan, the need to rebuild the American economy and the rise of new non-Western powers has all resulted in a new strategic environment in Europe. When it comes to central and eastern Europe the American role will be either enhanced or replaced by the EU, led by Germany and Poland. However the United States is still important and even crucial to maintaining stability in this region. Whether it will continue to see this as a major strategic interest will be central to stability in this part of Europe.

Russia will be a great challenge for the United States–German relationship during the remaining Putin years and beyond. As one German analyst points out, "Despite Germany being a key ally, there was, and is, a great deal of US mistrust in Germany over its perceived softness on Russia, its ties with Iran, and its close economic relations with China."[52] It will take statesmanship in both Washington and Berlin to contain the built-in differences over Russia and to shape a common strategy. As a report by the Bertelsmann Foundation already stated in 2008, "If the U.S. can acknowledge that Europe's perspectives on Russia start from a fundamentally different point of view, and can move on from there, they may find great utility in an open and candid trans-Atlantic exchange about what to do next with Russia."[53]

The end of the American reset will create a time of testing, especially given the limits to any German reset on Russia. The United States will have to continue to pursue a path of foreign policy restraint and realistic balance if it wants to stand a good chance of shaping a healthy new relationship with both Moscow and Berlin. However a mishandling of the United States–Russia relationship could severely test the United States–German relationship.

Future administrations will follow an approach which balances a bilateral relationship with Russia with a United States–European Union approach. Strategic arms control agreements will be bilateral and many of US interests with Russia are global. A weak, divided and ineffectual Europe will also make a bilateral approach more appealing in Washington. In some ways, the two great nuclear powers are closer in their strategic cultures than America is to Europe's. The United States still remains the primary point of reference for Russia's policies, not the EU, and this remains important to Russia's view of its status. However the key issues facing the United States with Russia, which concern Russia's role in its neighborhood, will require a joint approach with Germany, Poland, and the EU remaining the key players in Europe on Russia policy. As a German–American study group on Russia policy convened by the Friedrich Ebert Stiftung in 2012 concluded, "Neither Berlin nor Washington have discovered the 'silver bullet' when it comes to Russia policy. While the answer to the question 'what to do' remains elusive, one fact is clear: when Germany and the U.S. pursue divergent policy approaches toward Russia, on can seriously undermine the other."[54]

In the wake of the Ukraine crisis

The Russian annexation of Crimea and its destabilization attempts in Ukraine look like traditional geopolitics and have awakened references to a new Cold War, but this misses the transformation in the nature of international politics that has been brought about by the forces of globalization and its implications for Germany's relationship with Russia and the West. Russia's use and the threat of the use of military force in Crimea and Ukraine is only the opening of a much longer game, one in which economic interdependence will be decisive factors. Not only are the Western assumptions about dealing with Russia now bankrupt but so are the assumptions about where Germany will stand in this central challenge to the post-Cold War order in Europe. Germany emerged during the crisis as the key player in the shaping of Western policy toward Russia with some observers writing of a Russo-German Europe.[55] President Obama relied on Chancellor Merkel to take the lead in mediation attempts with Russian President Vladimir Putin and it was clear that whatever sanctions regime emerges will only go as far as Berlin permits.

Ukraine has pushed the tension between interests and values to its limits, with Merkel delivering a number of tough speeches and warning Putin that his actions risked "massive damage to Russia, both economically and politically," and has moved progressively closer to sectoral sanctions. However, it remains an open question over whether really biting sanctions will be supported by the German government over the long haul and without Berlin on board it is unlikely that the United States will be able to go very far in its sanctions policy without opening divisions in the West and penalizing its own companies to the benefit of European competitors. While Germany remains the key, the role of economics and finance in Russia's relationship with other European countries, including Britain (a magnet for rich Russian's money), France (going forward with the sale of Mistral-class amphibious assault ships to Moscow), Italy, and the Netherlands, means that this new geo-economic relationship goes far beyond Germany. Facile comparisons between the Cold War and this new Cold War ignore this geo-economic dimension and miss the new nature of the West's relationship, not only with Russia, but also with China and other emerging authoritarian economies.

Despite Russia's actions in Ukraine, including its absorption of Crimea, the security policy of Germany is unlikely to be substantially altered. Defense spending will not be increased. When Defense Minister Ursula von der Leyen suggested that NATO show more support for it members, which could face Russian military aggression, she quickly had to pull back in the face of substantial resistance from the German public, parliamentarians, and the Vice Chancellor, Sigmar Gabriel, who criticized her for contributing to the escalation of tensions. Yet the arguments about *Wandel durch Handel* and the need to continue to engage Russia have created a growing gap between the public statements of Merkel and others in her government and party and the continued prioritization of the economic relationship.

In the case of Ukraine, geo-economic Germany confronts a Russian use of military power with only economic tools with which to respond. Germany's Russia strategy is, like Washington's, now in tatters. Both capitals will have to come up with new approaches. The discussions in Washington seem to be between those who favor a new containment strategy with an incremental and conditional approach to targeting the Russian economy and those who would like to see a more aggressive sanctions policy and a more active use of arms shipments and NATO deployments.[56] In Berlin any idea of a containment strategy and writing off dealing with Putin is a nonstarter and would mark a reversal of its long-standing reluctance to use economic levers for political purposes in its dealings with Russia.

Geo-economic Germany assumes that economics will trump the use of military force over the medium term, if not immediately, and that Russia's dependence on outside markets will eventually draw it back from further confrontation. While the German public and the German media remain among the most critical of Putin in Europe, they also remain reluctantly realist regarding the use of sanctions, fearing they will harm the German economy.[57] Germany will continue to be dependent on Russian energy for the medium term as neither American gas or European sources can replace Russian sources for at least a decade. While there may be an adjustment to the *Energiewende*, it is unlikely that future German governments will reverse the move away from nuclear power as a means of lessening dependence on Russian energy. The CEO of engineering giant Siemens, Joe Kaeser, met with Putin in March 2014 to make a long-term commitment to continuing investments in Russia as Obama was in Europe meeting with Chancellor Merkel and calling for sanctions. Gazprom remains on track to take over leading German gas storage and distribution company Wingas.

While Chancellor Merkel has no illusions about Putin and has taken an increasingly tough line on Russia, Steinmeier and his party have always been more Russia-friendly. While Steinmeier himself has become more critical of Russia, barring a major escalation by Putin in Ukraine beyond Crimea, Germany will continue to look for ways to dampen down the split with Moscow. Its economic interests in Russia will continue to outweigh those it has with Ukraine and the Foreign Office is likely to get support from the Finance and Economics/Energy Ministries for a geo-economic approach. The Defense Ministry, as seen in the rebuff of von der Leyen on Ukraine, has not been a central player in this arena.

The Chancellor is increasingly limited, as well, by a growing anti-American climate in Germany over the fall-out from the Snowden revelations. The prospect of a serious split between Washington and Berlin over Russia remains very real. Following the Snowden revelations, many Germans have felt betrayed and have lost trust in American policies moving Germany more into a posture of equidistance between Moscow and Washington. The depth of anger and mistrust of the United States has been consistently underestimated in Washington and has made it very difficult for Merkel to support Obama on Russia policy.[58] Add to this the contrast in reactions to between Germany and Poland and the prospects for splintering of these key relationships becomes real. This confluence of factors and trends only enhances the danger that Ukraine may end up dividing Germany from both Washington and Warsaw at a time of testing for the West.

Conclusions: Germany the Shaping Power

Future scenarios for German–Russian relations

The future of German–Russian relations over the next decade to 15 years will depend on a number of key drivers.[1] First is the energy relationship. The recent energy revolution characterized by the shale gas boom and the development of renewal energy sources is still very new and the depths of it are uncertain as is the outcome of the German *Energiewende*. The initial indications from these trends point to a continued medium-term German dependence on Russian energy but a decrease in the long run. This trend poses serious challenges for Gazprom. These in turn have implications for the stability of the Putin system as well. The increasing Europeanization of energy policy will limit Germany's role to serve as an advocate for Russia within Europe and will dilute somewhat the centrality of the German–Russian relationship.

Second is the broader trade and investment relationship. The German economic stake in Russia will almost certainly remain substantial. The German finance and business sector will continue to be the main driver in German policy toward Russia, trumping concerns about the state of democracy and human rights. The key factor determining the future of this relationship will be the investment climate in Russia. German firms have been extraordinarily successful in the Russian market but the continued corruption and lack of a real rule of law in Russia will be a seriously inhibiting factor for future development of the German stake in Russia. The hope of German firms that they would modernize Russian and bring in a *Rechtstaat* have so far been illusory. The Putin government continues to believe that technological and economic modernization can be had without social and political modernization, a belief and practice that may finally undermine what remains of business confidence in Germany. Already the core of the German economy, the *Mittelstand*, is beginning to get out of the Russian market. Yet the Russian middle class has grown substantially and prospects for long-term growth in the consumer market are good. The spiral set off by German and western sanctions over Russia's actions in Ukraine and Crimea could deepen these trends toward disengagement.

The third driver will be political developments in Russia. As long as the Putin system continues as it has, there will be real limits to how close German relations with Russia will be. Not only are there the concerns of business, but the German public, the media, the NGO community, and part of the political leadership have a very negative view of Putin and the state of democracy and the rule of law in Russia. In addition, as Ukraine has demonstrated, there seems to be a direct link between the nature of the domestic political system and its foreign policies. The more Putin relies on appeals to nationalism and on a rural base of political support, the more he will stress an anti-Western and zero-sum approach to foreign policy. This system also is based on corruption and the maintenance of corrupt and interlocking networks of the state with oligarchs and organized crime. Any opening of this system would risk its demise. However after Putin real chances for change may emerge. If the new middle classes of Moscow and St Petersburg become more dominant, then an open and westward-oriented Russia may emerge and this would open up possibilities for an even closer German–Russian relationship. Modernization with the West is still Russia's best long-term strategic option and there is still a chance that Russia will return to this path after Putin.

Political developments in Germany will be a fourth driver, but not likely as significant as the first three. Given the stability and consensus-oriented nature of German politics, a major shift in Russia policy is highly unlikely. Any German government will be faced with the need to work with Russia, given the imperatives of geography and economics. Germany will continue to pursue a geo-economic strategy and will place exports and natural resources first and will limit the role of human rights and democracy concerns in its overall policies.

A fifth driver will be the geopolitical environment within which Germany will operate. A key uncertainty will be the role of more traditional strategic concerns. To what extent will economic interests override or define the German strategic approach to Russia-related policies as in the eastern neighborhood in particular? What will be the outcome of the conflict between an EU oriented region versus one dominated by the Russian-led Eurasian Economic Union? The shift of German policy from opposition to Ukrainian NATO membership to support for Ukrainian entry into the Trade Agreement with the EU and against Putin's Eurasian Union may prefigure a longer term shift in German priorities. How will the European Union and the eurozone develop and what role will the EU play in German policies in five to ten years? What will the United States–German relationship be like? Germany has begun to develop a serious debate over its strategic options, which the shift of the United States away from European security missions will only accelerate. Germany will not be able to outsource security policies as it did for most of the past six decades.

The following box outlines four possible future scenarios for German–Russian relations developed by a German–Russian team brought together in 2013 by the Friedrich Ebert Foundation, the Ural Federal University of Yekaterinburg and the University Viadrina in Frankfurt (Oder).

Four scenarios for the German Russian relations 2030

Scenario I: Cruise liner—A value-based alliance

In 2030, German–Russian relations are at their best in decades. Cooperation between the two countries is very close. Germany supports the Russian government in its political and economic modernization efforts. Both countries also work well together on security matters, particularly insofar as these are related to their common neighborhood.

Scenario II: Cargo vessel—A pragmatic partnership

Relations in 2030 are characterized by pragmatism: common interests dominate, whereas value-based policies have lost their importance. Germany is at the helm of a bloc of European states that survived the disintegration of the Eurozone. Russia succeeded in building a Eurasian Union. Because NATO has lost importance since the United States is more focused on the Asia-Pacific region, Moscow and Berlin maintain close economic relations and share common security interests centered on the Balkans and the Middle East.

Scenario III: Coast guard—A new ice age

Germany and Russia have turned their backs on each other by 2030. Russia is set on pursuing a decidedly anti-democratic track, having established a hardline foreign policy and have cut off strategic ties with the West. The EU—and Germany in particular—have become harsher and more outspoken in their criticism of the Kremlin. But, given the new geopolitical landscape, this has had little effect on Russia, which has shifted economically and politically toward Asia.

Scenario IV: Sailing boat—Business as usual

The character of relations and the set of issues at their center have remained essentially unchanged. A solid economic basis and fairly intensive societal contacts are still accompanied by a value divide between Russia and Germany. Relations are characterized by the usual ups and downs: minor crises bring value-related issues to the forefront and usually cause a downswing in relations, whereas interest-based realpolitik, although not uncontested, helps to overcome periods of more strained relations.

Source: *Germany and Russia in 2030: Scenarios for a Bilateral Relationship* (Berlin: The Friedrich Ebert Foundation, 2013)

The most likely scenarios are II and IV. The Sailing Boat scenario characterized state of relations up to the onset of the Ukraine crisis in 2014 and has shifted the relationship in the direction of the coast guard scenario but long term change can go in the direction of the pragmatic partnership given the changes it posits in the strategic environment, especially regarding the United States, or toward the Coast Guard scenario. The likelihood of the Eurasian Union taking off is minimal. The value-based alternative may have a chance in the post Putin era if the new Russian middle class emerges in a democratic direction.[2] There is very little prospect of the New Ice Age scenario, but it chances have increased after the crisis in Ukraine.

This new German strategic debate, which has already begun,[3] will include how to deal with Russia and the extent that the German approach to modernizing Russia through interdependence and engagement is still relevant. The strategy of modernization through interdependence was a version of the now traditional *Ostpolitik* approach, which has come to characterize German foreign policy. While the relevance of this approach in a radically different strategic environment from that of the Cold War has been questioned,[4] the Tutzing speech by Guido Westerwelle and his reference to *Wandel durch Handel* indicates that it is still alive in a morphed form. As Kundnani rightly points out, this is a realist approach that assumes that interests are more important than ideology. While the original Ostpolitik had as its goal the transformation of the division of Germany and in this sense was deeply revisionist, the new approach is not really aimed at changing Russia and other authoritarian powers or in using trade as leverage to secure concessions on human rights, but rather as trade for Germany's economic interests. In Hans Kundnani's words, "a perfect symbiosis between doing business and doing good."[5] Some discussion in Germany has already begun on decoupling from Russia and the Europeanization of Germany's Ostpolitik.[6]

Germany and the geo-economic world

The case of Russia is just part of a larger evolution of both Germany's role and that of the changing international environment in an era of globalization. As

Edward Luttwak observed, geo-economics is replacing geopolitics. Returning to Kundnani's typology of a geo-economic power, a geo-economic power has the following characteristics:[7]

- *A definition of national interest in economic terms*: As we have seen, while other interests are part of the German policy discussion on Russia, which has been characterized as a values versus interests or gas versus silence debate, the economic relationship has remained the dominant interest and has subordinated other interests in German policy. Only if this economic interest changes or the strategic environment in Europe is fundamentally altered will German policy change.

- *A shift from multilateralism to selective multilateralism*: Here the record is more mixed. Germany has moved from a more bilateral approach toward Russia to a more multilateral one in the Merkel years. Improvements in the German–Polish and German–American relationships have allowed Germany to coordinate its policies more with its allies and it seems to be more willing to allow a Europeanization of energy policy as well. Of course both the Polish and American resets of their Russia policies brought them closer to the German approach, but there has also been adjustments on the German side, which has also brought Berlin closer to its partners in Europe and Washington. The increasing authoritarianism and nationalism of Putin has pushed Germany and the other players closer to each other as well. The German role in coordinating European sanctions against Russia in the summer of 2014 are an important development in this regard. Yet elements of unilateralism or bilateralism remain, especially in the construction of the Nord Stream pipeline.

- *A predominant role of business and especially export oriented business in the shaping of German foreign policy*: This has clearly been the case with ample evidence of the leading role of German businesses and its major lobbies in driving Russia policy. The role of the Ost-Auschuss may have diminished in recent years but German policy remains very business friendly in its approach toward Russia. The Petersburg Dialogue is one example of the clout of German business in the relationship and the deep and extensive network of business relationships with Russia far exceeds those of the government and with over six thousand German firms active in Russia this is likely to continue. The CEO of engineering giant Siemens, Joe Kaeser, met with Putin in March 2014 to make a long-term commitment to continuing investments in Russia as Obama was in Europe meeting with Chancellor

Merkel and calling for sanctions. German business, included the Ost-Auschuss has lined up to support Merkel's tougher sanctions policies after the shoot down of the Malaysian airliner, but longer term policy remains open and Russia is a special case in this context.

- *The elevation of economic interests over human rights, democracy promotion and other non economic interests*: The discourse on human rights and the lack of democracy in Russia has clearly increased since the rigged Russian parliamentary elections of December 2011 and the return of Putin to the Presidency in 2012. The Schockenhoff resolution in the Bundestag and the tougher line taken by Merkel have raised the level of concerns about human rights clearly above where they were during the Grand Coalition years. Yet the arguments about *Wandel durch Handel* and the need to continue to engage Russia continue to prevail and these arguments tend to support the overriding German economic stake in Russia. The balance may have shifted but still favors economics interests.

- *The use of economic power to impose national preferences on others*: This had not been visible in the Russia case before the Ukraine crisis. German companies have pushed with some success for improvements in the rule of law regarding contract enforcement and other business-related areas, but neither German business nor the German government has used its large economic clout to push Russia to do what it says it wants it to do until the summer of 2014. The use of such economic instruments of power as tariffs, quotas, and rules that control access to markets, sanctions, the use of checkbook diplomacy and other means to make the other partner more dependent on you than you are upon them had not been employed.[8] This may be due to the fact that German companies are still making a lot of money despite the difficulties of working in Russia, but Germany has used its economic power closer to home in the eurozone and is likely to do so in the future. Germany has also allowed the EU Commission to take more coercive actions against Gazprom and may be hiding behind the EU and other national actors. Chancellor Merkel has imposed tough sanctions on Russia over Ukraine and but it is still to be seen if this becomes a long term German policy.

Over all the German approach to Russia has fit this geo-economic model, with the exception that it had not used its economic power to impose its preferences on Russia until very recently. While the case of Russia is close to an ideal type geo-economic relationship, it illustrates the general approach Germany takes to the outside world.

If we apply this typology beyond Russia we can expect that Germany will be driven by its economic interests and these will determine its definition of national interest. Security policy, which had been the anchor of German policy for most of the period since the end of World War II, will be defined more by German dependence on exports and raw materials. Multilateralism will be increasingly replaced by minilateralism, bilateral relations, or shifting networks rather than by alliances. Germany will be less likely to follow Moralpolitik and more likely to pursue commercial realism. Geo-economics should be regarded as the new form of realism with security now defined in economic terms.

The private sector will play an increasing role in setting the course that Germany takes in the world. Most studies of the evolving international system, including both those by the US National Intelligence Council and the EU Security Institute, conclude that private corporations will play a larger role in a post Westphalian world. As the EU Institute put it, "Non-state actors, in particular national and transnational civil society networks and private corporations, will play a critical role in the coming decades. Their power and influence will be greater than that of many states, and may lead to new forms of governance and civic action."[9] The *New York Times* columnist, Thomas Friedman has put this trend in vivid terms:

> There is an enormous gap between the way many C.E.O.s in America . . . look at the world and how the average congressman, senator or president looks at the world. . . . Politicians see the world as blocs of voters living in specific geographies—and they see their job as maximizing the economic benefits for the voters in their geography. Many C.E.O.'s, though, increasingly see the world as a place where their products can be made anywhere through global supply chains (often assembled with nonunion-protected labor) and sold everywhere. These C.E.O.'s rarely talk about "outsourcing" these days. Their world is now so integrated that there is no "out" and no "in" anymore. In their businesses, every product and many services now are imagined, designed, marketed and built through global supply chains that seek to access the best quality talent at the lowest cost, wherever it exists. They see more and more of their products today as "Made in the World" not "Made in America." Therein lies the tension. So many of "our" companies actually see themselves now as citizens of the world. But Obama is president of the United States.[10]

The former director of Policy Planning in the State Department under Hillary Clinton, Anne Marie Slaughter, has also made this point, "If you look at the role that companies are playing in the world . . . these are corporations that have to be part of the solutions of most of the top problems that are on the [US] secretary of state and president's list . . . Whether that is combating violent extremism, or climate change, or development of the global economy broadly, or global pandemics, those are not issues that can be solved only by governments . . . because they involve changing the individual behaviour on the ground. And who is on the ground? Well, foundations, [aid and advocacy groups] and corporations."[11]

In today's world the flag follows trade and investment. Politicians, both in democracies and autocracies, are rated by the performance of their economies more than by the performance of their armies. Influence no longer flows out of the barrel of a gun but rather from the power of money. This is even more apparent in the German case given the national aversion to the use of force. Economic power, however, is just as hard a power as military power. In World War II Germany conquered Greece militarily while today it influences key Greek economic, social, and political decisions through its economic clout. There is certainly a qualitative and moral difference but the impact on influence is not different. Talk of a post-American world is taking place in a time of unquestioned American military predominance, indicating this edge has limited usefulness in an era of globalization.

Joseph Nye has noted that economic power is difficult to wield on a global scale because the locus of decision making is diffuse, at the level of firms and households.[12] States are not powerless in the face of corporations. When Angela Merkel visited India just after announcing the *Energiewende*, with a large German corporate delegation, her Indian interlocutors requested help in developing their nuclear power industry. She responded that this was up to the businessmen not to the government and the energy CEOs had to demur given that their industries were being shut down at home. In addition the German government has gone along with the sanctions regime against Iran, despite a large German business stake in that country, although only after a long and sustained pressure from the U.S. and some of its European partners. Merkel also met with the Dalai Lama despite the protests of German business leaders. The sanctions on Russia over Ukraine and the way that German businesses have come to support them is another example.

While Merkel has been justly criticized for lacking strategic vision (in this she is characteristic of most of the German political class) and although German finance and business leaders live in a global environment every day, they also do not have a coherent and comprehensive view of the world. While they know what it takes to compete in a brutal global marketplace, their concerns are sectoral and limited. Many of the larger firms have to adopt a long-term planning perspective. Daimler, EADS, Siemens, and E.ON for example, are thinking at least 10 years out and in the case of aircraft up to 30 years. Energy and infrastructure projects require huge investments with long-term returns. This is especially important for an advanced industrial economy like Germany's rather than service and information technology based economies that tend to have much shorter time horizons. This is a double challenge for an economy like Germany's which integrates high tech into industrial production.[13] The exposure of firms to the world, both in terms of production and distribution chains, including the need to import almost all of its raw materials, makes them favor a careful approach to the world in which they create as few enemies as possible and maintain a reputation as a reliable business partner. In contrast, German politicians have a four-year-time perspective to match the length of a normal Bundestag term. But they have to give business interests top priority, given their centrality to German political and economic stability and to both Germany's influence and the outcome of elections.

This tension has created continual trade offs between values and interests and has resulted in priority being given to economic interests over all others. This opens firms up to the problems of corruption discussed earlier in this study. The approach to engage all comers, democratic or not, may change the engager as much as the engaged and can result in "reversed socialization" in which German firms are socialized by their Russian partners and result being corrupted.[14]

This is hardly a problem limited to Germany. One of the greatest global problems in this era of globalization is that of corruption.

> Too much friendliness with autocracies can also corrupt a democracy from within. The Thai military and police, for example, allegedly long have used their connections in Myanmar to exploit natural resources and profit from the cross-border drug trade. Brazilian construction companies with a large presence in Venezuela court Chavez's government with an enthusiasm that skirts outright bribery. Such interests exist in Western democracies, too, but longer-established democracies tend to have stronger human rights groups and independent media as a counterweight. In younger or weaker democracies, criticism of government policies—even anti-democratic ones—can be an excuse for a crackdown.[15]

Yet even a mature democracy, like Germany, has to worry about the corrosive effects of corruption. German closeness to Russia comes at a risk. It is not Bulgaria or some other weak central European state and it has either the upper hand in the balance with Russia or is at least an equal partner.[16] Yet as we have seen, Germany is importing more than just gas and oil from Russia. A number of German companies have been fined for bribery and other corrupt acts in the past. Russian mafia as well as the dubious practices of Gazprom have also exported corruption into Germany. As Transparency International has pointed out, the costs of corruption to both the country being bribed as well as the company doing the bribing can be high. A country like Russia pays a high cost in lost productivity and the Russian population pays a cost in terms of overpriced and bad quality products and services and market distortion.[17] There is evidence that Germany and German firms have learned that they need to do something about these risks in part due to heavy fines by the World Bank and the US Securities and Exchange Commission. A Transparency International Report on exporting corruption listed Germany along with the United States, United Kingdom, and Switzerland as "active enforcers of the OECD anti bribery convention, while such Scandinavian countries as Sweden, Norway, and Denmark are ranked in the lower category of limited enforcers. However, only about 32 percent of world exports were from countries that have been enforcing this convention.[18]

There remains the larger problem of Russian penetration of Germany. The use by Putin of former Stasi agents in Gazprom, the broader role of Gazprom in Europe and the impact of Russian organized crime should not be underestimated. To go back to Anne Applebaum's warning:

> . . . the members of the Russian elite may no longer aspire to launch international Communist revolution, as they did in the 1930s. But they do aspire to change the Western norms and behavior that they see as standing in their way: they want to make Americans and Europeans less interested in human rights, more accepting of corruption, and perhaps more amenable to Russian investment and Russian oligarchs. To some degree they can do so openly. Their money buys them the services retired Western officials, including a former German Chancellor, as well as access to public relations firms, advertising agencies, and lawyers.[19]

Corruption is not limited to monetary compensation but includes the corruption of language. It is one thing for firms to work in an inhospitable environment, but they do not have to go out of their way to gloss over these realities or to promote Russian interests and interpretations. Do large German firms or lobbying groups have to praise Putin's role in bringing stability to Russia or laud him as a "flawless democrat and award him prizes for his contributions to the German-Russian relationship?" This too, is hardly limited to Germany or Europe. Putin published an op-ed in The New York Times on September 11, 2013 challenging the concept of American exceptionalism, an article which was placed by an American PR firm Ketchum Washington, while Matthias Warnig, the allegedly former Stasi associated head of Gazprom Germania, has used a Washington law firm to help create a better image for Gazprom.[20] As the United States–Russian economic relationship grows, American firms would do well to learn from the German experience. A recent study of the George W. Bush Presidency reports that "Bush said Putin had even tried to lure him by offering a lucrative job in the Russian oil industry to Don Evans, the former commerce secretary and one of his closest friends. Putin asked me. 'Would it help you if I moved Evans to an important position?'"[21] Another example of the centrality of corruption to the Putin system as described by Gaddy and Hill and a carbon copy of the offer to Schröder to join Gazprom.

The German relationship with China will be another and perhaps more significant case in geo-economic strategy. The German economic stake in China dwarfs that with Russia. China is the second largest market for German exports outside the EU and will soon overtake the American market for German firms. The German approach to China is similar to its approach to Russia with an emphasis on *Wandel durch Handel, Einbindung* and a "community of responsibility."[22] Human rights have been downplayed. When Merkel received the Dalai Lama in the chancellery in 2007, then Foreign Minister Steinmeier reportedly sent a letter to his Chinese counterpart recognizing Tibet as part of Chinese territory. Despite repeated problems of cyber espionage and the violation of intellectual property rights, German business remains bullish on its prospects in China and German policy has tended to take a bilateral over a European approach to Beijing.

Germany as a shaping power

The head of the Policy Planning Staff of the Foreign Office under both Westerwelle and then Steinmeier, Thomas Bagger, is one of Germany's brightest minds on strategy. Bagger developed the concept of Germany as a Shaping Power (*Gestaltungsmacht*) during the Westerwelle years and this concept may emerge as the conceptual core of a new German strategy. A Gestaltungsmacht is a state that has the power to shape outcomes and events. The term reflects the end of a unipolar era when the US dominated the agenda. This thinking reflects the emergence of a polycentric, highly interdependent, world with rising non-Western powers playing a larger role in global and regional decision-making. As the official German government paper on this puts it, "these countries are economic locomotives which substantially influence regional cooperation and also have an impact in other global regions and play an increasingly important role in international decision making. . . . We see them as more than developing countries but as new shaping powers."[23] Germany will be a shaping power through the use of networks, shaping networks with new actors both at home and abroad. Germany has to develop networks alongside its traditional fora of the EU, NATO, and the G-8 to develop the global governance needed to deal with the new challenges of globalization.

Both the Chinese and Russian cases illustrate the dilemmas for Western democracies of dealing with semi-capitalist authoritarian systems. This is a world quite different than the one where Communist China and the Soviet Union were largely one-dimensional military powers with little economic strength. The future foreign policy of Germany Inc. is likely to be one with few allies but many customers. It will try to find a balance between interests and values but is likely to see its interests define its values. This will have major implications for the normative dimension of the new international order, which is emerging from the one shaped by the United States over the past seven decades. Germany will not be an ally in the Cold War sense of the term but an increasingly independent player, which will be both a partner and competitor for the European Union and the world beyond. Stability, predictability, and the reliability of Germany's reputation as a stable economic partner are paramount. In this sense risk aversion, already a deeply embedded trait in the German political culture, is reinforced.[24]

At the same time the German export economy remains highly vulnerable to forces beyond its control. The sanctions against Russia will cost Germany in terms of GDP growth. The continuing European economic crisis has accelerated a shift in the political economy of the Eurozone countries. In 2010 Eurozone countries, including Germany, exported mostly within the Eurozone. By 2013, 60 percent of eurozone country exports were going out of the eurozone including two-thirds of German exports.[25] The new German economic miracle could quickly turn and Germany could become the sick man of Europe, as it was viewed before the Schröder Agenda 2010 reforms. Export dependence has created severe strains within the Eurozone from the resulting trade and financial imbalances and the relatively weak German domestic demand and has resulted in serious strains between the US Treasury and the European Commission. Germany also faces major future risks in its demographic decline. Already many companies of the *Mittelstand* are having difficulties finding qualified workers, and this problem will only increase as Germany ages. Finally the energy revolution in the United

States and the *Energiewende* may undercut German competitiveness due to the high energy costs in Germany and the lowering costs in the United States.

Germany will have to also develop a far more effective decision-making process that integrates politics and economics. As noted, firms cannot provide a national strategy, only a sectoral one. They are profit maximizers and are responsible to their shareholders while governments have to think of the public interest and of the preferences of their voters. Germany has to find ways to better link the private with the public sectors and to do so with the speed necessary to deal with a rapidly changing global environment. As the chapter on policymaking pointed out, the traditional foreign policy ministries, the Foreign Office and Defense, are not capable of doing this any longer given the diffusion of power. The geo-economic ministries of Finance, Economics/ Energy and Technology, and Development Assistance, need to be better integrated into an overall strategy. The large gap between universities and other research institutions from government and to some extent business, needs to be narrowed. The weakness of the German university system is beginning to be addressed but is clearly a drag on German competitiveness. This will be especially difficult in Germany given the strong independence of Ministries in the German system and the still small capacity for the Chancellery to coordinate these varying elements.[26] Thomas Bagger argues that the Foreign Office should play the role of the coordinator of new networks but Germany could consider other options, including the creation of a National Economic Security Council, which would integrate both governmental and private sector perspectives. The area of cyber security is one area where this should be a priority.

Germany is well placed to play a leading role in this globalized network system. It now is the most popular country in the world according to a recent poll.[27] This reflects not only its economic success but its leadership style, which is consensual and geared at creating coalitions. Its political system is decentralized and its private sector is in many dimensions a global leader. It is a medium-sized power that downplays the use of military force and is not a threat to be a hegemon. Finally it is a strange combination of both a status quo power that has benefited from globalization and a revisionist power that sees the global order still overly reflective of the power distribution which existed at the end of World War II and one that still disadvantages Germany. In this respect it may be more open to change than the United States.

The twentieth century could have been the German rather than the American century if Germany had had the leadership and the mature democratic system it now possesses. It has learned from its horrible Nazi past and is poised to be the kind of power that is suited to the twenty-first century. But geo-economic Germany is an advanced case of a bigger and important political and moral dilemma facing all countries in a globalized world, and that is the problem elaborated by the philosopher, Michael Sandel, of market economies becoming market societies. As Sandel points out, while markets and market thinking have resulted in a prolonged period of economic growth and even prosperity, market economies have become market societies with market values and economics becoming primary. He argues that, market reasoning empties public life of moral argument as markets don't pass judgment on preferences. "This nonjudgmental stance toward values lies at the heart of market reasoning, and explains much of its appeal. But our reluctance to engage in moral and spiritual argument, together with our embrace of markets, has exacted a heavy price: it has drained public discourse of moral and civic energy, and contributed to the technocratic, managerial politics afflicting many societies today."[28]

This is the great danger of geo-economics and why it has a tendency to undermine a value based approach to politics. Germany is especially vulnerable to being not only a market economy but a market society. It rebuilt its identity after World War II on economics and the Deutsche mark. Since unification it has continued to pursue economic prosperity and measures politics and society by market measures. Politicians and policies are judged on the basis of their economic success. To be sure the German social market economy has tried to balance market forces with social concerns to a far greater degree than have the neo liberal Anglo-Saxon economies, but developments since the adoption of Agenda 2010 have begun to weaken this social element. All of this is heightened by its dependence on the outside world for its prosperity as one of the world's greatest trading states. During the euro-zone crisis it has also fallen into a tendency to judge weaker European economies as somehow morally deficient because they have been economically weak. In its dealings with Russia and other nondemocratic nations it has tended to withhold judgment applying the morality of market values. In this respect it represents the larger spirit of the global age and clarifies the choices other democratic states will have to make as they weigh the conflict between values and economic interests in a materialist era.

Notes

Chapter 1

1   Koni has his own Wikipedia page http://en.wikipedia.org/wiki/Koni_(dog) This is how the Merkel incident was reported in *Der Spiegel* A popular anecdote is of when the chancellor of Germany Angela Merkel met Vladimir Putin, Putin brought Koni to their meetings. On January 21, 2007, the two leaders met at Bocharov Ruchei, the president's summer residence in Sochiand; at the beginning of their meeting, Koni wandered into the room, leading Putin to ask Merkel, who was afraid of dogs, "The dog does not bother you, does it? It's a friendly dog and I'm sure it will behave itself." Merkel responded in Russian, a language in which she is fluent, "It doesn't eat journalists, after all."(24). Koni then proceeded to sniff the German chancellor and sat at her feet. Merkel was reported to have shown "apparent discomfort," but the two quickly became friends. "Germany and Russia Try to Smooth Over Energy Tensions." *Der Spiegel*. January 22, 2007. Retrieved 12-21-2008.

2   Sol Sauders, "Germany Follows Money in Drive to East," http://www.washingtontimes.com/news/2010/jul/18/germany-follows-money-in-drive-to-east/

3   Melana K. Zyla, "The New Ostpolitik: America's German Problem," *The Weekly Standard*, February 16, 2009.

4   Quoted by John Vinocur, "German Vote a Turning Point on Russia and its Energy," *International Herald Tribune*, March 9, 2009.

5   Edward Lucas, "Bearhugged by Uncle Vlad," *LSE Standpoint*, January 2009; John Vinocur, "German Vote a Turning Point on Russia and its Energy."

6   Philip Stephens, "Testing Times for the West's Odd Couple," *The Financial Times*, August 4, 2011.

7   Peter Watson, *The German Genius: Europe's Third Renaissance, the Second Scientific Revolution and the Twentieth Century* (New York: Harper Collins, 2010).

8   Charles Maier, *The Unmasterable Past: History, Holocaust and the German National Identity* (Cambridge, MA: Harvard University Press, 1988).

9   John Kornblum, "Germany: From the Middle to the Center," www.aicgs.org June 30, 2010.

10 Germany's per capita exports are $13,681 compared with $3,439 for the United States, $4,559 for Japan, and $6,785 for Italy. Daniel Schäfer, "Germany on a Roll," *The Financial Times*, August 15, 2010.

11 US Department of Treasury, Office of International Affairs, *Report to Congress on International Economic and Exchange Rate Policies (October 30, 2013)*; http://www.treasury.gov/resource-center/international/exchange-rate-policies/Documents/2013–10–30_FULL%20FX%20REPORT_FINAL.pdf

12 See KOF Swiss Economic Institute, 2010; http://globalization.kof.ethz.ch/ Weber 2007; OSW 2010; Financial Times, August 16, 2010.

13 Horst Köhler, President of the Bundesrepublik Deutschland, in interview with Deutschlandradio May 22, 2010.

14 See Hans Kundnani, "Germany as a Geo-economic Power," *The Washington Quarterly* (Summer 2011), 31–45; see also Rawi Abdelal, "The Profits of Power: Commercial Realpolitik in Europe and Eurasia," Harvard Business School, Unpublished paper, September 20, 2010.

15 Edward Luttwak, "From Geopolitics to Geoeconomics," *The National Interest*, 17 (Summer 1990); for a broad survey of the concept, see Paul Aligica, "Geo-economics As A Geo-Strategic Paradigm: An Assessment," The Hudson Institute, August 9, 2002.

16 Pascal Lorot, *Introduction a la geoeconomie* (Paris: Economica, 1999) quoted in Aligica, "geo-Economics."

17 Robert Cooper, *The Postmodern State and the World Order* (London: Demos, 2000).

18 See Hans Kundnani, "Germany as a Geo-economic Power," pp. 31–45.

19 For more on Germany as a normative power, see Beverly Crawford, "The Normative Power of a Normal State," in Jeffrey Anderson and Eric Langenbacher, eds, *From the Bonn to the Berlin Republic:Germany at the Twentieth Anniversary of Unification* (New York: Berghahn Books, 2010), pp. 287–305.

20 Abraham L. Newman, "Flight from Risk: Unified Germany and the Role of Beliefs in the European Response to the Financial Crisis," in Anderson and Langenbacher, *From the Bonn to the Berlin Republic*, pp. 306–18.

21 Edward Luttwak, "From Geopolitics to Geoeconomics," pp. 17–24; see also Kundnani, "Germany as a Geo-economic Power."

22 See Gideon Rachman, *Zero Sum World: Politics, Power and Prosperity after the Crash* (London, 2011).

23 Joachim Bitterlich, "Berlin and Paris Need a Revitalized Relationship," *Financial Times*, January 22, 2013, p. 11.

24 Interview in *Cicero*: http://www.cicero.de/97.php?ress_id=1&item=4955 Mai 2010.

Chapter 2

1 http://www.sueddeutsche.de/politik/2.220/deutsch-russische-vorurteile-die-ruepel-kommen-1.262601

2   Judy Dempsey, "Exhibition Traces Ties Between Germany and Russia," *New York Times*, December 20, 2012, http://www.nytimes.com/2012/12/21/arts/21iht-russgerman21.html?ref=judydempsey

3   Klaus Liedtke, ed., *Der Neue Flirt: Russen und Deutsche auf dem Weg zu Veränderten Beziehungen* (Berlin: Stern, 1989), p. 7.

4   Gerd Koenen, *Der Russland Komplex: Die Deutschen und der Osten 1900–1945* (Munich: C.H. Beck, 2005), p. 9.

5   Angela E. Stent, *Russia and Germany Reborn:Unification, the Soviet Collapse and the New Europe* (Princeton, NJ: Princeton University Press, 1999), p. 5.

6   Stent, *Russia and Germany Reborn*, p. 7.

7   Koenen, *Der Russland Komplex*, pp. 10–11: on the historians debate see Charles Maier, *The Unmasterable Past: History, Holocaust, and German National Identity* (Cambridge, MA: Harvard University Press, 1988).

8   Anthony Read and David Fisher, *The Deadly Embrace: Hitler, Stalin and the Nazi-Soviet Pact 1939–1941* (New York: Norton, 1988). p. 9.

9   Stent, *Russia and Germany*, p. 13.

10 In 2011, there were 2.4 million people living in Germany with a so-called "migration background," who arrived from the former USSR. This included 566,000 "real" immigrants, that is people still holding their original citizenship and 380,000 naturalized citizens. The majority, however, were ethnic Germans (so-called Spätaussiedler), that is, the descendants of Germans who had emigrated to Russia as early as the eighteenth century. The ethnic Germans' return to Germany and their right to citizenship is guaranteed under the German constitution. At the end of the cold war, hundreds of thousands of Spätaussiedler arrived from the USSR, Poland, and Romania to Germany. However, the inflow from Poland and Romania quickly fell to a few thousands per year, while Russlanddeutschen kept arriving in large numbers until 2005. Besides ethnic Germans, Jews also enjoyed a special standing in German immigration law, and therefore represent a distinct category. Between 1990 and 2005, approximately 200,000 Jews arrived to Germany from the former USSR. Unlike ethnic Germans, Jews did not receive citizenship upon arrival, but until 2005 they enjoyed a privileged quota status.

11 Statistics from the Federal Agency for Tourism, Ministry of Culture of the Russian Federation, http://www.russiatourism.ru/en

12 There are a number of polls measuring how Germans perceive Russia and what they think about its current state of affairs. The following discussion refers to data from The Transatlantic Trends (TT) Survey, commissioned annually by the German Marshall Fund of the United States, which measures public opinion in the United States, in 12 European countries, and recently in Turkey and Russia as well. The Pew Research Global Attitudes Project, includes among a whole array of other questions, a survey on opinions of Russia. Besides these well-known and regularly repeated surveys, a few other relevant studies will be mentioned below as

well. For example, in 2008, a German public opinion organization, the Allensbach Institute conducted a special survey on behalf of the German–Russian Forum on how people in the two countries view each other. More recently the Bertelsmann Stiftung conducted a survey on German public views of Poland and Russia, Jacek Kucharczyk, et al., *Im Osten was Neues? Das Bild Polens und Russlands in Deutschland 2013* (Berlesmann Stiftung, 2013).

13 Bertelsmann study, *Im Osten was Neues.*

14 Matthias Kolb, "Die Rüpel kommen," *Sueddeutsche Zeitung*, January 1, 2008, http://www.sueddeutsche.de/politik/deutsch-russische-vorurteile-die-ruepel-kommen-1.262601

15 Pew Research, Global Attitudes Project, "Global Opinion of Russia Mixed," http://www.pewglobal.org/2013/09/03/global-opinion-of-russia-mixed/

16 In a Pew poll taken 20 years after the fall of the Berlin Wall, 48 percent of West Germans and 40 percent of East Germans viewed Russia's influence in Germany as negative. Forty-four percent of East compared to 42 percent of West Germans thought the United States had a negative influence on their country. The Pulse of Europe 2009: 20 Years After the Fall of the Berlin Wall. http://pewglobal.org/2009/11/02/end-of-communism-cheered-but-now-with-more-reservations/

17 Those holding the most negative views of Russia in the 2011 edition of Transatlantic Trends (60% negative compared to 36% positive) were in the 25–34-year cohort (born between 1977 and 1986) and were socialized during the Putin era. The oldest cohort (65 years and older) held the least negative views, but here only 54 percent had a positive view compared to 39 percent negative.

18 Dr Renate Köcher, *The Russlandbild der Deutschen-das Deutschlandbild der Russen* (Berlin: Institut für Demoskopie Allensbach, September 18, 2008).

19 On the energy dependence issue, the Allensbach surveys found that 67 percent of Germans feared that Russia would use its energy resources to push through its goals with Germany while in the TT a robust 38 percent approve of the notion of increasing cooperation with energy producers even if they are undemocratic, with 35 percent looking to reduce energy dependence and 22 percent for increasing diplomatic pressure. While 35 percent of Europeans in the survey would agree to continue dependence, only 23 percent of Americans would.

20 Thirty-five percent of Germans were very concerned compared to an EU 12 average of 21 percent and a US average of 32 percent. They were also more supportive than the European average of the idea of the EU increasing support for democratic forces in Russia (34% approving very much in Germany, compared to 25% in the Euro 12 and 21% in the United States). See *Transatlantic Trends 2008* (www.transatlantictrends.org).

21 "European Worries About Reliance on Russia Energy Were Already High," Pew Research Center Publications, January 9, 2009.

22 www.transatlantictrends.org q.4.4

23 *Transatlantic Trends 2011*, www.transatlantictrends.org

24 http://www.worldpublicopinion.org/pipa/articles/views_on_countriesregions_
bt/660.php?lb=btvoc&pnt=660&. Among Americans, negative views dropped by
18 points bringing it below half (down to 46%, from 64%). Among Germans,
negative views fell by 16 points (to 54%, down from 70%), and among the French
by 11 points (to 55%, down from 66%).

25 According to the Transatlantic Trends survey, following Putin's return for a
third term as president and the recent crackdown on civil society, both in the
United States and in 11 out of the 12 European countries participating in the
survey showed a very significant worsening of views on Russia. The EU-12
average of unfavorable views jumped from 39 to 55, the US figure increased
from 42 to 48 percent. Germans reacted even stronger with an increase from 45
to 63 percent. Germans seemed to be especially concerned about the elections
in Russia: only 11 percent of them were confident that the results represent
the will of Russian voters. Europeans in general were slightly more confident
(16%), while in the United States one-third trusted the democratic process in
Russia.

26 "Troubled by Loss of Standing in the World, Americans Support Major Foreign
Policy Changes," (Chicago: The Chicago Council on Global Affairs, 2008).

27 Ibid., p. 6. Only 17 percent in the Chicago survey considered democracy promotion
as a very important goal in American foreign policy.

28 "Unsere Russen: Unsere Deutschen: Das Russland Bild des Deutschen?" (Forsa,
December 2007); http://www.wintershall.com/fileadmin/download/presse/
pressemeldungen/2007/Charts_PK_Druckversion.pdf

29 Jan Peters, "Russland in den Augen deutscher Experten," in Agnieszka Lada, ed.,
et al., *Russland heute und morgen: Meinungen deutscher und polnischer Experten*
(Warsaw: Institut für Öffentliche Angelegenheiten, 2010), p. 96.

30 http://www.wintershall.com/pi-forsa-071207.html?&L=0

31 Quoted in Judy Dempsey, "Exhibition Traces Ties Between Germany and
Russia."

32 Ibid.

33 Ost-Auschuss der Deutschen Wirtschaft, *Geschäftsklima Russland 2013: 10.
Umfrage des Ost-Ausschusses der Deutschen Wirtschaft und der Deutsch-Russischen
Auslandshandelskammer* (Berlin, 2013).

34 *Rede von Aussenminister Guido Westerwelle, "Ostpolitik im Zeitalter der
Globalisierung" vor dem Politischen Club der Evangelischen Akademie Tutzing*,
June 29, 2013.

35 *Rede von Aussenminister Guido Westerwelle, "Ostpolitik im Zeitalter der
Globalisierung"* p. 3.

36 Alexander Rahr, *Russland gibt Gass: Die Ruckkehr einer Weltmacht* (Munich:
Hanser, 2008), p. 49.

37 The German public is surprisingly open to democracy promotion. The Transatlantic Trends 2011 survey asked a number of questions about democracy promotion in the wake of the Arab Spring and found that 60 percent believed that we should promote democracy even if it leads to periods of instability as opposed to 32 percent with the opposite view. This view held consistently across the political spectrum. However 67 percent believed that it is not possible to export democracy compared to only 32 percent who thought it was possible.

38 Jan Peters, "Russland in den Augen deutscher Experten," p. 81.

39 Ibid., pp. 83–6.

40 Dr Lars Peter Schmidt, Johan Bölts, "Wandel durch Ahnährung-Utopie oder Wirklichkeit?: Russland und Deutschland im 21. Jahrhundert," (KAS Moskau)—November 4, 2010, http://www.kas.de/wf/doc/kas_21026–1522–1–30.pdf?101104131040

41 Bernhard Kastner, MdB (CDU)—March 2011 [http://www.kas.de/wf/doc/kas_22504–1522–1–30.pdf?110412163602

42 Gernor Erler, MdB, in Interview mit der Saarbruecker Zeitung: http://www.saarbruecker-zeitung.de/sz-berichte/politik/Schulterschluss-trotz-Verstimmung-Erler-Politik-droht-in-Rituale-zu-verfallen;art2815,3854872#.Tjl3D2FRW1s

43 Interview mit Sascha Tamm, Leiter des Moskauer Büros der Naumann-Stiftung—March 13, 2011, http://www.dw-world.de/dw/article/0,,6473973,00.html; for the work of the Böll Foundation see: Pressemitteilung der Böll-Stiftung zum Petersburger Dialog: Für freie Wahlen in Russland—July 19, 2011, http://www.boell.de/presse/presse-fuer-freie-wahlen-in-russland-12618.html; The Böll-Foundation has its own blog to cover to current human rights situation as well as special occurrences, http://blog.boell-net.de/blogs/russland-blog/default.aspx

44 The Human Rights Watch keeps a periodically updated list of NGOs targeted by the "Foreign Agents" Law here: http://www.hrw.org/news/2013/05/14/russia-foreign-agents-law-hits-hundreds-ngos-updated-july-8–2013

45 Daniel Brössler, "Russische Staatsanwälte ermitteln gegen deutsche Stiftungen"—*Süddeutsche Zeitung* March 26, 2013, http://www.sueddeutsche.de/politik/strenges-vorgehen-gegen-nichtregierungsorganisationen-russische-staatsanwaelte-ermitteln-gegen-deutsche-stiftungen-1.1633479

46 Lang, Susanne; Härtel, Alexandra und Bürsch, Michael: Zivilgesellschaft und bürgerschaftliches Engagement in Russland—April 2010, http://library.fes.de/pdf-files/id/07173.pdf

47 In the period from October 2010 to August 2011, the Foreign Office issued 16 interviews and statements on human rights in Russia compared to 19 on Belarus.

48 Speech of Chancellor Merkel to the annual meeting of the Ost-Ausschusses der Deutschen Wirtschaft, October 14, 2010 in Berlin.

49 Statement on the need to clarify the murder of a Russian human rights activist, July 15, 2010.

50 Cited by Deutche Welle, http://www.dw-world.de/dw/article/0,,15581878,00. html

51 Speech by Guido Westerwelle, Federal Minister for Foreign Affairs, to the Political Club of the Protestant Academy Tutzing on June 29, 2013 "Ostpolitik in the age of globalization." http://www.auswaertiges-amt.de/EN/Infoservice/Presse/ Reden/2013/130629-BM-EA_Tutzing.html

52 Steltzenmüller, Constanze (2009): Germany's Russia Question, in: *Foreign Affairs*, 88(2), 89–100.

53 Johannes Voswinkel, "Menschenrecht in Russland," *Bundeszentral für Politische Bildung*, October 12, 2009; Information provided by the Bundeszentrale fuer politische Bildung, http://www.bpb.de/themen/IVYKPD,0,0,Menschenrechte_in_ Russland.html

54 Ivan Krastev, "Paradoxes of the New Authoritarianism," *Journal of Democracy*, 22(2) (April 2011), 8.

55 For the classic study of the German democratic idea, see Leonard Kreeger, *The German Idea of Freedom:History of a Political Tradition* (Chicago: The University of Chicago Press, 1957).

56 *Society and Democracy in Germany.* New York & London: W. W. Norton & Company, 1967.

57 Interview with political foundation representative, August 2013.

58 Ibid.

59 Krastev, "Paradoxes of the new Authoritarianism," p. 13.

Chapter 3

1 Stefan Meister, *An Alienated Partnership: German-Russian Relations After Putin's Return, FIFA Briefing Paper 105* (The Finnish Institute of International Affairs, May 10, 2012), p. 3.

2 See Lilia Shevtsova and David Kramer, "Germany and Russia: The End of Ostpolitik?" *The American Interest*, November 13, 2012.

3 For details see Stephen F. Szabo, *Parting Ways: The Crisis in German-American Relations* (Washington: Brookings Institution Press, 2008).

4 See Hans-Joachim Spanger, "Die deutsche Russlandpolitik, in: Thomas Jäger/ Alexander Höse/ Kai Oppermann (Hg.), Deutsche Außenpolitik, Wiesbaden, 2010, p. 652.

5 Interview with author May 2013.

6 Bundeskanzler Gerhard Schröder (SPD) hat Rußlands Präsident Wladimir Putin vor Vorwürfen in Schutz genommen, demokratische Grundsätze zu mißachten. Schröder antwortete in der ARD-Sendung "Beckmann" laut vorab veröffentlichten

Interview-Auszügen auf die Frage, ob Putin ein lupenreiner Demokrat sei: "Ja, ich bin überzeugt, daß er das ist." Er sei sicher, daß Putin Rußland "zu einer ordentlichen Demokratie machen will und machen wird," meinte Schröder. Das Land habe 75 Jahre kommunistischer Herrschaft hinter sich sowie zehn Jahre, in denen alle Staatlichkeit zerfallen sei. "Putin schafft es jetzt, den Staat wieder in seine Funktion zu setzen." Es sei klar, "daß dabei nicht alles idealtypisch laufe." "Schröder: 'Putin ist lupenreiner Demokrat'"*Hamburger Abendblatt*, November 23, 2004. Auf die Frage, ob er Russlands Präsidenten immer noch als "lupenreinen Demokraten" sehe, sagte Schröder im Deutschlandfunk: "Ich habe nichts daran abzustreichen. Ich glaube, dass er ernsthaft sein Land auf eine wirkliche Demokratie hin orientiert. Dass da noch eine Menge zu tun ist, weiß niemand besser als er selber. Auch die Leute, die um ihn herum sind, wissen das." http://www.tagesschau.de/inland/schroederputin100.html

7 Quoted in *Spiegel Online*, November 20, 2007.

8 Comments at a public presentation of a Germany–Russia Scenrio exercise at the Friedrich Ebert Stiftung in Berlin, June 26, 2013. http://www.youtube.com/watch?v=sYKr0w2y1RM&feature=youtu.be

9 Jochen Franzke, "Wertepolitik versus Realpolitik: Die Russlandpolitik ser Regierung Merkel/Steinmeier," *Zeitschrift für Internationale Politik*, 67 (2009), 92.

10 Hannes Adomeit, *German-Russian Relations: Balance Sheet since 2000 und Perspectives until 2025* (Paris: IFRI: October 2012), p. 6.

11 Franzke,"Wertepolitik versus Realpolitik," p. 93.

12 Interview with the author.

13 Hans-Joachim Spanger, "Die deutsche Russlandpolitik," p. 655.

14 http://www.cablegatesearch.net/cable.php?id=06BERLIN3354

15 Meister, *An Alienated Partnership*, p. 4.

16 Quoted in Spanger, "Die deutsche Russlandpolitik," p. 654.

17 Constanze Steltzenmüller, "Germany's Russia Question," *Foreign Affairs*, 88(2) (2009), 89–100.

18 CDU-Wahlprogramm, http://www.cdu.de/doc/pdfc/090628-beschluss-regierungsprogramm-cducsu.pdf, Ein gutes nachbarschaftliches Verhältnis zu Russland liegt im Interesse Deutschlands und seiner europäischen Partner und Verbündeten. Wir wollen so enge Beziehungen zu Russland wie möglich. Die Tiefe und Breite dieser Beziehungen hängt insbesondere davon ab, ob und wieweit Russland bereit ist, seinen Verpflichtungen im Rahmen der Vereinten Nationen, der OSZE, des Europarats und der Europäischen Energie-Charta sowie aus den Vereinbarungen mit der Europäischen Union nachzukommen. Wir treten für eine zuverlässige, in der Europäischen Union eng abgestimmte Energie-Zusammenarbeit mit Russland auf der Grundlage transparenter und nicht diskriminierender Bedingungen ein. Grundsatzprogramm: http://www.spd.de/linkableblob/1778/data/hamburger_programm.pdf. Die strategische Partnerschaft

mit Russland ist für Deutschland und die Europäische Union unverzichtbar. Die Öffnung Russlands sichert Frieden und Stabilität auf unserem Kontinent. Allgemeine Auffuehrung der Menschenrechtsproblematik, allerdings ohne konkreten Bezug zu Russland.

19 Lilia Shevtsova and David Kramer, "Germany and Russia: The End of Ostpolitik?" *The National Interest*, November 13, 2012, http://www.the-american-interest.com/article.cfm?piece=1344

20 See John Vinocur, "German Vote a Turning Point on Russia and its Energy," *International Herald Tribune*, March 9, 2009.

21 Interview, July 1, 2013.

22 See his comments at a public presentation of a Germany–Russia Scenrio exercise at the Friedrich Ebert Stiftung in Berlin, June 26, 2013. http://www.youtube.com/watch?v=sYKr0w2y1RM&feature=youtu.berview July 1, 2013.

23 The German Foreign Office, *Deutschland Nachrichten*, "Bundesaussenminister Steinmeier in Moskau," February 17, 2014.

24 Shevtsova and Kramer, "Germany and Russia."

25 As Rudolf notes, the German "debate stays very much within the broad parameters of a strategy of integration." Rudolf, "Toward a Common Transatlantic Strategy in Dealing with Russia?" p. 3.

26 William E. Paterson, "Foreign Policy in the Grand Coalition." Paper presented to the annual meeting of the American Political Science Association, Boston, August 2008, p. 10.

27 Ralf Neukirch, "German Foreign Ministry Fights to Stay Relevant," *Spiegel Online*, May 4, 2012.

28 Ralf Neukirch and Matthias Schepp, "German-Russian Relations Enter a New Ice Age," *Spiegel Online*, May 30, 2012; http://www.spiegel.de/international/germany/german-and-russian-relations-are-at-an-impasse-a-835862.html

29 Susan Stewart, *Germany's Relationship with Russia: Buisness First?* (Berlin:Stiftung Wissenschaft und Politik, May 2012), p. 11.

30 Condoleezza Rice, *No Higher Honor: A Memoir of My Years in Washington* (New York: Crown, 2011), p. 672.

31 Steven Erlanger and Steven Lee Meyers, "NATO Allies Oppose Bush on Georgia and Ukraine," *The New York Times*, April 3, 2008, http://www.nytimes.com/2008/04/03/world/europe/03nato.html?pagewanted=all&_r=0

32 Interview with the author, May 2013.

33 Condoleezza Rice reported that while Steinmeier made the argument about the weakness of the Ukrainian coalition and also that NATO should not grant MAP to a country with a frozen conflict and that he received strong counter arguments from Radek Sikorski and other Central European Foreign Ministers. Steinmeier later said it was "the most brutal experience of his time as foreign minister." Condoleezza Rice, *No Higher Honor*, p. 674. She credits Merkel with shaping the

compromise and producing the language, which promised NATO membership in
the future.

34   Ralf von Beste, Susanne Koebl and Dirk Kurbjuweit, "Wandel durch Bestürzung,"
Der Spiegel, August 25, 2008, http://www.spiegel.de/spiegel/print/d-59403006.
html; "Merkel, Medvedev Clash Over Russia's War in Sochi Talks," *Deutsche Welle*,
August 15, 2008. http://www.dw.de/merkel-medvedev-clash-over-russias-war-in-
sochi-talks/a-3567243-1

35   "German Leaders Split on Placing Blame in Caucasian War," *Deutsche Welle*,
August 10, 2008. http://www.dw.de/german-leaders-split-on-placing-blame-in-
caucasian-war/a-3551206-1

36   "SPIEGEL Interview with Gerhard Schröder: 'Serious Mistakes by the West,'"
Spiegel Online, August 18, 2008. http://www.spiegel.de/international/world/spiegel-
interview-with-gerhard-schroeder-serious-mistakes-by-the-west-a-572686.html

37   "Berlin's Shifting Policy: Has Merkel Changed her Tune on Georgia?—Part 2: 'Are
We Prepared to Escalate?'" Spiegel Online, August 25, 2008, http://www.spiegel.
de/international/world/berlin-s-shifting-policy-has-merkel-changed-her-tune-on-
georgia-a-574227-2.html

38   von Beste, et al., "Wandel durch Bestürzung."

39   Chivvis, Christopher S. and Rid, Thomas, "The Roots of Germany's Russia Policy,"
Survival, 51(2) (2009), 105–22.

40   Steve Coll, "Hard on Obama," *The New York Review of Books*, July 11, 2013, 10.

41   Hannes Adomeit, *German-Russian Relations: Balance Sheet since 2000 und
Perspectives until 2025* (Paris: IFRI: October 2012), p. 29.

42   *Natural gas.* The Nord Stream gas pipeline is to be completed; EU financial resources
for that purpose are to be tapped; Gazprom and German partners, mainly E.ON
and Wintershall with its parent firm BASF, are to cooperate more closely; Germany
should participate in the construction of gas pipelines other than Nord Stream; and
joint ventures for marketing Russian gas in Germany should be created.
Nuclear Energy. Implementation of the framework agreement concluded between
Rosatom, the Russian Nuclear Energy State Corporation, and Siemens AG on the
foundation of a joint venture to modernize nuclear power plants and to pool efforts
in marketing.
Energy Efficiency. The activities of the Russian–German Energy Agency are to be
broadened and projects planned with Siemens in Yekaterinburg and in Krasnodar
for the construction of a wind park to be implemented.
Design and Construction of Aircraft. Airbus, EADS EFW and their Russian partners,
United Aircraft Corporation (UAC) and IRKUT, should carry out the agreement
for the construction of the Airbus A-350 transport aircraft on the basis of the
Airbus A-320.
Automobiles. Volkswagen, Daimler, and BMW are to develop and produce
components for automobiles of these firms.

Railway Transport. The Russian Railways, the Deutsche Bahn and Siemens should cooperate in the construction of high-speed trains and the improvement of railway connections between Europe and Russia's Asian-Pacific region.*Laser and Heavy Ions Technology.* Russia should participate as the main partner in the development of x-ray laser technology on the basis of free electrons (XFEL) in Hamburg and the creation of a European Centre for the Acceleration of Heavy Ions (FAIR) in Darmstadt. Cited in Hannes Adomeit, *German-Russian Relations: Balance Sheet since 2000*, p. 27.

43 Interview with author, June 2013.

44 Michael Birnbaum, "In Germany, Campaigns are just Beginning for Sept. 22 Parliamentary Election." *The Washington Post*, August 18, 2013, A 16.

45 Lobby Control, *Lobby Report 2013* (Cologne, 2013).

46 "SPD Chancellor Candidate Discloses Pay: Steinbrück Fends Off Criticism *of* His Extra Income," Spiegel International Online, October 30, 2012, http://www.spiegel. de/international/germany/spd-candidate-peer-steinbrueck-reveals-income-to-end-controversy-a-864263.html

47 Benjamin Bidder and Ralf Neukirch, "Mixed Messages from Berlin on Russia Human Rights," *Speigel Online*, August 8, 2012, http://www.spiegel.de/international/world/germany-russia-dialogue-group-silent-on-human-rights-and-pussy-riot-a-848442.html

48 Quoted in Stefan Meister, An Alienated Partnership: German-Russian Relations After Putin's Return (The Finnish Institute for International Affairs, Briefing Paper 105, May 10, 2012, 5.

49 Benjamin Bidder and Ralf Neukirch, "Mixed Messages from Berlin on Russia Human Rights."

50 The DAX-30 is the stock market index that consists of the 30 largest companies trading on the Frankfurt Stock Exchange. Eighteen of these companies—Allianz, BASF, Bayer, Commerzbank, Daimler, Deutsche Bank, Deutsche Börse, Deutsche Telekom, Lufthansa, E.ON, Fresenius, HeidelbergCement, K+S, RWE, SAP, Siemens, and Volkswagen—are either listed as members or are represented by their senior executives or board members in the Forum.

51 "German Businessmen on Prospects of Economic Relations with Russia," *Strategic Culture Foundation*, February 18, 2012; http://www.strategic-culture. org/news/2012/02/18/german-businessmen-prospects-economic-relations-with-russia.html; see also Benjamin Bidder, "Deutsche Wirtschaft setzt auf Putin," *Spiegel Online*, December 5, 2011, http://www.spiegel.de/wirtschaft/unternehmen/russland-wahl-deutsche-wirtschaft-setzt-auf-putin-a-801760.html

52 Benjamin Bidder, "Deutsche Wirtschaft setzt auf Putin."

53 See Steve Coll, *Private Empire,* for a look at how a major American multinational has dealt with these challenges.

54 Valentina Pop, "Germany wants EU visa free travel for Russian citizens," *EU Observer*, June 3, 2013. http://euobserver.com/foreign/119304

55 Valentina Pop, "Germany wants EU visa free travel for Russian citizens."

56 "German authorities have refused to grant William Browder, the leader of the global campaign for justice for Sergei Magnitsky, safe passage to Germany from a politically motivated Russian arrest warrant, resulting in the cancellation of the European Magnitsky Law event, scheduled in Berlin on May 27, 2013. In the latest development concerning the Magnitsky sanctions, the German government has informed the event organizers that Germany is not able to guarantee the safe passage of Mr Browder to Berlin, in light of the recent actions from the Russian government who are seeking assistance from police worldwide to "locate" Mr Browder in retaliation for his campaigning for sanctions on Russian officials. William Browder was a keynote speaker at the "Time for European Magnitsky Law" event, on the invitation of European Parliament deputy Kristiina Ojuland, and the Institute for Cultural Diplomacy. The event was to be held in Germany next week within the framework of the Symposium on Cultural Diplomacy and Human Rights 2013 (www.bhrc.de), which has freedom of expression on the agenda. "It is remarkable that the German authorities, who have refused calls to sanction Russian officials responsible for torturing and killing 37-year-old Sergei Magnitsky, are now effectively sanctioning the person fighting for justice for Mr Magnitsky. By doing so, the German authorities are, for all intents and purposes, becoming an accessory to the Russian cover-up of Magnitsky's killers in Europe," said a Hermitage Capital representative. "The actions of the German authorities are in contrast to actions from the UK, Belgian, and Norwegian governments, who undertook not to act on political and abusive requests from the Russian government in relation to Mr Browder." Statement of Kristiina Oujuland, MEP, http://lawandorderinrussia. org/2013/major-event-in-germany-promoting-european-magnitsky-sanctions-cancelled-because-german-government-refuses-to-grant-safe-passage-to-william-browder-from-politically-motivated-russian-arrest-warrant/

57 Andrew Rettmann, "EU and Russia in visa talks despite Magnitsky 'regret,'" *EU Observer*, March 21, 2013. http://euobserver.com/foreign/119519

58 Hannes Adomeit, *German-Russian Relations: Balance Sheet since 2000 and Perspectives until 2025* (Paris: IFRI, October 2012), p. 9.

59 Peters, "Russland in den Augen deutscher Experten," p. 88.

60 Reiner Veser, "Kein Partner: Deutsch-russische Beziehungen," *FAZ*, November 13, 2012. http://www.faz.net/aktuell/politik/ausland/deutsch-russische-beziehungen-kein-partner-11959659.html; See also Ralf von Beste, Susanne Koebl and Dirk Kurbjuweit, "Wandel durch Bestürzung," August 25, 2008. http://www.spiegel.de/spiegel/print/d-59403006.html

61 Susan Stewart, *Germany's Relationship with Russia: Buisness First?* p. 12.

62 http://www.german-foreign-policy.com/en/fulltext/56359

63 From the website of the Valdai Club; http://valdaiclub.com/europe/52040.html

64　"Deutchlands Ostpolitik hat die Balance verloren," *Spiegel Online*, March 18, 2013, http://www.spiegel.de/politik/ausland/alexander-rahr-deutschlands-ostpolitik-hat-die-balance-verloren-a-889270.html

65　See, for example, his critique, "Die vielen Irrtümer der deutschen Russland Politik," http://www.zeit.de/politik/ausland/2012–10/Deutschland-Russland

66　Hannes Adomeit, *German-Russian Relations: Balance Sheet since 2000*, p. 17; note the reference to propagandists for Moscow is to Rahr.

67　Susan Stewart, *Germany's Relationship with Russia: Buisness First?* p. 12.

68　See Hans Kundnani, "Germany as a Geo-economic Power," *The Washington Quarterly* (Summer 2011), 31–45.

69　Susan Stewart, *Germany's Relationship with Russia: Buisness First?* p. 12.

70　Timothy Garton Ash, "The New German Question," *The New York Review of Books*, August 15, 2013, 54.

Chapter 4

1　Hans-Joachim Spanger, "Die deutsche Russlandpolitik, in: Thomas Jäger/ Alexander Höse/ Kai Oppermann (Hg.), Deutsche Außenpolitik, Wiesbaden, 2010, p. 661.

2　See Stent, *Russian and Germany Reborn*, p. 28.

3　Ibid., p. 148.

4　Ibid., p. 189.

5　Gazprom and Wintershall have had joint natural gas trading activities since 1990 through the German–Russian joint ventures of WIEH, WIEE, and WINGAS. The Vertrag über die gaswirtschaftliche Zusammenarbeit (agreement on gas-industry partnership), which was signed shortly before the German reunification, formed the basis for something completely unprecedented in the gas industry, cooperation between partners from the Russian and German energy industries. As a result, Wintershall and WINGAS are among the biggest German importers of Russian gas. The jointly operated natural gas trading company WINGAS has sold more than 250 billion cubic meters of gas since it was established. "Our partnership with Gazprom is unique: It extends from natural gas exploration and production in Western Siberia to transporting the gas through Nord Stream and distributing it through our gas pipeline network in Germany and other European countries," explains Dr Rainer Seele, Chairman of the Board of Wintershall. Taken from the Wintershall website: http://www.wintershall.com/en/worldwide.html

6　Stent, *Russia and Germany*, pp. 178–9.

7　Hans-Joachim Spanger, "Die deutsche Russlandpolitik," pp. 661–2.

8　Ibid., p. 662.

9　Bundeszentrale für politische Bildung http://www.bpb.de/internationales/europa/russland/

10　Deutsche Bundesbank (2011): Bestandserhebung ueber Direktinvestitionen, S.16.

11　Ibid.

12　Bundesministerium fuer Wirtschaft und Technologie (2010): Energie in Deutschland. Trends und Hintergruende zur Energieversorgung, Berlin, S.15ff.

13　Fiona Hill and Clifford Gaddy, *Mr. Putin: Operative in the Kremlin* (Washington, DC: The Brookings Institution, 2013), p. 239.

14　Hill and Gaddy, *Mr. Putin*, p. 240.

15　Ibid., p. 225.

16　Andrew Wood, "Russia's Business Diplomacy," *Chatham House Briefing Paper* (London: Chatham House, May 2011).

17　Andrew Wood, "Russia's Business Diplomacy."

18　Hill and Gaddy, *Mr. Putin*, p. 248.

19　See Uwe Klussmann, "Russian Mafia an International Concern for US Diplomats," *Spiegel Online*, December 2, 2010.

20　Moises Naim, "Mafia States," *Foreign Affairs*, May/June 2012.

21　Naim, "Mafia States."

22　Heinz Eggert, Interior Minister of Saxony, quoted in Stephen Kinzer, "Ivan in Berlin: The Long Shadow of the Russian Mob," *The New York Times*, December 11, 1994.

23　Stefan Nicola, "Berlin a Russian mafia hub," UPI, November 26, 2008.

24　Andrew Wood, "Russia's Business Diplomacy."

25　Rainer Lindner, "Kooperation statt Konfrontation," *Ost-auschuss informationen*, October 2012, p. 8.

26　Sonia Schinde, "Korruption mit System," *Handelsblatt*, August 5, 2006.

27　Asheesh Goel and Michael Y. Jo, "Recent Anti-Corruption Developments in Germany," in Asheesh Goel, *International Bribery and Corruption Trends and Developments* (Ropes and Gray, Washington, DC) http://www.ropesgray.com/files/upload/20120521_ABC_Book.pdf

28　9Anette Dowideit, *Korruption kostet Deutschland 250 Milliarden Euro*, DIE WELT, March 16, 2012, *available at* http://www.welt.de/wirtschaft/article13924503/Korruption-kostet-Deutschland-250-Milliarden-Euro.html.; cited by Goel and Jo, Recent Anti-Corruption Developments in Germany,"

29　Goel and Jo, "Recent Anti-Corruption Developments in Germany."

30　Jens Hartmann and Eduard Steiner, "Wie Siemens in Russland im Alleingang modernisiert," *Die Welt,* December 25, 2010, http://www.welt.de/wirtschaft/article10520015/Wie-Siemens-Russland-im-Alleingang-modernisiert.html

31　Eric Lichtblau and Carter Dougherty, "Siemens to Pay $1.34 Billion in Fines," *New York Times*, December 15, 2008, *available at* http://www.nytimes.com/2008/12/16/business/worldbusiness/16siemens.html; Samuel Rubenfeld, "Greece Settles with

Siemens over Bribery Charges," *The Wall Street Journal*, March 8, 2012, available at http://blogs.wsj.com/ corruption-currents/2012/03/08/greece-settles-with-siemens-over-bribery-charges/

32 "Siemens to pay $100m to fight corruption as part of World Bank Group settlement," Press Release No:2009/001/EXT, July 2, 2009. http://web.worldbank. org/WBSITE/EXTERNAL/NEWS/0,,contentMDK:22234573~pagePK:64257043~pi PK:437376~theSitePK:4607,00.html

33 Hawranek, Dietmar, "'Useful Payments': US Investigators Crack Down on Daimler's Culture of Corruption," *Spiegel,* March 30, 2010, available at http://www.spiegel.de/international/business/useful-payments-us-investigators-crack-down-on-daimler-s-culture-of-corruption-a-686238.html

34 Crawford, David. "H-P Executives Face Bribery Probes," *The Wall Street Journal*, April 14, 2010, available at http://online.wsj.com/article/SB1000142405270230334 8504575184302111110966.html; Palazzolo, Joseph. "H-P Bribe Probe Widens", *The Wall Street Journal,* September 10, 2010, available at http://online.wsj.com/article/S B10001424052748704644404575481961121687910.html

35 "US Justice Department Accusations: Daimler Charged with Systematic Bribery," *Spiegel*, March 24, 2010, available at http://www.spiegel.de/international/business/us-justice-department-accusations-daimler-charged-with-systematic-bribery-a-685408.html; Hawranek, Dietmar. "'Useful Payments': US Investigators Crack Down on Daimler's Culture of Corruption," *Spiegel*, March 30, 2010, available at http://www.spiegel.de/international/business/useful-payments-us-investigators-crack-down-on-daimler-s-culture-of-corruption-a-686238.html; Hawranek, Dietmar, "Trapped in the US Web: Daimler Upset with Over-Eager American Oversight," Spiegel, December 13, 2011, available at http://www.spiegel. de/international/business/trapped-in-the-us-web-daimler-upset-with-over-eager-american-oversight-a-803350.html

36 Debevoise & Plimpton LLP. "FCPA Update" 1(9), April 2010. Available at: http:// www.debevoise.com/newseventspubs/publications/detail.aspx?id=0ba57376–052a-48e3-aa86–107980556ca5. See also, Mauldin, William, "Russia Investigates Daimler Bribery Claims," *The Wall Street Journal*, November 3, 2010, available at http://online.wsj.com/article/SB10001424052748704658204575610442043886702. html

37 "Ausländische Firmen Started Intiative gegen Korruption in Russland," *Sueddeutsche Zeitung*, April 21, 2010, 18.

38 Quoted in Gregory Feifer, "Too Special a Friendship."

39 George Haynal of Bombadier in written comments to the author, September 2013.

40 http://www.census.gov/foreign-trade/balance/c4280.html

41 See Judy Dempsey, "German Business Moves Beyond Russia to China," *The New York Times*, July 13, 2010; and Judy Dempsey, "Russia and Germany Bolster Trade Ties," *The New York Times*, July 19, 2011.

42 The Bruegel think tank reported that the percentage of German GDP
    coming from exports to non-EU countries rose from around 8 percent in
    2000 to around 18 percent by 2013 while the euro area accounted for around
    15 percent and the non-euro ten countries for about 8 percent of German
    GDP. Zsolt Darvas, "The German trade surplus may widen with the euro
    area recovery," Bruegel, November 7, 2013, http://www.bruegel.org/nc/blog/
    detail/article/1189-the-german-trade-surplus-may-widen-with-the-euro-area-
    recovery/?utm_source=Bruegel+Update&utm_campaign=0aa0c64710–131109_
    Bruegel+Update&utm_medium=email&utm_term=0_cb17b0383e-
    0aa0c64710–273942062

43 Dempsey, "Russia and Germany Bolster Trade Ties."

44 Bundesministerium fuer Wirtschaft und Technologie (2010): Energie in
    Deutschland. Trends und Hintergruende zur Energieversorgung, Berlin, S.15ff.

45 "Gazprom: Russia's Wounded Giant, *The Economist*, March 23, 2013. (from the
    print edition).

46 Heidi Brown, "Igor Sechin: The Kremlin's Oil Man," http://www.forbes.
    com/2009/11/09/igor-sechin-rosneft-leadership-power-09-oil_print.html

47 "Stanislav Belkovsky, a political analyst and critic of Putin, is one of the most
    outspoken. He claims Putin could be worth as much as $70bn, a figure that would
    make him the richest man in the world. This extraordinary sum is based on claims
    that Putin owns shares in three major oil and gas companies: 4.5% of national
    gas giant Gazprom, 37% of oil supplier Surgutneftegas and a major shareholder
    of a company that cannot be named for legal reasons. That company strenuously
    denies any links to Putin. "The figure of $40bn emerged in 2007. That figure could
    now have changed, I believe at the level of $60–70bn," Belkovsky says. Maeve
    McClenaghan, Putin the Richest Man on Earth? Open Society, April 19, 2012,
    http://www.thebureauinvestigates.com/2012/04/19/putin-the-richest-man-on-
    earth/

48 For a detailed account of the variety of criminal and other corrupt dealings of
    Gazprom see Jürgen Roth, *Gazprom-Das Unheimliche Imperium* (Frankfurt:
    Westend, 2012).

49 Jürgen Roth, *Gazprom-Das Unheimliche Imperium*, p. 12.

50 Andreas Heinrich Koszalin, "Gazprom's Expansion Strategy in Europe and the
    Liberalization of EU Energy Markets," *Russian Analytic Digest*, 34/08, 8, 9.

51 The text of 2009/73/EC, Article 11: "Where Certification is Requested by a
    Transmission System Owner or a Transmission System Operator which is
    Controlled by a Person or Persons from a Third Country or Third Countries, the
    Regulatory Authority shall Notify the Commission."

52 Roland Oliphant, "Gazprom Vows to Fully Comply in EU Raids," *The Moscow
    Times*, September 29, 2011.

53 Koszalin, "Gazprom's Expansion Strategy," p. 11.

54 Vladimir Socor, "Gazprom Seeks Expansion Into Germany's Electricity Sector," *Eurasia Daily Monitor*, July 15, 2011, Washington: The Jamestown Foundation. http://www.jamestown.org/programs/edm/single/?tx_ttnews[tt_news]=38183&cHa sh=659ec4661bb2802d799a8e04523eba11

55 Socor, "Gazprom Seeks Expansion Into Germany's Electricity Sector."

56 Cited in Juergen Roth, *Gazprom-Das Unheimliche Imperium*, p. 87.

57 David Hoffman, "Putin's Career Rooted in the Russia's KGB," *The Washington Post*, January 30, 2000, A1, http://www.washingtonpost.com/wp-srv/inatl/longterm/russiagov/putin.htm

58 Guy Chazan and David Crawford, "A Friendship Forged in Spying Pays Dividends in Russia Today," *The Wall Street Journal*, February 23, 2005, http://online.wsj.com/article/0,,SB110911748114361477,00.html; this article provides an extensive account of the Warnig-Putin relationship. See also *The Telegraph*, October 2, 2012, http://www.telegraph.co.uk/finance/newsbysector/industry/mining/9580243/Rusal-hires-former-Stasi-agent-Matthias-Warnig-as-chairman.html

59 Guy Chazan and David Crawford, "A Friendship Forged in Spying Pays Dividends in Russia Today," http://online.wsj.com/article/0,,SB110911748114361477,00.html

60 Gazprom holds a 51 percent stake in the joint venture. BASF SE/Wintershall Holding GmbH and E.ON Ruhrgas each hold 15.5 percent, and Gasunie and GDF SUEZ each have a 9 percent share. For more on Warnig's role while with the Dresdner bank see, Tom Parfitt, "Putin's Enemies Call for Investigation for Links with Stasi Agent," *The Telegraph*, Feburary 27, 2005, http://www.telegraph.co.uk/news/worldnews/europe/russia/1484535/Putins-enemies-call-for-investigation-into-links-with-Stasi-agent.html

61 Hill and Gaddy, *Mr. Putin*, p. 247.

62 Roman Kupchinsky, "Gazprom's Loyalists in Berlin and Brussels," *Eurasia Daily Monitor*, 6(100), http://www.jamestown.org/single/?no_cache=1&tx_ttnews%5Btt_news%5D=35034

63 Ibid.

64 Roman Kupchinsky, "Gazprom's Loyalists in Berlin and Brussels"; see also Dirk Banse and Uwe Müller, "Gazprom-Manager im Visier der deutschen Justiz," *Welt Online*, May 6, 2008, http://www.welt.de/wirtschaft/article1970576/Gazprom-Manager-im-Visier-der-deutschen-Justiz.html

65 Roman Kupchinsky, "Gazprom's Loyalists in Berlin and Brussels."

66 Stefan Steinberg, "Gerhard Schröder, Gazprom and German Foreign Policy," http://www.wsws.org/articles/2006/apr2006/schr-a14.shtml

67 "Gerhard Schröder's Sell Out," *The Washington Post*, December 13, 2005, http://www.washingtonpost.com/wp-dyn/content/article/2005/12/12/AR2005121201060.html

68 Lantos Raps Former European Leaders (Axis of Weasels) Associated Press, June 13, 2007, http://www.freerepublic.com/focus/f-news/1850361/posts

69 Quoted in Gregory Feifer, "Too Special a Friendship:Is Germany Questioning Russia's Embrace?" *Radio Free Europe/Radio Liberty*, July 11, 2011.

70 Quoted in Guy Chazan and David Crawford, "A Friendship Forged in Spying Pays Dividends in Russia Today."

71 Guy Chazan and David Crawford, "A Friendship Forged in Spying Pays Dividends in Russia Today."

72 Gregory Feifer, "Too Special a Friendship:Is Germany Questioning Russia's Embrace?" *Radio Free Europe/Radio Liberty*, July 11, 2011, http://www.rferl.org/content/germany_and_russia_too_special_a_relationship/24262486.html

73 Nicolas Kulish, "German Group That Cited Putin as "Role Model" Cancels Prize After Outcry," *The New York Times*, July 16, 2011; http://www.nytimes.com/2011/07/17/world/europe/17germany.html?_r=0

74 Anne Applebaum, "In the New World of Spies," *The New York Review of Books*, October 25, 2012, 56. As the investigative journalist, Jürgen Roth has concluded, "Thus the Russian government can use OC elements for intelligence, sabotage and even diplomatic service abroad. This also gives the Kremlin plausible deniability, since OC's actions are always extrajudicial and are assumed—but rarely proven—to be directly linked to the state. Central Europe, where Russian OC often 'negotiates' deals with local politicians on Moscow's behalf, is full of examples of this. Russian OC's influence also extends domestically by allowing the Kremlin to use OC to pressure regional politicians, businessmen or journalists without using government organs." Jürgen Roth, "Organized Crime in Germany," *Flare Network*, March 1, 2010, http://www.flarenetwork.org/report/enquiries/article/organised_crime_in_germany.htm

75 Jürgen Roth, "Organized Crime in Germany," *Flare Network*, March 1, 2010, http://www.flarenetwork.org/report/enquiries/article/organised_crime_in_germany.htm

76 Ognyan Minchev, "Russia's Energy Monopoly Topples Bulgarian Government," *Transatlantic Take*, German Marshall Fund, March 4, 2013.

77 "The Czech counterintelligence service warned in June 2010 that Russian industrial espionage was growing aggressively in the country's energy sector." John Lough, "Russia's Energy Diplomacy," *Chatham House Briefing Paper* (London: Chatham House, May 2011), p. 13.

78 For a detailed description of the Commission's actions, see Alan Riley, "Commission v. Gazprom: The Antitrust Clash of the Decade?" *CEPS Policy Brief*, No. 285, October 31, 2012 (Brussels: Centre For European Policy Studies) www.ceps.eu

79 Oil continues to be the main source of energy in Germany although it has declined markedly since the early 1970s. It now represents approximately 32 percent of

Germany's total primary energy supply (TPES) with Russia supplying 38 percent of that total. The trend of decreasing oil consumption is expected to continue, with the German Petroleum Industry Association forecasting a 14 percent decrease in oil consumption for the period 2010–2025. The share of natural gas in the country's TPES is 22 percent in 2010, down from 24 percent in 2009 and also down from nearly 24 percent in 2005. On the other hand dependence on coal has increased dramatically, going from 22,722 tons in 1999 41,561 tons in 2011 with Russia supplying 23 percent. Source: Statistik der Kohlenwirtschaft eV http://www.kohlenstatistik.de/files/silberbuch_2011.pdf; see also "Negotiations between Germany's E.ON and Gazprom result in lower gas prices," *OSW:Centre for Eastern Studies*, July 11, 2012.

80 John Lough, "Russia's Energy Diplomacy," *Chatham House Briefing Paper* (London: Chatham House, May 2011), p. 15.

81 "Gazprom: Russia's Wounded Giant," *The Economist*, March 23, 2013; see also Anders Aslund, "Gazprom's Demise Could Topple Putin," *Bloomberg News*, June 9, 2013.

82 Anders Aslund, "Gazprom's Demise Could Topple Putin."

83 Gregory Feifer, "Too Special a Friendship."

84 In addition to Applebaum see Jurg Gerber, "On the Relationship between Organized and White-Collar Crime: Government, Business, and Criminal Enterprise in Post-Communist Russia," *European Journal of Crime, Criminal Law and Criminal Justice*, 8(4) (2000), 337.

Chapter 5

1 Edward Luttwak, "From Geopolitics to Geoeconomics," *The National Interest*, 17 (Summer 1990); for broad survey of the concept see Paul Aligica, "Geo-economics As A Geo-Strategic Paradigm: An Assessment," The Hudson Institute, August 9, 2002.

2 Robert Cooper, *The Postmodern State and the World Order* (London: Demos, 2000); for an American version of this argument see Thomas P. M. Barnett, *The Pentagons New Map: War and Peace in the Twenty-First Century* (New York: Putnam, 2004).

3 Luttwak cited in Aligica.

4 James J. Sheehan, *Where Have All the Soldiers Gone? The Transformation of Modern Europe* (Boston: Houghton Mifflin, 2008), p. 201.

5 Ibid., p. 221.

6 Aligica, "Geo-economics."

7 Edward Luttwak, *Turbo-capitalism: Winners and Losers in the Global Economy* (New York: Harper Collins, 1999).

8 Luttwak, *Turbo-capitalism*.

9   Pascal Lorot, *Introduction a la Geoeconomie* (Paris: Economica, 1999) quoted in
     Aligica, "geo-Economics." On the rise of geo-economics see Richard Rosecrance,
     The Rise of the Trading State (New York: Basic Books, 1986).

10   Rawi Abdelal, "The Profits of Power:Commercial *Realpoltitik* in Europe and
     Eurasia," Working Paper, Harvard Business School, September 20, 2010.

11   Joseph S. Nye Jr, *The Future of Power* (New York: Public Affairs, 2011), p. 53.

12   Gideon Rachman, *Zero Sum Future: American Power in an Age of Anxiety*
     (New York: Simon & Schuster, 2011).

13   Christian Mölling, "Deutsche Verteidigungspolitik," *SWP-Aktuell*, #18 (Berlin:
     Stiftung Wissenschaft und Politik, March 2012).

14   Q. 34.2, Transatlantic Trends 2013, http://trends.gmfus.org/files/2013/09/
     TT-TOPLINE-DATA.pdf

15   Q 43.1, Transatlantic Trends 2013, http://trends.gmfus.org/files/2013/09/
     TT-TOPLINE-DATA.pdf

16   Jos Boonstra, "What Legacy for Security and Defense?" in Anna Martiningui and
     Richard Youngs, ed., *Challeges to European Foreign Policy in 2012: What Kind of
     geo-economic Europe?* (Madrid: FRIDE, 2011).

17   "The New Normalcy in German Foreign Policy," *German Politics*, 21 (December
     2012), 515, 520.

18   See Jochen Bittner, et al., "Wir tun doch nix..." *Die Zeit*, March 21, 2013, p. 2.

19   Ulrich Speck, "Pacifism Unbound: Why Germany Limits EU Hard Power," *Policy
     Brief* (Madrid: FRIDE, May 2011), 4.

20   "Jörg Lau, Die deutsche Liebe zu den Dikatoren," *Die Zeit*, February 21, 2013;
     http://blog.zeit.de/joerglau/2013/02/21/schurken-die-wir-brauchen_5889

21   Lutz Feld, Carlo Masala, Hans-Joachim Stricker, and Konstantinos Tsetsos, "Kein
     Land in Sicht?" *Frankfurter Allgemeine Zeitung*, April 2, 2013, 11.

22   The National Intelligence Council, *Global Trends 2030: Alternative Worlds*
     (Washington, DC: December 2012); www.dni.gov/nic/globaltrends, p. 31.

23   Philip Andrews Speed, et al., *The Global Resource Nexus: The Struggles for Land,
     Energy, Food, Water and Minerals* (Washington, DC: The Transatlantic Academy,
     May 2012). Chapter 3.

24   Anna Kwiatkowska-Drozdz, "The Natural Resources Deficit: The Implications for
     German Politics," Centre For European Studies, Warsaw, Poland, February 8, 2011;
     http://www.osw.waw.pl/en/publikacje/osw-commentary/2011–02–08/natural-
     resources-deficit-implications-german-politics

25   Bundeswehr Transformation Centre, Future Analysis Branch, *Armed Forces,
     Capabilities and Technologies in the 21st Century Environmental Dimensions of
     Security: Sub-Study 1: Peak Oil: Security policy implications of scare resources*
     (Strausberg, Germany: Bundeswehr Transformation Centre, Future Analysis
     Branch, November 2010).

26   Stefan Schulz, "'Peak Oil' and the German Government: Military Study Warns of
     a Potentially Drastic Oil Crisis," *Spiegel Online*, September 1, 2010, http://www.

spiegel.de/international/germany/peak-oil-and-the-german-government-military-study-warns-of-a-potentially-drastic-oil-crisis-a-715138–2.html

27 Bundeswehr Transformation Centre, *Peak Oil: Security policy implications of scare resources,* p. 73.

28 Ibid., p. 74.

29 *Positionspapier,* "Chinesische Aktivitäten in Osteuropa—Erfolg durch marktaggressive Finanzierungsangebote," Ostauschuss, October 2010, 8, http://www.ost-ausschuss.de/sites/default/files/pm_pdf/Positionspapier-China-Ost-Ausschuss_2.pdf

30 Gerrit Wiesmann, "Merkel strikes Kazakh rare Earth Accord," *The Financial Times,* Feburary 8, 2012, 3.

31 Steve Coll, *Private Empire: Exxon Mobil and American Power* (New York: Penquin Press, 2012), 19–20.

32 Ibid., pp. 93–121.

33 Bundeswehr Transformation Centre, *Peak Oil: Security Policy Implications of Scare Resources,* p. 37.

34 Lutz Feld, Carlo Masala, Hans-Joachim Stricker, and Konstantinos Tsetsos, "Kein Land in Sicht?"

35 Kristina Kausch, "A Geo-economic Germany?" in Martiningui and Youngs, *Challenges to European Foreign Policy in 2012,* p. 48.

36 Spiegel Staff, "How the Merkel Doctrine is Changing Berlin Policy," *Spiegel Online,* December 3, 2012, http://www.spiegel.de/international/germany/german-weapons-exports-on-the-rise-as-merkel-doctrine-takes-hold-a-870596.html

37 This case is based on reporting in *Spiegel Online* by Holger Stark, "Tank Exports to Saudi Arabia Signal German Policy Shift," October 14, 2011, http://www.spiegel.de/international/world/the-merkel-doctrine-tank-exports-to-saudi-arabian-signal-german-policy-shift-a-791380.html; all the quotes in this case are taken from this article.

38 Holger Stark, "Tank Exports to Saudi Arabia."

39 Ibid.

40 "Merkel Seeks to Ease German Arms Exports," *Spiegel Online,* November 8, 2011, http://www.spiegel.de/international/germany/letter-to-brussels-merkel-seeks-to-ease-german-arms-exports-a-796541.html

41 Lobby Control, *Jahresberich 2013* (Cologne, 2013), p. 11, https://www.lobbycontrol.de/wp-content/uploads/jahresbericht-13-lobbycontrol-140519-screen.pdf

42 Spiegel, "The Merkel Doctrine." Employment figures taken from Jürgen Grässlin, *Schwarzbuch Waffenhandel: Wie Deutschland am Krieg vedient* (Munich: Wilhelm Heyne: 2013), p. 16.

43 *SIPRI Yearbook 2013* (Stockholm: Stockholm International Peace Research Institute, 2013), p. 10, http://www.sipri.org/yearbook/2013

44 Spiegel, "The Merkel Doctrine."

45 Nicolas Kulish, "Germany, For Decades a Pacifist Power, Faces the Need to Play a Military Role," *The New York Times*, January 6, 2013, 12.

46 http://www.nytimes.com/2012/10/12/business/global/missteps-doomed-merger-of-eads-and-bae-news-analysis.html?pagewanted=all

47 Christian Mölling, *Europe without Defence,*" *SWP Comments* 38 (Berlin: Stiftung Wissenschaft und Politik, November 2011), 1.

48 Christian Mölling, *Deutsche Verteidigungspolitik ,*" *SWP Aktuell 18* (Berlin: Stiftung Wissenschaft und Politik, March 2012), 4.

49 The question reads: "As you may know, unmanned aircraft, or drones (aircraft that are piloted remotely), are being used more extensively to find and kill suspected enemies in places like Afghanistan and Pakistan. Do you approve or disapprove?" Q 20 Transatlantic Trends 2013, Topline Data, http://trends.gmfus.org/files/2013/09/TT-TOPLINE-DATA.pdf

50 "German Defense Minister to Face Grilling Over Eurohawk Debacle," Deutche Welle, July 22, 2013; http://www.dw.de/german-defense-minister-to-face-grilling-over-euro-hawk-debacle/a-16964646

51 Judy Demsey, "Germans Play for Time in the Debate on Drones," *The New York Times*, July 22, 2013; http://www.nytimes.com/2013/07/23/world/europe/23iht-letter23.html?_r=0

52 Hans Monath, "Koalition streitet über Rüstungsexporte," *Der Tagesspiegel*, September 19, 2013, 5.

53 http://www.theblaze.com/stories/2013/03/26/nr-draft-how-important-are-guns-to-the-u-s-economy-for-starters-the-firearms-industry-employs-twice-as-many-americans-as-bailed-out-gm/

54 Jürgen Grässlin, *Schwarzbuch Waffenhandel: Wie Deutschland am Krieg vedient* (Munich: Wilhelm Heyne: 2013), p. 415.

55 Christian Mölling, "Fur eine sicherheitspolitische Begründung deutscher Rüstungsexporte," *SWP—Aktuell*, 66, November 2013 (Berlin: Stiftung Wissenschaft und Politik), p. 2.

56 Ibid., pp. 3, 4.

57 Annegret Bendiek, *European Cyber Security Policy*, SWP Research Paper, RP 13 (Berlin: Stiftung Wissenschaft und Politik, October 2012), 5.

58 For details see, Annegret Bendiek, *European Cyber Security Policy*, p. 13; and Klaus Dieter Fritsche, *Cyber-Sicherheit: Die Sicherheitsstrategie der Bundesregierung*, Analysen und Argumente 89 (Sankt Augustin: Konrad Adenauer Stiftung, March 2011).

59 Cited in Annegret Bendiek, *European Cyber Security Policy*, p. 10.

60 Joseph S. Nye, *The Future of Power* (New York: Public Affairs, 2011), p. 113.

61 Ibid., p. 137.

62 http://www.defensenews.com/article/20130709/DEFREG01/307090008/Across-Europe-Nations-Mold-Cyber-Defenses

63 Interview October 2013.

64 Annegret Bendiek, *European Cyber Security Policy*, p. 7.

65 A study conducted by the German Chamber of Commerce in China found that protection of intellectual property rights was one of the biggest challenges facing German businesses there. Forty five percent of the respondents said it was a serious problem and another 29 said it was a problem. Judy Dempsey, "German Buisness Moves Beyond Russia to China," *The New York Times*, July 13, 2010; http://www.nytimes.com/2010/07/14/business/global/14trade.html?_r=0

66 *Datenklau: Neue Herausforderungen für deutsche Unternehmen* (Eschborn, Germany: Ernst and Young, 2013); for an article summarizing the main findings, see Chris Bryant, "Germans' fear of US spying surges," *The Financial Times*, August 6.

67 David Sanger, "'In Spy Uproar,' Everyone Does It' Just Won't Do," *The New York Times*, October 26, 2013, A1; see also Richard McGregor and James Politi, "Snowden Factor Hampers Trade Bargaining and Foreign Policy," *Financial Times*, October 26/27, 2013, 2.

68 "This affair has released highly contaminated fall-out on German–American relations, because it came as a wake-up call in the middle of a German dream of partnership—even friendship—without the typical, nasty fine print. More than in any other European country, the German media is still chewing on the realization that American interests differ from those defined in Berlin—that Washington is pursuing its own agenda, irrespective of sensitivities or even vital interests "over there." On top of all that, Snowden is being granted political asylum in Moscow. US Attorney General Eric Holder has since assured the Russians that—if extradited—Snowden will not be tortured, but in Germany, this promise is received as an ugly echo of Abu Ghraib and Guantanamo. The image of Washington as the ever-benign friend and vanguard of human rights has morphed into the Big Brother, not only watching, but also twisting the arms of friends and allies and openly talking about the unspeakable. Obamania is definitely over. Heinrich Vogel, "After Snowden: The Impact of PRISM in Russia and Germany," *AICGS Commentary*, August 19, 2013, http://www.aicgs.org/issue/after-snowden-the-impact-of-prism-in-russia-and-germany/

69 Quoted in Daniel Castro, "How Much Will PRISM Cost the U.S. Cloud Computing Industry? p. 3.

70 Margarete Klein, *Russlands Militärpotential zwischen Grossmachtanspruch und Wirklichkeit*, SWP Studie (Berlin: Stiftung Wissenschaft und Politik: October 2009), p. 6.

71 Ibid., pp. 13–14.

72 Justyna Gotkowska, "The Current State, Problems and Future of Germany's Air and Missile Defence," *OSW Commentary* (Warsaw: Center For Eastern Studies, April 10, 2013, http://www.osw.waw.pl/en/publikacje/osw-commentary/2013-04–10/current-state-problems-and-future-germany-s-air-and-missile-def

73 Justyna Gotkowska, "The Current State, Problems and Future of Germany's Air and Missile Defence."

74 Miriam Elder and Luke Harding, "Cyprus Bailout Threatens Germany's 'Special Relationship' with Russia," *The Guardian*, March 29, 2013, http://www.theguardian.com/world/2013/mar/29/cyprus-bailout-germany-russia-relationship

75 Markus Dettmer and Christian Reiermann, "Bailing Out Oligarchs: EU Aid for Cyrpur a Political Minefield for Merkel," *Spiegel Online*, November 5, 2012; http://www.spiegel.de/international/europe/german-intelligence-report-warns-cyprus-not-combating-money-laundering-a-865451.html

Chapter 6

1 Samuel Charap (Rapporteur), "Developing a More Comprehensive Russia Policy: Lessons Learned from the German and US Experiences," Fredrich Ebert Stiftung, Washington, DC office, July 2012, p. 4.

2 Robert Cooper, *The Postmodern State*, http://fpc.org.uk/articles/169; for a fuller version see *The Breaking of Nations: Order and Chaos in the Twenty First Century* (London: Atlantic Books, 2003).

3 See Derek Chollet and James Goldgeier, *America Between the Wars: From 11/9 to 9/11* (New York: Public Affairs, 2008).

4 Daniel Brössler, "Zu Besuch im Aufbruch," *Süddeutsche Zeitung*, February 5, 2009.

5 Q 1-c, *Transatlantic Trends 2013*.

6 Q 4.4, *Transatlantic Trends 2013*.

7 On a thermometer rating, Germans rated Russia at 49 degrees with 0 being cold and 100 being warm (favorable). Americans came in at 48 and the EU 12 at 43. Even Poles came in at 40 degrees.

8 "Troubled by Loss of Standing in the World, Americans Support Major Foreign Policy Changes," (Chicago: The Chicago Council on Global Affairs, 2008).

9 Q 17, *Transatlantic Trends 2013;* for earlier results on this issue, see Troubled by Loss of Standing in the World, Americans Support Major Foreign Policy Changes," (Chicago: The Chicago Council on Global Affairs, 2008), p. 6. Only 17 percent in the Chicago survey considered democracy promotion as a very important goal in American foreign policy.

10 US Census Bureau figures: http://www.census.gov/foreign-trade/balance/c4621.html#2008

11 US Department of State, "2012 Investment Climate Statement-Russia," http://www.state.gov/e/eb/rls/othr/ics/2012/191223.htm

12 http://www.usrussiatrade.org/

13 See press releases from the Coalition for U.S.–Russia Trade, http://www.usrussiatrade.org/facts.php?content=exports

14 William J. Burns, "Keynote Remarks at the Annual Meeting of the U.S.-Russia Business Council," October 3, 2011, Washington: U.S. Department of State, http://www.state.gov/s/d/2011/174958.htm

15 Samuel Charap, "Beyond the Russian Reset," *The National Interest*, July/August 2013.

16 Washington Post Editorial Board, "Trouble at the Core of U.S. Foreign Policy," *The Washington Post*, September 25, 2013.

17 Ellen Berry, "A Crossroad for Russia and America," *The New York Times*, January 11, 2009, Week in Review.

18 Ellen Berry, "A Crossroad for Russia and America." As Jackson Diehl describes this second, pessimistic school: "Former secretary of state Condoleezza Rice, a longtime student of Russia, liked to point out that, historically, deepening Russian domestic repression has correlated with greater external belligerence. Will this era be an exception? The Obama administration and European governments seem to hope so; the latest Moscow political murders have not slowed their rush to "reset." Yet the cheery Russian response has covered a series of policy moves that are, at best, ambiguous." Jackson Diehl, "A Reset that Doesn't Compute," *The Washington Post*, February 23, 2009, A19. See also Constanze Stelzenmüller, "Germany's Russia Question," *Foreign Affairs* (March/April 2009), 96.

19 John Thornhill, "A Russia United by Anti-westernism," *The Financial Times*, February 4, 2009, 9.

20 Peter Rudolf, "Toward a Common Transatlantic Strategy in Dealing with Russia?" *SWP Comments* 22 (Berlin: Stiftung Wissenschaft und Politik, October 2008), p. 1.

21 Ibid., p. 2.

22 Henry A. Kissinger and George P. Shultz, "Building on Common Ground With Russia," *The Washington Post*, October 8, 2008, A19.

23 Joseph Biden, "Speech at the 45th Munich Security Conference," www.securityconference.de; in the speech Biden contended that the NATO–Russia relationship was not a zero-sum game, and that it was time to press the reset button. He listed counter terrorism and loose nukes and nuclear arms reductions as the key issues for the bilateral relationship while rejecting the acceptance of a Russia sphere of influence in the Caucuses. The White House, Office of the Vice President, REMARKS BY VICE PRESIDENT BIDEN AT 45TH MUNICH CONFERENCE ON SECURITY POLICY, February 7, 2009, http://www.whitehouse.gov/the-press-office/remarks-vice-president-biden-45th-munich-conference-security-policy

24 See Samuel Charap, "Beyond the Russian Reset," and Samuel Charap, *Assessing the 'Reset' and the Next Steps for U.S. Russia Policy* (Washington, DC: Center for American Progress, April 2010).

25 Frances G. Burwell and Svante E. Cornell, "Rethinking the Russian Reset," *Issue Brief* (Washington, DC: The Atlantic Council, March 2012).

26 Charap comments to the author, November 2013; SPD officials comment in an Interview with author, August 2013.

27 Fred Weir, "Putin and Merkel Set for a Prickly Russian-German Summit?" *The Christian Science Monitor*, April 5, 2013; http://www.csmonitor.com/World/Europe/2013/0405/Putin-and-Merkel-set-for-a-prickly-Russian-German-summit

28 As early as 2007 the European Council on Foreign Relations published *A Power Audit of EU-Russia Relations*, which came up with five distinct EU member state approaches to Russia ranging from Trojan Horses (Greece and Cyprus), Strategic Partners (France, Germany, Italy and Spain), Friendly Pragmatists (Austria, Belgium, Bulgaria, Finland, Hungary, Luxembourg, Malta, Portugal, Slovakia, and Slovenia), Frosty Pragmatists (Czech Republic, Denmark, Estonia, Ireland, Latvia, The Netherlands, Romania, Sweden, and the United Kingdom), and Cold Warriors (Poland and Lithuania). These splits also overlayed those of weak states that have been penetrated substantially by Russian businesses and organized crime, most notably Cyprus, Bulgaria, the Czech Republic, Croatia, and Hungary. Mark Leonard and Nico Popescu, *A Power Audit of EU- Russia relations*, European Council on Foreign Relations, November 7, 2007.

29 Thomas Gomart, "France's Russia Policy: Balancing Interests and Values," *The Washington Quarterly*, 30(2) (Spring 2007), 147–55.

30 "How do you Solve a Problem Like Russia?" *Europa*, October 17, 2013; http://www.theguardian.com/world/2013/oct/17/problem-russia-syria-greenpeace-kremlin-europe-eu

31 http://www.dailymail.co.uk/news/article-2412831/Just-small-island-pays-attention-Russias-astonishing-attack-Britain.html

32 Ben Judah, "UK Russia Reset Reluctance," European Council on Foreign Relations, September 12, 2011; http://ecfr.eu/blog/entry/uk_russia_reset_reluctance

33 Mark Leonard and Nico Popescu, *A Power Audit of EU-Russia Relations*, November 7, 2007, p. 48.

34 https://dgap.org/en/node/20055

35 Interview with the author, May 2013. When Kaczynski visited Georgia in the aftermath of its war with Russia, polls found that while 50 percent of Poles blamed Russia for the war, one-third viewed his visit to Tbilisi as a "provocation." Andrew Curry, "Will Poland Split EU Over Russia Policy?" *Spiegel Online*, August 14, 2008.

36 Edward Lucas, "Essay: Russia's Reset and Central Europe," Center for European Policy Analysis, March 1, 2011, 9; http://cepa.org/content/essay-russias-reset-and-central-europe

37 https://ip-journal.dgap.org/en/ip-journal/topics/polish-german-relations-good-better-sidelined

38 Q 4.4 http://trends.gmfus.org/files/2013/09/TT-TOPLINE-DATA.pdf

39 Jacek Kucharczyj, *Im Osten was Neues? Das Bild Polens und Russlands in Deutschland 2013*, pp. 4, 5, http://www.bertelsmann-stiftung.de/cps/rde/xbcr/SID-539C3372–693DB141/bst/xcms_bst_dms_38167_38168_2.pdf

40 Pawel Sweiboda, "Poland Votes for Continuity in Germany," *Carnegie Europe*, September 12, 2013, http://www.carnegieeurope.eu/2013/09/12/poland-votes-for-continuity-in-germany/gmxp

41 See Andrez Turkowski, "The Polish-German Tandem," *Carnegie Europe*, November 17, 2011.

42 Edward Lucas, "Essay: Russia's Reset and Central Europe," p. 12.

43 Comment to author, November 2013.

44 Elzbieta Kaca and Agnieszka Lada, "What Policy towards Russia? The Polish and German Points of View," Warsaw: The Institute of Public Affairs, No. 12/113, September 2010.

45 "How do you Solve a Problem Like Russia?" *Europa*, October 17, 2013.

46 Elzbieta Kaca and Agnieszka Lada, "What Policy towards Russia?"

47 Jan Cienski, "Polish-Russian Relations Still Strained," *Beyond BRICs, FT.com*, April 20, 2012; http://blogs.ft.com/beyond-brics/2012/04/20/poland-russia-relations-still-strained/#axzz2ikAhrc6k

48 Andrew Michta, "Back to the Frontier," *The American Interest*, November/December, 2013.

49 Edward Lucas, "Essay: Russia's Reset and Central Europe," p. 11.

50 Elzbieta Kaca and Agnieszka Lada, "What Policy towards Russia?"

51 See Dmitri Trenin, ed, Maria Lipman and Alexey Malashenko, *The End of an Era in EU-Russian Relations* (Moscow: The Carnegie Moscow Center, May 2013), p. 12.

52 Jan Techau quoted in Peter Spiegel, "Merkel Eyes New Intelligence Sharing Agreement with US," *The Financial Times*, October 26/27, 2013, p. 2.

53 Bertelsmann Foundation, *Transatlantic Briefing Book: Managing Expectations, Expanding the Partnership, Shaping the Agenda for 2009* (Washington, DC: Bertelsmann Foundation, 2008), pp. 46 and 47.

54 Samuel Charap (Rapporteur), "Developing a More Comprehensive Russia Policy," pp. 6, 7.

55 Mitchell A. Orenstein, "Get Ready for a Russo-German Europe," *Foreign Affairs*, Snapshot, March 9, 2014.

56 Peter Baker, "In Cold War Echo, Obama Strategy Writes off Putin," *The New York Times,* April 20, 2014, 1.

57 Katherina Peters, "Umfragen zur Krim-Krise: Deutsche zweifeln an Sanktions-Strategie," *Spiegel On Line,* March 20, 2014, http://www.spiegel.de/politik/deutschland/umfragen-zur-krim-krise-deutsche-zweifeln-an-sanktions-strategie-a-959679.html

58 The May 2014 survey of the German public on foreign policy found that when asked which countries were most important for Germany to cooperate with, 61 percent listed China, 56 percent listed the United States, and 53 percent listed Russia. See *Die Sicht der Deutschen auf die Aussenpolitik* (Berlin: Körber Stiftung, May 6, 2014).

Chapter 7

1 For an example of a cooperative German–Russian scenario building exercise see *Germany and Russia in 2030: Scenarios for a Bilateral Relationship* (Berlin: The Friedrich Ebert Foundation, 2013).

2 As one of the toughest German critics of Russia, Hannes Adomeit observes, "In fairness, however, German business leaders, despite their apparent 'value' aversion and open rejection of any 'interference' of politics with business, too, are insisting on the transformation of Russia from, in the dual sense of the word, 'state' of 'legal nihilism' to a *Rechtsstaat*—if only for the narrow sake of the security of their investments. The German effort, therefore, is much more broadly conceived than the Kremlin desires. Despite evidence of waning interest in Russia ('Russia fatigue') and declining expertise on Russian affairs … German federal and *Länder* institutions, the German business community, the foundations attached to the major political parties and a plethora of nongovernmental institutions continue to be engaged in manifold activities to promote not only social and economic but also political change in Russia. Much of this is based on the conviction that, ultimately, as the Russian middle class will expand, change will come and the 'spillover' from the manifold activities at local and regional levels in the social and economic spheres from 'low politics' to 'high politics' will finally occur." Hannes Adomeit, *German-Russian Relations: Balance Sheet since 2000 and Perspectives until 2025* (Paris: IFRI, October 2012).

3 See, for example, the joint German Marshall Fund, Stiftung Wissenschaft und Politik paper, *Neue Macht: Neue Verantwortung*/ or *New Power, New Responsibility: Elements of a German foreign and security policy for a Changing World* (English version) and the speeches of German President Gauck, Foreign Minister Steinmeier and Defense Minister von der Leyen at the 2014 Munich Security conference. https://www.securityconference.de/en/activities/munich-security-conference/msc-2014/reden/

4 See Hans Kundnani, "The Ostpolitik Illusion," *Internationale Politik Journal*, October 17, 2013, https://ip-journal.dgap.org/en/ip-journal/topics/ostpolitik-illusion.

5 Kundnani, "The Ostpolitik Illusion."

6 Sabine Fischer, "Neuw Impulse für die deutsche Russlandpolitik, SWP Kurzgesagt," November 13, 2013, http://www.swp-berlin.org/de/publikationen/kurz-gesagt/neue-impulse-fuer-die-deutsche-russlandpolitik.html

7   Hans Kundnani, "Germany as a Geo-economic Power," *The Washington Quarterly* (Summer 2011), 31–45.

8   Joseph Nye, *The Future of Power* (New York: Public Affairs, 2011), p. 54.

9   http://www.espas.europa.eu/espas-report/detail/article/part-iii-a-polycentric-world-but-a-growing-governance-gap/

10 Thomas L. Friedman, "Made in the World," *The New York Times*, January 29, 2012, Sunday Review, 11.

11 Quoted in Shawn Donnan, "Think Again," *Financial Times Magazine*, July 8, 2011; http://www.ft.com/cms/s/2/b8e8b560-a84a-11e0–9f50–00144feabdc0. html#axzz2dBHhvnKe

12 Joseph S. Nye Jr, *The Future of Power* (New York: Public Affairs, 2011), p. 53.

13 I owe this insight to a conversation with Ewald Boehlke, the Director of the Beitz Center at DGAP.

14 Susan Stewart, "Prämissen hinterfragen: Plädoyer für eine Neugestaltung der deutschen Russlandpolitik," *SWP Aktuell* 50 (Berlin: Stiftung Wissenschaft und Politik, August 2012, p. 3 and 4.

15 Joshua Kurlatzik, "Are the New Democracies Pro Democracy?" *The Boston Globe*, December 16, 2012; http://www.bostonglobe.com/ideas/2012/12/16/are-new-democracies-pro-democracy/4x0aF4QLhi4ZNme9q2zUcI/story.html

16 "Vulnerability produces more power in relationships than does sensitivity. The less vulnerable of two countries is not necessarily the less sensitive, but rather the one that would incur lower costs from altering the situation." Joseph S. Nye Jr, *The Future of Power*, p. 55.

17 http://www.transparency.org/news/feature/turning_a_blind_eye_to_bribing_foreign_officials

18 Transparency International, *Exporting Corruption: Progress Report 2013* (Transparency International: 2013) http://www.transparency.org/news/feature/turning_a_blind_eye_to_bribing_foreign_officials

19 Anne Applebaum, "In the New World of Spies," *The New York Review of Books*, October 25, 2012, p. 56.

20 Vladimir V. Putin, "A Plea for Caution from Russian," *The New York Times*, September 11, 2013, A31.

21 Peter Baker, *Days of Fire: Bush and Cheney in the White House* (New York: Doublday, 2013); quoted in Peter Baker, "The Seduction of George W. Bush," Foreign Policy.com, November 6, 2013. http://www.foreignpolicy.com/articles/2013/11/05/the_seduction_of_george_w_bush_by_vladimir_putin

22 Hans Kundnani and Jonas Parello-Plesner, *China and Germany: Why the Emerging Special Relationship Matters for Europe*, Policy Brief, European Council on Foreign Relations, May 2012, p. 3.

23 Die Bundesregierung, *Globalisierung gestalten- Partnerschaften ausbauen- Verantwortung teilen: Konzept der Bundesregierung* (German Foreign Office, 2012),

p. 4. See also Thomas Bagger, "The Networked Diplomat," *Internationale Politik*, August 3, 2013; and *Neue Macht: Neue Verantwortung*.

24 Abraham L. Newman, "Flight from Risk: Unified Germany and the Role of Beliefs in the European Response to the Financial Crisis," in Anderson and Langenbacher, *From the Bonn to the Berlin Republic*, pp. 306–18.

25 Claire Jones, "Stuttering Growth Casts Doubt on German-led Exports Drive," *The Financial Times*, November 15, 2013, p. 2.

26 See the *Neue Macht: Neue Verantwortung* study on this challenge, pp. 7–8 and 39–40.

27 "BBC Poll: Germany most popular country in the world," *BBC Europe*, May 23, 2013. http://www.bbc.co.uk/news/world-europe-22624104

28 Michael J. Sandel, "What Isn't for Sale?" *The Atlantic*, February 27, 2012, http://www.theatlantic.com/magazine/archive/2012/04/what-isnt-for-sale/308902/

Select Bibliography

Abdelal, R., 2010. *The Profits of Power:Commercial Realpoltitik in Europe and Eurasia*, Cambridge: Harvard Business School.

Adomeit, H., 2012. *German-Russian Relations: Balance Sheet since 2000 and Perspectives until 2025*, Paris: IFRI.

Aligica, P., 2002. *Geo-economics as a Geo-Strategic Paradigm: An Assessment*, Washington, DC: The Hudson Institute.

Andrews-Speed, P., Bleischwitz, R., Kemp, G., Vandeveer, S., Boersma, T., and Johnson, C., 2012. *The Global Resource Nexus: The Struggles for Land, Energy, Food, Water and Minerals*, Washington, DC: The Transatlantic Academy.

Bagger, T., 2013. "The Networked Diplomat." *Internationale Politik*, August 3. https://ip-journal.dgap.org/en/ip-journal/topics/networked-diplomat

Baker, P., 2013. *Days of Fire: Bush and Cheney in the White House*, New York: Doublday.

Bendiek, A., 2012. *European Cyber Security Policy*, Berlin: Stiftung Wissenschaft und Politik.

Bertelsmann Foundation, 2008. *Transatlantic Briefing Book: Managing Expectations, Expanding the Partnership, Shaping the Agenda for 2009*, Washington, DC: Bertelsmann Foundation.

Boonstra, J., 2011. "What Legacy for Security and Defense?" In A. Martiningui and R. Youngs, eds, *Challeges to European Foreign Policy in 2012: What Kind of geo-economic Europe?* Madrid: FRIDE, pp. 4–9.

Bundesregierung, 2012. *Globalisierung gestalten-Partnerschaften ausbauen-Verantwortung teilen: Konzept der Bundesregierung*, Berlin: German Foreign Office.

Burwell, F. G. and Cornell, S. E., 2012. *Rethinking the Russian Reset*, Washington, DC: The Atlantic Council.

Charap, S., 2010. *Assessing the "Reset" and the Next Steps for U.S. Russia Policy*, Washington, DC: Center for American Progress.

— 2013. "Beyond the Russian Reset." *The National Interest*, (126) (July/August), 39–48.

Chivvis, C. S. and Rid, T., 2009. "The Roots of Germany's Russia Policy." *Survival*, 51(2), 105–22.

Chollet, D. and Goldgeier, J., 2008. *America Between the Wars: From 11/9 to 9/11*, New York: Public Affairs.

Coll, S., 2012. *Private Empire: Exxon Mobil and American Power*, New York: Penquin Press.

Cooper, R., 2000. *The Postmodern State and the World Order*, London: Demos.

Debevoise & Plimpton LLP., 2010. *FCPA Update*, 1(9).

Fisher, D. and Read, A., 1988. *The Deadly Embrace: Hitler, Stalin and the Nazi-Soviet Pact 1939–1941*, New York: Norton.

Fritsche, D., 2011. *Cyber-Sicherheit: Die Sicherheitsstrategie der Bundesregierung*, Sankt Augustin: Konrad Adenauer Stiftung.

Gaddy, C. and Hill, F., 2013. *Mr. Putin: Operative in the Kremlin*, Washington, DC: The Brookings Institution.

Goel, A. and Jo, M. Y., n.d. "Recent Anti-Corruption Developments in Germany." In G. Asheesh, ed. *International Bribery and Corruption Trends and Developments*. Washington, DC: Ropes and Gray, pp. 3–34.

Gomart, T., 2007. "France's Russia Policy: Balancing Interests and Values." *The Washington Quarterly*, 30(2), Spring, 147–55.

Gotkowska, J., 2013. *The Current State, Problems and Future of Germany's Air and Missile Defence*, Warsaw: Center For Eastern Studies.

Grässlin, J., 2013. *Schwarzbuch Waffenhandel: Wie Deutschland am Krieg vedient*, Munich: Wilhelm Heyne.

Hans-Joachim Spanger, Die deutsche Russlandpolitik, in: Thomas Jäger/ Alexander Höse/ Kai Oppermann (Hg.), Deutsche Außenpolitik, Wiesbaden, 2010.

Jones, C., 2013. "Stuttering Growth Casts Doubt on German-led Exports Drive." *The Financial Times*, November 5, 2.

Kaca, E. and Lada, A., 2010. *What Policy towards Russia? The Polish and German Points of View*, Warsaw: The Institute of Public Affairs.

Kausch K., 2011. "A geo-economic Germany?", In A. Martiningui and R. Younges (eds), *Challenges for European Foreign Policy in 2012, What kind of geo-economic Europe?*, Fride: Madrid.

Klein, M., 2009. *Russlands Militärpotential zwischen Grossmachtanspruch und Wirklichkeit*, Berlin: Stiftung Wissenschaft und Politik.

Köcher, D. R., 2008. *The Russlandbild der Deutschen-das Deutschlandbild der Russen*, Berlin: Institut für Demoskopie Allensbach.

Koenen, G., 2005. *Der Russland Komplex: Die Deutschen und der Osten 1900–1945*, Munich: C.H. Beck.

Koszalin, A. H., n.d. "Gazprom's Expansion Strategy in Europe and the Liberalization of EU Energy Markets." *Russian Analytic Digest*, 34(8), 8–10.

Kramer, D. and Shevtsova, L., 2012. "Germany and Russia: The End of Ostpolitik?" *The American Interest*, http://www.the-american-interest.com/articles/2012/11/13/germany-and-russia-the-end-of-ostpolitik/

Krastev, I., 2011. "Paradoxes of the New Authoritarianism." *Journal of Democracy*, 22(2), 5–16.

Kreeger, L., 1957. *The German Idea of Freedom: History of a Political Tradition*, Chicago: The University of Chicago Press.

Kundnani, H., 2011. "Germany as a Geo-economic Power." *The Washington Quarterly*, 34(3), Summer, 31–45.

— 2013. "The Ostpolitik Illusion." *Internationale Politik Journal*, October 17, https://ip-journal.dgap.org/en/ip-journal/topics/ostpolitikillusion.

Kundnani, H. and Parello-Plesner, J., 2012. *China and Germany: Why the Emerging Special Relationship Matters for Europe*, London: European Council on Foreign Relations.

Kupchinsky, R., n.d. "Gazprom's Loyalists in Berlin and Brussels." *Eurasia Daily Monitor*, 6(100), http://www.jamestown.org/single/?tx_ttnews%5Btt_news%5D=35034#.U950ByfD-Pw

Kwiatkowska-Drozdz, A., 2011. *The Natural Resources Deficit: The Implications for German Politics*, Warsaw: Centre For European Studies.

Leonard, Mark and Popescu, Nico, 2007. *A Power Audit of EU-Russia Relations*, London: European Council on Foreign Relations.

Liedtke, K., 1989. *Der Neue Flirt: Russen und Deutsche auf dem Weg zu Veränderten Beziehungen*, Berlin: Stern.

Lipman, M., Malashenko, A., and Trenin, D., 2013. *The End of an Era in EU-Russian Relations*, Moscow: The Carnegie Moscow Center.

Lobby Control, *Jahresbericht 2013* (Cologne, 2013), p. 11. https://www.lobbycontrol.de/wp-content/uploads/jahresbericht-13-lobbycontrol-140519-screen.pdf

Lough, J., 2011. *Russia's Energy Diplomacy*, London: Chatham House.

Lucas, E., 2011. *Russia's Reset and Central Europe*, Washington, DC: Center for European Policy Analysis.

Luttwak, E., 1990. "From Geopolitics to Geoeconomics." *The National Interest*, 17, 17–24.

— 1999. *Turbo-capitalism: Winners and Losers in the Global Economy*, New York: Harper Collins.

Maier, C., 1988. *The Unmasterable Past: History, Holocaust, and German National Identity*, Cambridge: Harvard University Press.

Meister, S., 2012. *An Alienated Partnership: German-Russian Relations After Putin's Return*, Helsingfors: The Finnish Institute for International Affairs.

Michta, A., 2013. "Back to the Frontier." *The American Interest*, November/December.

Mölling, C., 2011. *Europe without Defence*, Berlin: Stiftung Wissenschaft und Politik.

— 2012. *Deutsche Verteidigungspolitik*, Berlin: Stiftung Wissenschaft und Politik.

— 2013. *Fur eine sicherheitspolitische Begründung deutscher Rüstungsexporte*, Berlin: Stiftung Wissenschaft und Politik.

Naim, M., 2012. "Mafia States." *Foreign Affairs*, May/June, http://www.foreignaffairs.com/articles/137529/moises-naim/mafia-states

Newman, A. L., 2010. "Flight from Risk: Unified Germany and the Role of Beliefs in the European Response to the Financial Crisis." In J. Anderson and E. Langenbacher, eds, *From the Bonn to the Berlin Republic*. New York: Berghahn Books, pp. 306–18.

Nye, J. S., 2011. *The Future of Power*, New York: Public Affairs.

Paterson, W. E., 2008. *Foreign Policy in the Grand Coalition*, Boston, American Political Science Association.

Peters, J., 2010. "Russland in den Augen deutscher Experten." In A. Łada, ed. *Russland heute und morgen:Meinungen deutscher und polnischer Experten*. Warsaw: Institut für Öffentliche Angelegenheiten, pp. 81–108.

Rachman, G., 2011. *Zero Sum Future: American Power in an Age of Anxiety*, New York: Simon & Schuster.

Rahr, A., 2008. *Russland gibt Gass: Die Ruckkehr einer Weltmacht*, Munich: Hanser.

Rice, C., 2011. *No Higher Honor: A Memoir of My Years in Washington*, New York: Crown.

Roth, J., 2012. *Gazprom-Das Unheimliche Imperium*, Frankfurt: Westend.

Rudolf, P., 2008. *Toward a Common Transatlantic Strategy in Dealing with Russia?* Berlin: Stiftung Wissenschaft und Politik.

Sandel, M. J., 2012. "What Isn't for Sale?" *The Atlantic*, February 27, http://www.theatlantic.com/magazine/archive/2012/04/what-isnt-for-sale/308902/

Sheehan, J. J., 2008. *Where Have All the Soldiers Gone? The Transformation of Modern Europe*, Boston: Houghton Mifflin.

Speck, U., 2011. *Pacifism Unbound: Why Germany Limits EU Hard Power*, Madrid: FRIDE.

Steltzenmüller, C., 2009. "Germany's Russia Question." *Foreign Affairs*, 88(2), 89–100.

Stent, A. E., 1999. *Russia and Germany Reborn: Unification, the Soviet Collapse, and the New Europe*, Princeton: Princeton University Press.

Stewart, S., 2012a. *Germany's Relationship with Russia: Buisness First?* Berlin: Stiftung Wissenschaft und Politik.

— 2012b. *Prämissen hinterfragen: Plädoyer für eine Neugestaltung der deutschen Russlandpolitik*, Berlin: Stiftung Wissenschaft und Politik.

Sweiboda, P., 2013. "Poland Votes for Continuity in Germany." *Carnegie Europe*, September 12, http://carnegieeurope.eu/publications/?fa=52934&reloadFlag=1

Szabo, S. F., 2008. *Parting Ways: The Crisis in German-American Relations*, Washington, DC: Brookings Institution Press.

The Chicago Council on Global Affairs, 2008. *Troubled by Loss of Standing in the World, Americans Support Major Foreign Policy Changes*, Chicago: The Chicago Council on Global Affairs.

The National Intelligence Council, 2012. *Global Trends 2030: Alternative Worlds*, Washington, DC: The National Intelligence Council.

Trenin, Dmitri, ed., Maria Lipman and Alexey Malashenko, 2013. *The End of an Era in EU-Russian Relations*. Moscow: The Carnegie Moscow Center.

Turkowski, A., 2011. "The Polish-German Tandem." *Carnegie Europe*, November, http://carnegie.ru/publications/?fa=46059

Watson, P., 2010. *The German Genius: Europe's Third Renaissance, the Second Scientific Revolution and the Twentieth Century*, New York: Harper Collins.

Wood, A., 2011. *Russia's Business Diplomacy*, London: Chatham House.

Index